PENN'S GREAT TOWN

PENN'S GREAT TOWN

By GEORGE B. TATUM

The Philadelphia Art Alliance and The College

PHILADELPHIA • UNIVERSI

50 YEARS OF PHILADELPHIA ARCHITECTURE
ILLUSTRATED IN PRINTS AND DRAWINGS

Foreword by Theo. B. White

Fellows of the American Institute of Architects

PENNSYLVANIA PRESS

Title page is a view of Chestnut Street near Fifth Street looking east, from a drawing attributed to William Strickland, now in the collection of the Atwater Kent Museum.

Grateful acknowledgment is made of generous contributions by the following to the planning, preparation, and publication of *Penn's Great Town:*

The Atwater Kent Museum

The College of Fellows of the American Institute of Architects

The Fairmount Park Art Association

The Philadelphia Art Alliance

. . . having taken w^t Care you can for the Peoples good . . . let the Rivers and Creeks be sounded on my side of the Delaware River, especially Upland, in order to settle a great Towne, and be sure to make your choice where it is most navigable, high, dry and healthy.

William Penn to his commissioners on the eve of their departure for the new province of Pennsylvania, September 30, 1681.

FOREWORD

THIS IS A BOOK THAT HAS LONG BEEN NEEDED TO TELL THE STORY OF PHILADELPHIA ARCHITECTURE.

It is a need not limited to Philadelphia, for it is manifest in all American metropolitan areas where the traditional architectural design reflects an early society and then merges into the bold, imaginative expressions of the later nineteenth century, again reflective of social changes. And, finally, come the sometimes frantic searchings for a new and satisfying interpretation of the present century. This need has not hitherto been satisfied in the Philadelphia story.

Thus *Penn's Great Town* in its comprehensiveness fills a void and in its manner of composition satisfies the need in a twofold fashion. Dr. Tatum has written of Philadelphia buildings and the men who built them. He has supplemented his text with illustrations of prints and drawings and in the *Notes to the Illustrations* he has provided the layman—and the scholar—with helpful information on the buildings and the material illustrating them. These notes are certain to prove a valuable source of reference.

It has been stated that this is the first history of Philadelphia architecture. This statement is made with the awareness and, indeed, admiration of those many charming and often scholarly books on Philadelphia, which have covered in detail certain phases of the city's architecture. But there is always a gap between them or an overlapping that detracts from each. This is inevitable since any two books covering succeeding phases of Philadelphia history by the same author are a rarity, if they exist at all.

This book is not intended to fill those gaps nor to eliminate the overlaps. Rather, it seeks to tell the story of the continuous architectural endeavor of a great town from its inception to the present. It does not concern itself with charming anecdotes of its more illustrious (or not so illustrious) citizens except where these people have left their mark on the architecture of the city. It is a warm mantle gathering in its folds the many facets of architectural expression of a society that has nourished its exceptional culture for some two hundred and fifty years.

It is altogether proper that the publication of *Penn's Great Town* should coincide with a comprehensive exhibition of the material represented by its illustrations and certain supplemental material at the Philadelphia Art Alliance. Indeed, it is a heartening fact that the book is sponsored by the Art Alliance, which has made available the necessary financial assistance for the preparation of the manuscript and the hanging of the exhibition.

This book had its origin in the planning of the annual convention of the American Institute of Architects in Philadelphia in the third week of April, 1961. The A.I.A. Committee for the convention requested the Art Alliance Committee on Architecture to present to its Board of Directors a request for an architectural exhibition to be held during

7

the convention week. The Board readily consented and referred the whole matter back to its Committee on Architecture to determine the theme and content of the exhibition. This was a challenge, delivered early in the spring of 1959. The Committee eyed this challenge, not joyously, for the answer was not easily forthcoming. Committee deliberations produced a number of varied and exciting subjects before it finally achieved its resolution.

After all, we thought, the Convention will bring to Philadelphia several thousand architects and their wives from the western and middle states, the southern and the northern states. Some of these visitors might have a vague acquaintance with this city; only a few would possess an intimate knowledge of its architectural history. Indeed, such intimacy is probably enjoyed by few persons even among those who count themselves Philadelphians by birth or adoption. Therefore, we reasoned that in the absence of a comprehensive history of architecture of the greatest of the eighteenth century American metropolitan centers, and the second largest city in the British empire of the same period, an exhibition of its architecture from the late seventeenth to the middle years of the twentieth century should be as comprehensive a show of historical building as any ever held in the country.

From the first the exhibition was conceived as a polished mirror of architecture from the very beginnings of Philadelphia. It should be a reflection of the taste of Philadelphians in architecture, period by period, phase merging into succeeding phase and culminating in the year before the exhibition. It could show the charming, amusing, and sometimes frightening paradoxy of Philadelphia architecture: a Frank Furness' Provident Life and Trust Company staring in its imaginative boldness across Chestnut Street at the quiet of Strickland's Second Bank; the starkness of Louis Kahn's University laboratory towering on the skyline above the Jacobean lacework of Cope & Stewardson's dormitories. It could be an exciting show, and the book, we hoped, would lead the reader to a deeper knowledge of Philadelphia architecture.

The Art Alliance Committee, having determined the character of the exhibition, felt that a complete and accurate catalogue should also be compiled and published. We were fortunate in having two distinguished art historians as members of the committee, Dr. George B. Tatum and Dr. David M. Robb. The preparation of the catalogue and the selection of exhibition material was delegated to Dr. Tatum, Dr. Robb, and the Chairman of the Committee.

The more the subcommittee for the catalogue talked about its contents and scope, the repositories wherefrom we might expect to draw illustrative material and its format, by that much and more we became aware that a catalogue would be a compromise. Assuredly, an accurate catalogue of an exhibition is a fine medium for its purpose, but it has severe limitations in content, warmth, and above all in its restrictions in dealing with the architecture of a society. Thus, we discarded the idea of a catalogue and talked, thereafter, of a book: a history book of close to three hundred years of Philadelphia architecture. There was a unanimity of opinion between Dr. Robb and the Chairman of the Committee that the book should be written by Dr. Tatum. He gracefully accepted the authorship. At this point the College of Fellows of the A.I.A. joined the Art Alliance as one of the sponsors of the proposed book and exhibition. This was September, 1959.

It soon became obvious that in selecting the illustrative material for the book and the exhibition we must rely on prints and drawings, for many of the actual structures of the eighteenth and nineteenth centuries had been destroyed. This was brought home to us by, among other things, the disappearance of many buildings in the short seven-year period since the publication of our earlier volume *Philadelphia Architecture in the Nineteenth Century* (University of Pennsylvania Press, 1953). In view of the necessity of using prints and drawings as illustrations for those periods of architecture where the buildings were not extant, we felt that this pattern of illustration should be maintained throughout the book as a matter of visual continuity and pleasant book-making. Moreover, there is a warm intimacy in examining a building through the eyes of an artist rather than the mechanical eye of the camera. The engravers or etchers of the early periods and the lithographers of the nineteenth century possessed the feeling of the artist anxious to transmit to the public and the collector the character of the architecture even if frequently with the license of the poet.

Exploratory searchings in archives in Washington, Philadelphia, and New York assured us a wealth of material. Searching deeper with care and patience, we were amazed and inspired by the amount of material available and by the number of prints and drawings that had never been published nor probably exhibited. Archivists have been kind to Philadelphia. In one collection we were shown better than a dozen extremely fine lithographs of later nineteenth-century Philadelphia subjects so newly found and procured that they had not been recorded in its catalogue. This search for illustrative material was a continuing task through the winter of 1959-60 and was maintained to the time we went to press in July, 1960. There was frustration when a particular item became the needle in newly mown hay and there was pure joy when it was uncovered. It is quite accurate to state that thousands of items were examined and discarded. One whole morning in a great and voluminous collection in New York produced precisely six items of which, in the final selection, only one or two were included. Our culling process was highly discriminatory.

We cannot be too appreciative of the courtesy and cooperation shown us in our search for illustrative material in many places. When we mentioned our plans for an exhibition and a book on Philadelphia architecture, we invariably encountered an enthusiasm to match our own. Dr. Edgar Breitenbach, Chief of the Prints and Photographs Division, and his assistant Mr. Milton Kaplan furnished us a delightful day in the print rooms of the Library of Congress and supplied us with a number of exceptional lithographs from the nineteenth century. Dr. Karl Kup, Chief of the Art Division of the New York Public Library, kindly put the riches of the Stokes Collection at our disposal; it was a rewarding day. The New-York Historical Society lent us several extremely interesting items, as did the Metropolitan Museum and the Philadelphia Athenaeum. Dr. Emerson Greenaway, Director of the Free Library of Philadelphia, offered us thousands of prints to choose from. Mr. Nicholas Wainwright, President of the Library Company of Philadelphia, and Mr. Edwin Wolf, 2nd, Librarian, encouraged us in our search for prints and drawings and supplied many rare and unusual items. Mr. R. Norris Williams, 2nd, Director of the Historical Society of Pennsylvania, made available to us the unique collections of the Society.

Mr. M. Joseph McCosker, Director of the Atwater Kent Museum, and his assistant, Mr. Charles T. Bryan, spent many hours segregating pertinent material for us. Mr. Lessing J. Rosenwald has shared our enthusiasm and given generously of his interest and advice. We owe to Mr. Penrose Hoopes, Chairman of the Library Committee, and Mr. John P. McGowan, Librarian, appreciation for their assistance in our search for drawings in the collections of the Franklin Institute. The Pennsylvania Academy of the Fine Arts, the Academy of Music, the Kean Archives, and the Grand Lodge, Free and Accepted Masons of Pennsylvania have all lent material from their collections.

All of us who have had anything to do with the publication of *Penn's Great Town* are especially appreciative of the encouragement and assistance that we have received from the staff of the University of Pennsylvania Press and from its director, Mr. Thomas Yoseloff. We have been especially heartened by the willingness of the Press to undertake a project of this magnitude while under the severe restriction of time and without any guarantee of financial assistance from either individuals or foundations. In all our plans for the book Mr. Yoseloff and his associates have moved with us when they were not already ahead of us.

This Foreword also presents a welcome opportunity to acknowledge the part played by the other members of the Committee, especially in preparing for the exhibition. These are: Mr. Paul C. Harbeson, Mrs. Marion Mitchell, Mr. Beryl Price, Dr. David M. Robb, and Dr. George B. Tatum. Our only regret is that, since this book must go to press almost a year before the opening of the exhibition, it is not possible to express in print our appreciation for the contribution of others upon whom we may still call for assistance. These, we hope, will find their satisfaction in the success of the completed show.

I am aware that personalities have little place in a foreword; I beg special privilege. I have worked closely with Dr. George Tatum through the winter and spring of 1959-60, offering what small assistance I could in the preparation of the book and the earmarking of items for the exhibition. The book is a monument to his scholarly dedication to his subject. The association has been a fine and rewarding experience to me and has rendered a warm friendship an even deeper thing.

Theo. B. White, Chairman
Committee on Architecture
The Philadelphia Art Alliance

CONTENTS

PENN'S GREAT TOWN

INTRODUCTION

THE GREAT TOWN THAT WILLIAM PENN HAD FOUNDED ON THE WEST BANK OF THE DELAWARE was not yet half a century old on the Sunday in 1723 when Benjamin Franklin first entered it by way of the Market Street wharf. A search for work as a journeyman had brought the young printer to Philadelphia, but doubtless he elected to remain because he sensed there an intellectual climate more in sympathy with his inquiring mind than anything he had known in New York or his native Boston. History, much of it of his own making, has proved the wisdom of his choice. Medicine, law, banking, prison reform, publishing, the theater, and, above all, individual freedom divorced from considerations of race and religion are but a few of the American institutions and traditions whose origins have been traced to Franklin's adopted city.

Nor, surprisingly enough, was Philadelphia to neglect the visual arts, its Quaker origins notwithstanding. In 1782 Charles Willson Peale built his portrait gallery adjacent to his house at Third and Lombard streets, and this was followed in 1805 by the founding of the Pennsylvania Academy of the Fine Arts, one of the first institutions in the United States established solely for the teaching of art. And what was true of painting and sculpture was even more applicable to architecture. The story of the great buildings of Philadelphia and of the men who built them is, in fact, a kind of history of American architecture. Perhaps a similar statement might be made about any city that had been a cultural and commercial center for more than two hundred years, but whereas the buildings of New York or Boston must usually be regarded simply as mirroring in their style the shifting tides of American taste, the architects and architecture of Philadelphia in a remarkable number of instances helped to create new styles or led the way to their acceptance. Even when due weight is given to the importance of regional differences, it is the buildings of Philadelphia, more than those of any other city, that must be taken into account in any general discussion of American culture.

To this estimate of the significance of Philadelphia architecture at least two relevant qualifications should be added. Since Philadelphia was not founded until 1682, the seventeenth-century buildings in the English colonies are best studied either in the wooden structures of Massachusetts or in their brick counterparts in the towns and rural areas of Virginia. Exception must also be made of the twentieth century, for although it will be found that Philadelphia played a greater part in the development of modern architecture than is commonly supposed, it can hardly claim pre-eminence in this period.

Unfortunately, Philadelphians, like most of their countrymen, have not always been alert to preserve their distinguished architectural heritage. For every important structure that remains, at least a score of equally important ones have been destroyed or altered to

15

a point where much of their original character has been lost. Not all forms of architecture have suffered equally, of course. Because of their different roles in the changing pattern of urban life, it is to be expected that religious buildings would fare the best and commercial and domestic ones the worst. The more comprehensive the discussion of Philadelphia architecture, the less it is possible to disregard the sweeping changes that time, neglect, and the hand of man have made in the appearance of the city.

No one knows better than the architectural historian that the past cannot be recovered, much less recreated. Yet through the medium of prints and drawings it is often possible to recapture something of the spirit of the great buildings of Philadelphia as they appeared to a variety of artists, professional and amateur, celebrated and unknown, over a span of more than two centuries. To this extent the old may be said to be made new again, and the forgotten or half-remembered is brought once more to mind.

THE EARLY YEARS (1682-c.1725)

WITHIN A FEW MONTHS AFTER CHARLES II HAD CONFIRMED HIM AS PROPRIETARY, WILLIAM Penn, in September, 1681, dispatched commissioners to the vast region of the New World that was to bear his family name. Little was then known of Pennsylvania beyond the fact that it was inhabited by the Lenape Indians (sometimes called the Delaware), with whom Penn was resolved to deal fairly, and that it was said to have a generally temperate climate and to abound in fresh water, wild game, fertile soil, and rich forests. At first probably few persons realized that, by reason of its central location on the Atlantic seaboard, the new colony would find it natural to assume the cultural and economic leadership of its neighbors; the "Keystone" among the states of the new American republic, it would one day be called. Necessary preparations for his colonial venture delayed Penn's own sailing until the spring of the following year, but in his place he sent his cousin William Markham with instructions to select as promptly as possible the most suitable site for the great town he was planning.

In his letters Penn makes it clear that from the first he had looked upon the grant of lands in America as an opportunity to conduct a kind of "holy experiment" for which he believed there might yet be a place in the New World, even if there had been none in the Old. It was probably its Greek meaning of "city of brotherly (or sisterly) love," rather than prominence of the Lydian city of the same name, that led the idealistic young Quaker to select the name "Philadelphia" for the capital of his new province. Here he proposed to found a society based upon tolerance and justice, and since the hazards and hardships of a colonist's life were hardly likely to appeal to many of the rich or well born, he sought to interest in his plans for Pennsylvania those whose position was "low in the world" or who were "men of universal spirits." By the former he meant principally farmers and craftsmen who found themselves unable to make a decent living in Europe, as well as the younger members of a family who must depend upon the "elder brother's table and charity"; among the latter he included those men of good will who, like himself, were desirous of promoting "good discipline and just government among a plain and well-intending people." Long before the Fourierists or Shakers had founded their ideal communities in America, William Penn had sought in his way to establish a more perfect society, and although it does not usually find a place in the literature on that subject, Philadelphia also deserves mention as a kind of early Utopia founded on Quaker principles. Certainly few, if any, of the later communities regularly cited in this connection were as carefully planned in advance for the health and happiness of the citizens.

William Crispin, Penn's first Surveyor-General, died on his way to America, and to replace him Thomas Holme sailed from London on April 23, 1682. When he reached Penn-

17

sylvania he found that the commissioners had not been idle; at their direction Thomas Fairman had already taken soundings of the river channel and had "placed Philadelphia" at the narrowest part of the relatively high and well-drained peninsula formed by the Delaware and Schuylkill rivers (Fig. 1).* Extending south along the Delaware was the settlement of Wicaco, later included in the District of Southwark. Settled early by Swedes, this was the oldest part of the county and the first to develop extensively beyond the limits of the city. Further to the south and west were the areas known, then as now, by their Indian names Passyunk and Moyamensing, which would be organized as townships at an early date. To the north and west of the city lay a tract of land that William Penn had originally intended to include within the boundaries of his great town and which, when that proved impracticable, he set aside as "the liberty land of free lots" to be divided as a kind of dividend among the first purchasers of property in the new colony. This appears to be the origin of the term "Liberties" as applied to this tract and, by extension, to much of the area outside the city proper. In 1854 all these outlying districts were made a part of Philadelphia when the county was consolidated with the city.

The final form given by the new Surveyor-General to Penn's "Capitall Citty" did not differ essentially from that indicated on the Scull and Heap map of 1777, noted above. Acting upon his instructions "to Settle the figure of the Towne so as that the streets hereafter may be uniforme downe to the Water from the Country bounds," Holme based his plan for Philadelphia upon a rigid grid system. In lieu of the 10,000 acres that Penn had envisaged, however, the commissioners contented themselves with a rectangle approximately two miles long and one mile wide, bounded on the east and west by the two rivers, and covering about 1,280 acres. Along each of the rivers ran a Front Street, and through the approximate center of the town, bisecting it from east to west and from north to south, were two main thoroughfares, each one double the fifty-foot width of the other streets, labeled respectively High and Broad streets (Fig. 2). Somewhat later the streets that ran east and west were given the names of the principal trees found in "Penn's Woods," and those running north and south were numbered consecutively from both rivers to the center of the city. As an aid to remembering the sequence of the major east-west streets, Philadelphians early evolved a useful jingle:

> High, Mulberry, Sassafras, Vine
> Chestnut, Walnut, Spruce, and Pine.

The second line still applies well enough, but later changes have made the first badly out of date; High is now called Market, Mulberry has become Arch, and Sassafras is known as Race. As time went on, the large original blocks were also subdivided by the numerous small streets and alleys that exist today, and in 1839 the streets west of Broad were renumbered to continue the sequence of those on the east.

In the center of his plan, at the junction of High and Broad streets, Holme designated an area of ten acres as the site of the market and town hall that Penn had mentioned in

---

* A description of the prints and drawings, together with additional facts concerning the subjects represented, will be found in the *Notes to the Illustrations* that appear at the end of the text.

his instructions, and, in all the quadrants thus formed, slightly smaller areas of eight acres each were set aside after the pattern of the open common in London known as the "Moorfields." Holme does not identify any of the squares, but they were later named for five of the men most prominently associated with the early history of Philadelphia: William Penn (Center Square), George Washington (Sixth and Walnut), David Rittenhouse (Eighteenth and Walnut), James Logan (Eighteenth and Race) and Benjamin Franklin (Sixth and Race). As finally constructed, Penn, Logan, and Rittenhouse squares appear to have been located somewhat further to the west than indicated on the Holme Plan. During the eighteenth century Logan Square was the site of public executions, and both Washington and Franklin squares served for a time as cemeteries. In the twentieth century, however, all these areas (except of course for Penn Square, which since the late nineteenth century has been occupied by the City Hall) were restored to their original purpose as commons set aside for the use and enjoyment of the citizens of Philadelphia.

Holme does not give names to any of the streams that he shows flowing through the city, but that in the southeast corner is certainly the Dock Creek that figures prominently in the early history of Philadelphia and today lies beneath the street bearing its name. South of the creek, along the Delaware, was a high point of land belonging to the Free Society of Traders, a company organized in London to promote the settlement and development of Pennsylvania. Although the Society was dissolved in 1723 and its lands sold, its name continued to be associated with the southeast corner of the city and came again into prominence in the 1950's when the architectural distinction of many of the old houses on "The Hill" began to attract public notice.

Whatever its European antecedents—and they are at least as old as the military camps of the Roman Empire—the plan of Philadelphia that Thomas Holme made following the Proprietary's instructions was essentially a conservative one. In it are none of the dramatic diagonals characteristic of French practice or that a few years earlier had been included in the plans of John Evelyn and Sir Christopher Wren for the rebuilding of London after the fire of 1666. Throughout the nineteenth century, visitors frequently commented upon the monotonous arrangement of Philadelphia streets; ". . . a city laid down by a square and rule, a sort of habitable problem—a mathematical infringement on the rights of individual eccentricity—a rigid and prosaic despotism of right angles and parallelograms," was the way Thomas Hamilton expressed it in *Men and Manners in America,* published at Edinburgh in 1843. But the designs of more modern planners who have sought to introduce a measure of variety into the old city have usually met with only qualified success, seldom appearing other than foreign intruders on conservative Quaker soil. It is the simple and direct form which William Penn first gave to his great town that is still memorialized by present-day Philadelphians when they characteristically measure distances in their city in terms of "squares."

Cities planned in advance of the construction of the first buildings are comparatively rare in any country at any period. Throughout his instructions to his commissioners, William Penn stressed the extent of his plans for his new city and his fear lest persons who already occupied land upon the site refuse to adjust their claims and thus thwart his

19

"great and good Contrivance." In words that have a curiously modern ring, Penn in 1681 as part of "Certain Conditions, or Concessions" directed that "great roads from city to city, not to contain less than forty feet in breadth, shall be first laid out and declared to be for highways, before the dividend of acres be laid out for the purchaser; and the like observation to be had for the streets in the towns and cities, that there may be convenient roads and streets preserved, not to be encroached upon by any planter or builder, that none may build irregularly to the damage of another." Together with one or two towns that do not appear to have been planned in such detail (Charleston, South Carolina, may have been planned on the grid system as early as 1670, and New Haven, Connecticut, was given that form in 1638), Philadelphia represents one of the earliest important American cities planned on a comprehensive scale in advance of its establishment. In fact, modern city planners might fairly claim William Penn as among the first to practice their profession in the New World.

Of the Swedes who had settled in Pennsylvania before the coming of the English or of the log construction that they are believed to have introduced into the Colonies, little or nothing remains in the Philadelphia area. The old brick house on Penrose Ferry Road, known as "Cannon Ball Farm" from a misadventure with a shot intended by Revolutionary soldiers in Fort Mifflin for a nearby British battery, is in a ruined condition, even could it be shown that any considerable part of the visible fabric goes back to the house built by Peter Cock in the late 1600's. On the other hand, the well-preserved woodwork in Bellaire, the city-owned and now restored house in Passyunk, is of such quality that it is difficult to accept for it a date prior to 1700. More probably, the small brick structure to the northwest, later the kitchen for the main dwelling, was the building erected by Thomas Jacobs, Jr., about 1675. There is growing evidence, in fact, that in the eighteenth century the wings and other dependencies of American mansions were more often erected prior to construction of the main block than is usually recognized.

Although the first houses that gradually replaced the caves along the Delaware in which the first settlers had found shelter must have been largely of wood, the type of half-timber construction descended from the Middle Ages is also known to have been employed in Philadephia at an early date. Soon, however, brick was available in sufficient quantity to permit the construction of all-brick dwellings similar to those the colonists had left behind in Europe and today regarded as characteristic of the colonial city. By the end of the seventeenth century contemporary writers boast that the citizens of Philadelphia had increased from a few hundred to nearly twenty thousand, many of whom lived in substantial houses two or three stories high and frequently built of brick.

It has long been a popular notion that bricks for Philadelphia buildings were imported from England and West Jersey. Perhaps a few paving tile and other special items may have been brought in, but conditions in the early eighteenth century make any very heavy traffic in such a commodity most unlikely. England was several thousand miles from America and cargo space was at a premium; there were no bridges over the Delaware and travel over dirt roads with a heavy load became nearly impossible during many seasons of the year. But more important, there was no need to import building brick. About 1800 the architect Latrobe called the clay of Philadelphia "excellent brick earth," an observation confirmed by the map of the city drawn by John Hills a year or two before on which may be distinguished at least twenty-five brickyards. In many cases a small kiln was probably set up at the construction site and bricks were burned from the clay removed from the excavation for the cellar.

Although the majority of the early dwellings of Philadelphia were necessarily modest in size and adornment, here and there in the new city we hear of more substantial houses that must have compared favorably with anything being built in any other colonial city at this time. Unfortunately, nothing remains of the double house built by Edward Shippen on the west side of Second Street below Dock Creek, of Clarke Hall with its famous gardens at the southwest corner of Third and Chestnut streets, or of Richard Whitpain's mansion, which was so large that in 1687 William Penn suggested that, although "too big for a private man," it might serve well enough "for all the offices of State." The generous proportions of Joshua Carpenter's house on Chestnut between Sixth and Seventh streets are suggested, however, by the drawing reproduced as Figure 3. Especially noticeable is the pent or overhanging roof between the first and second stories, a form popularly associated with the early architecture of the Philadelphia region. In the view of some historians, this device originated in Europe, where it served to protect wood and plastered walls from sun and weather. According to this theory, the disappearance of original pents may be explained by the fact that Philadelphians realized that they were no longer necessary on all-brick houses and so failed to renew them when they fell into disrepair. As an alternative, it might be suggested that the pent was essentially a medieval form that was dropped, along with the casement window and leaded glass, when it went out of fashion. In matters of this kind the simplest explanation often has the best chance of being the right one.

The house that perhaps as early as 1687 the British architect James Porteus had built for Samuel Carpenter on the southeast corner of Second and Norris' Alley (now Sansom) was one of the most important buildings of the period by reason of its architectural form as well as for the people and events associated with it. Known by its most prominent and—for that time—unusual feature as the "Slate Roof House," it was rented as his town house by William Penn during his second visit to Philadelphia (1699-1701); here he drew up his Charter of Privileges and here his son John, called the "American," was born. After Penn's return to England, James Logan made the Slate Roof House the seat of the colonial government until 1704, when Samuel Carpenter sold it, over Logan's protests, to William Trent, the future founder of the city of Trenton in neighboring New Jersey. In later years the house served variously as a boarding house (said to have numbered among its guests such prominent figures as Washington and Hancock), a girls' school, and a place of business for jewelers and silversmiths. It was finally pulled down in the nineteenth century but not before the new process of photography had confirmed the general accuracy of old prints and drawings such as the one reproduced as Figure 4.

Originally the Slate Roof House seems to have had casement windows composed of small leaded panes, but except for one or two features of this kind, even the earliest Philadelphia houses (unlike those of Virginia and New England) appear to have exhibited few elements that could be characterized as survivals from medieval architectural practice. The

21

absence of a medieval style in Philadelphia is explained by the fact that the first settlers took for models the new buildings recently constructed in London after the Great Fire of 1666: buildings which, in turn, were based upon classic canons of taste as interpreted by the Italian architects of the fifteenth and early sixteenth centuries.

However much they might have been captivated by their dream of antiquity, those Florentines who first gave direction to the new style of architecture had no thought of reproducing in detail any aspect of the buildings of the past. In common with artists and scholars in other fields, they sought a renewal of the spirit of classic art rather than the accurate revival of any of its specific forms, a fact that was taken by John Addington Symonds and other early historians as sufficient justification for the use of the term "Renaissance" (meaning "rebirth") to describe the period as a whole. In their efforts to adapt the classic architectural vocabulary to the needs of their own day, such early Renaissance architects as Leon Battista Alberti (1404-1472) received welcome assistance from the rediscovery in 1414 of the *Ten Books on Architecture* written early in the first century of the Christian era by the Roman architect Marcus Vitruvius Pollio. Henceforth until the time of Michelangelo (d. 1564), the use of classical forms in the architecture of the Italian Renaissance was based upon Roman practice and very largely regulated by the rules laid down by Vitruvius.

Eventually the Renaissance in architecture, as in the other arts, spread from Italy to all but the most remote areas of the civilized portions of the Western Hemisphere. The lag in time between the revival of classicism in Italy in the early decades of the fifteenth century and the appearance of the new style in England two hundred years later is to be explained partly by the geographical distance involved, partly by the break with the Church of Rome that had occurred in 1534 under Henry VIII, and partly by the vitality of the Gothic tradition in the northern countries. The classical elements that were employed by architects such as John Thorpe during the reigns of Elizabeth (1558-1603) and James I (1603-25) had usually to be learned at second hand, frequently through Dutch and Flemish sources. However refreshing we may find the architectural vagaries of such great "Jacobean" mansions as Kirby Hall, Hardwick, or Hatfield House, the complication of the classical forms and the naïveté with which they are handled make it clear that their designers were as yet unable to free themselves completely from the Tudor Gothic idiom in which they had been trained.

The first building in England to which the adjective "Renaissance" may be applied without reservation is usually considered to be the banqueting house for the Palace of Whitehall that Inigo Jones (1573-1652) built for James I in 1619-22. As studiously correct in his handling of classical forms as other Jacobean architects were arbitrary, Jones understood the essentials of Renaissance style to a degree unknown by his English predecessors. To the interpretation of classical forms as they evolved in England and her colonies the name "Georgian" has been given, although their earliest appearance antedated the accession of George I by at least a century. (Even though the practice of identifying periods by the names of persons is not entirely satisfactory, it has achieved such wide usage that it is difficult to substitute other labels. Perhaps this system has no more disadvantages than any other provided it is understood that, as far as the history of art is concerned, the reference is to a *style*, the beginning and end of which may have had little or nothing in common with the dates of a monarch's reign.) But by whatever name it is called, the Renaissance approach to architecture in England, as elsewhere, is as much at variance with that of the Middle Ages, which it followed, as it is with that of the modern period, which it precedes. In the designs of Jones and his successors the expression of function and construction, characteristic of medieval style, gives way to rigid symmetry in both plan and elevation. The high-pitched roof of the northern buildings of Tudor times is flattened to emulate Italian models; horizontal elements predominate over vertical, and the site is made to conform to the building, rather than the building to the site. The nature of the material counts for little in Georgian buildings, and at every point considerations of convenience and utility yield to the demands of formal elegance. In his application of Renaissance principles to architectural design, Jones, like most English architects, took as his models the works and writings of Italian architects, particularly Andrea Palladio, whose consequent influence has made the name "Palladian" synonymous with Renaissance architecture, especially in England and America (Fig. 5).

After the artistic vacuum caused by the Puritan Revolution (1642-60), the Renaissance style continued to flourish in England under the restoration of the Stuarts. But now to the Palladian architectural vocabulary favored by Inigo Jones and his contemporaries was added the more robust and dramatic interpretation of classic forms characteristic of much of the art of the seventeenth century, usually termed "Baroque." Perhaps nowhere was a happier blend of the Baroque and Palladian achieved than in the spires with which Sir Christopher Wren (1632-1723) adorned the more than fifty churches that he built in London after the Great Fire of 1666. The fact that many of the Royalists had sought refuge in Holland while the Puritans were in power also helps to explain the preference for red brick buildings ornamented with light trim of either stone or wood often found in the work of Wren and his followers.

This English combination of Baroque and Palladian styles is reflected in the Slate Roof House of Philadelphia. The half-timber construction characteristic of the Middle Ages has here given way to walls of brick with contrasting light trim. Also of Renaissance inspiration are the symmetrical spacing of doors and windows, the balance of the H-plan with its two projecting wings, and the horizontal emphasis of the cornice and the belt course marking the division between the floors. The hipped roof, like any classical detail given to the dormers, may also be regarded as a modification of an essentially northern medieval form inspired by southern canons of Renaissance taste imported, through England, from Italy. Rare in the American colonies at this date were such features of the Slate Roof House as the gabled hood over the central doorway, the interior paneling that seems to have adorned at least the principal room, and whatever classic moldings may have decorated the cornice along the eaves of the roof. Together with a very few other buildings like the College of William and Mary (1695-1702), Stoughton Hall at Harvard (1699), and the first City Hall in New York (1699), Samuel Carpenter's house provides an important early example of a building—among the first of its kind in British America—that clearly shows the influence of Renaissance style. Of these important examples known to

23

have been begun before 1700, only the first building of the College of William and Mary remains standing today.

Early descriptions of the principal houses of Philadelphia make it clear that we should think of many of them as adjoined by fine and often extensive gardens. This was as Penn had envisaged his capital, for in words that have often been quoted he wrote his agents of his hope that the houses in the new city might be placed in the middle of the lots to the end that Philadelphia appear "a greene Country Towne, which will never be burnt and will allwayes be wholsome." But Penn failed to reckon with man's innate conservatism and the persistent drive for economic gain to which even the more idealistic Quakers were not immune. Inspired partly by a desire to reproduce in the New World the homes they had left in the Old, and partly by the rising value of land in the city, Philadelphians more and more tended to build their houses in continuous rows directly on the street, leaving the rear for back buildings, yards, and gardens. No contemporary prints have been found that give a clear impression of a Philadelphia street in the early eighteenth century. Perhaps if we discount such later features as the curbing, paving, and street lights, the character and arrangement of the houses would differ little in essentials from those represented in the views engraved between 1798 and 1800 by William and Thomas Birch (Fig. 23). In these we see row upon row of brick dwellings, their attics lit by dormers and their façades broken by the horizontal line of nearly continuous pents.

In its simplest form the Philadelphia house consisted of one room on each of two or three floors. A winding stairway, usually enclosed and located beside the chimney, led to the cellar as well as to the upper floors. Built frequently for speculative profit or as housing for servants, these simple "Bandbox" houses, as they are sometimes called, were often grouped together along the small alleys or "courts" mentioned in old fire insurance surveys and still surviving here and there in the modern city.

When a larger house was desired, a second room might be added behind the first, as in the case of the small brick dwelling now standing somewhat incongruously alone in Fairmount Park, but originally built sometime before 1715 as one of a number of houses on Letitia Street near the Delaware River (Fig. 6). In this example the entrance is in the center of the façade and the stair rises in the corner of the front room. It was perhaps more customary, however, to place the front door at one side, as it appears in the contemporary Benezet House (Fig. 7). When placed at the side, the front door usually (but not invariably) gave access to a narrow hall that led to stairs located in a passage between the front and rear parlors. Following the usual Georgian practice, the first floor of all but the earliest Philadelphia houses was raised a few feet above ground level and service access to the cellar was through a bulkhead opening directly onto the sidewalk. At first the cooking seems to have been done in a shed or back building, for it was not much before the end of the eighteenth century that the more familiar cellar kitchen had become popular.

The Quakers who comprised the majority of the early settlers in Philadelphia held their first meetings in private houses such as that of Thomas and Elizabeth Fairman at Shackamaxon (Kensington) near the large elm reputed to be the site of Penn's treaty with the Indians. Later, meetings were held from 1684 until 1698 in a wooden building erected

24

for that purpose on Front Street, north of Arch, and known as the Bank Meeting House. About 1687 a more substantial brick structure, 60 by 40 feet, was erected on the southwest corner of Center Square. This was intended for morning meetings; for those in the evening a second building was constructed on Front Street above Sassafras (Race). When it became apparent that in the foreseeable future the city was not going to spread westward from the Delaware toward Center Square as Penn and his agents had first expected, the Center Square building was dismantled and the materials were used to build the Second Bank Meeting House, which stood from 1702 until 1791. As early as 1696 construction had also been begun on a meeting house more conveniently located at Second and Market streets and known from its size as the Great Meeting House. Built of red brick relieved only by modest wooden trim, and containing a large bare meeting room sparsely furnished with rude pine benches, the Great Meeting House conformed to the sound but plain type of architecture favored by the Society of Friends. After more than half a century during which it remained the largest of the Quaker meeting houses, the Great Meeting House was replaced in 1755 by a still larger building (Fig. 8), known appropriately as the Greater Meeting House. This stood on High Street until early in the nineteenth century when it, too, was dismantled and its materials were used, in the thrifty Quaker tradition, to erect yet another meeting house in West Philadelphia.

Except possibly for their larger size and the simplicity of their architectural lines, there was little to distinguish a Quaker meeting house from any of the more substantial private residences of the day. Most Friends would have considered vain and worldly even so tiny a steeple as that which adorned the new brick church at Wicaco, begun in 1698 by the Swedish congregation and, like its log predecessor, known as "Gloria Dei" (Fig. 9). The entrance on the south side, together with the vestry that balances it on the north, was added in 1703 to serve as buttresses when the walls showed signs of spreading under the weight and thrust of the vaulted ceiling within. Although the specific architectural elements that make up this oldest of Philadelphia churches appear to owe their origins to the English sources discussed above, the steep roof, the diminutive belfry, and the bold details unite to give "Old Swedes'" a distinctive flavor. Not as clear is whether these characteristics that set Old Swedes' apart from other churches in the Philadelphia area are attributable to the Scandinavian background of its builders or simply to its early date. In 1845 the congregation of Gloria Dei was admitted into the Convention of the Protestant Episcopal Diocese of Pennsylvania.

If exception be made for the numerous inns and taverns such as the famous Blue Anchor, which was at least as old as the city and perhaps older, there were few public buildings in Philadelphia before the beginning of the eighteenth century. In fact, it was not until 1707 that Philadelphians got around to constructing a building specifically for their government, and then it was not in Center Square, as the planners of the city had intended, but in the middle of High Street, north of the Great Meeting House and facing east. The form of the Town Hall as it appears in old prints and drawings (Fig. 8), with its balcony for public proclamations and addresses, was clearly based on English models, and European also was the practice of having the ground floor serve as a public market. Soon market

25

sheds extended behind the Town Hall down the center of High Street to Third, and in front of it, the Jersey Market stretched from Second to Front Street. The first market stalls were doubtless of wood, but these were soon supplanted by the massive brick piers that figure prominently in several of Birch's best-known engravings (Fig. 23). In the nineteenth century the brick piers were, in their turn, replaced by supports of cast iron, a new material just coming into general use about 1836 when the market was again renewed and extended. As part of these renovations the old Town Hall was demolished in 1837.

Although other markets were also established in Callowhill Street, Spring Garden, and North Second Street, the stalls in the middle of High Street continued to grow in number as the population of the city increased, until by 1850 they extended a full eleven blocks. Even before the middle of the eighteenth century High Street had become known as "Market" in popular parlance, but change has always come slowly in Philadelphia; it was not until 1858 that the new name was officially recognized, and then seemingly only just in time, for the following year the Select and Common Councils of the city passed an ordinance abolishing the sheds that had given Market Street its name.

As the division of lots on the Holme plan (Fig. 2) makes clear, Penn and his commissioners expected that settlement would take place simultaneously along both rivers and and spread thence toward the center of the city. Instead, the colonists built almost exclusively along the Delaware in order to be near the harbor, which had proved deep enough to permit the largest merchant vessels to come alongside the docks, even at low tide, and was to make of Philadelphia one of the great ports of the world. Penn had intended also that nothing be built on the east side of Front Street that might block the view of the river, but in this as in many of his hopes for the city he was destined to be disappointed. Soon merchants leased the land down to the water's edge and beyond for wharves and warehouses, until it was necessary to include between Front and the River another street that took from its location the name Water.

It is this thriving harbor scene that an otherwise unknown artist named Peter Cooper sought to represent in a view of the city from the southeast, presumably painted about 1720 (Fig. 10). Although a number of the details that Cooper included in his panorama seem to be imaginative touches of his own, the painting still deserves attention as the earliest known view of the city. Here the "brave brick houses" described to Penn by Robert Turner are shown grouped closely, but comfortably, along the waterfront. A majority of the buildings have three or four stories, although part of the apparent height of structures in the background is probably attributable to high ground along the river. The dwellings that supplanted the caves of the first settlers were often built against this bank so that one more story was visible in the rear than in front. Examples of such hill-houses survive today in the area along the river, still referred to by Philadelphians as "the Bank." In several places in the Cooper view can also be distinguished the balconies mentioned as commonplace in early accounts but now entirely disappeared, except possibly for such a rare example as that on the façade of Bellaire, the house in League Island Park discussed previously for its connection with the early Swedish community of Philadelphia.

26

THE GOLDEN AGE (c.1725-c.1775)

DURING THE EIGHTEENTH CENTURY WILLIAM PENN'S GREAT TOWN CONTINUED TO PROSPER until on the eve of the war with Britain it was first in importance among the cities of the American colonies and second in size only to London among those of the British Empire. To many it has seemed, in retrospect, that the quarter-century prior to the Revolution constituted for Philadelphia a kind of Golden Age. To be sure, most of the streets remained unpaved through much of the period, and it was not until the middle of the century that a serious attempt was made to provide illumination at night on even the major thoroughfares of the city. But these were also the years that saw the construction of one of the earliest and most distinguished public buildings in the Colonies, of probably the most elaborate Palladian church in British America, and of several of the most important mansions of the Georgian Era. Though Philadelphia would continue through the nineteenth century to produce buildings of the greatest historic and architectural importance, never again would her political and cultural leadership seem as clearly without peer or rival.

The extent of the building activity in Philadelphia during the second quarter of the eighteenth century is readily suggested by a comparison of the Cooper painting (Fig. 10) with the engraving published by Scull and Heap in 1754 and used, in part, as the end papers of this volume. In the latter view the buildings numbered 6 and 7 are, respectively, the Town Hall (shown without the sheds of the Jersey Market) and the Great Meeting House at Second and Market streets; both were completed early in the history of the city and have been discussed briefly in the preceding section. But most of the five spires of varying heights that give a new and distinctive appearance to the skyline were erected in the decade between 1745 and 1755. Number 5 is the polygonal German Reformed (Dutch Calvinist) Church that stood on Race Street, near Fourth, from 1747 until about 1772 when it was demolished to make way for a new and larger structure better suited to the growing congregation. Number 4 identifies the Second Presbyterian Church, begun in 1750 on the northwest corner of Third and Arch. The unusually tall spire was added in 1753 and until rotting timbers required it to be taken down in 1803 remained one of the most prominent landmarks in the city. In planning so tall a steeple for their new church the Arch Street congregation doubtless had in mind the architectural distinction achieved by the Episcopalians at nearby Christ Church. John Fanning Watson quotes, in this connection, a few lines of contemporary doggerel which suggests that to some, at least, the spire of the Arch Street Church seemed too pretentious for a Calvinist sect:

> The Presbyterians built a church, and
> fain would have a steeple;
> We think it may become the *church*,
> but not become the people.

27

Perhaps the satirist was right; in any case, it was some time before the Presbyterians in Philadelphia built another church with more than the most modest of belfries.

The lowest of the spires, numbered 3, marks the meeting house built on Fourth south of Arch Street in 1740-42 by the followers of the Wesleyan revivalist George Whitefield (the "New Lights") when their religious views made them no longer welcome in the First Presbyterian Church (the "Old Light"). Unfortunately, contributions failed to provide sufficient funds to meet the cost of constructing what was then one of the largest buildings in the city, and the property was sold in 1749 to a group headed by Benjamin Franklin. Here under his leadership was established the following year the Academy of Philadelphia, later called the College of Philadelphia, the forerunner of the University of Pennsylvania. In this way the trustees obtained a valuable site for the new academy at probably not more than half its cost, but the original objectives of Whitefield were not entirely ignored, for it was agreed as a condition of sale that the new owners would continue to provide a room for itinerant preachers and that a school would be opened for the free instruction of the children of the poor. In accordance with this stipulation, the Charity School was opened Sept. 16, 1751.

Of the buildings given prominence in the Scull and Heap View, all have disappeared except the two that have the greatest historical and architectural importance: the State House (numbered 2) and Christ Church (numbered 1) whose tall spire, rising to a height of nearly two hundred feet, has been given such prominence by the engraver. The history of the State House, or Independence Hall, as it later came to be known, is a somewhat complicated one that may appropriately be deferred until Christ Church has been examined more closely.

In response to a petition from more than thirty citizens of Philadelphia, acting under Article XXII of Penn's charter, the Bishop of London in 1695 sent the Rev. Thomas Clayton to organize the first Anglican church in Pennsylvania. So well did the new parish prosper that within two generations of its founding the original building had been enlarged at least once and the congregation was ready to set about replacing it entirely with the handsome Palladian church that still stands on Second Street above Market (Fig. 11). Construction of the new Christ Church began in 1727 as an expansion of the west end of the old nave, and by 1744 the new building was complete except for the steeple, which for lack of funds was not finished until 1754. At that time was hung a peal of eight bells imported from England, and since there was "always something to be chimed," Philadelphia in 1783 impressed at least one European traveler as "almost . . . an Imperial or Popish city." In the years following its completion, Christ Church numbered among its worshipers on occasion such men as Benjamin Franklin, Robert Morris, Benjamin Rush, and George Washington, and within its walls at the General Convention of 1789 the Episcopal Church in America, as distinct from the Church of England, was first established as part of the Anglican Communion.

Of even greater interest, however, is the fact that at this comparatively early date Philadelphians produced in Christ Church one of the handsomest and certainly one of the most elaborate Palladian churches in America. Here, both within and without, we meet a full repertory of Palladian forms as they had been used by Wren and Gibbs. In the dark brick walls the glazed "headers" are laid in Flemish bond, creating a pattern that enhances the contrast with the light wooden trim; and throughout, molded bricks are extensively used for window frames, pilaster bases, and water tables. Along the exterior side walls, brick pilasters in two stories separate the round-topped windows and support a wooden cornice decorated with Roman modillions. At the east end the nave projects beyond the side aisles and is pierced in the center by a great Palladian window enframed by pilasters resting on a high brick base and supporting a double entablature that continues the horizontal line of the roof balustrade. The latter feature serves to conceal the slope of the separate gallery roofs and is, in turn, crowned by flame-topped urns whose swelling curves help to account for that Baroque flavor that sets Christ Church apart from the majority of eighteenth-century buildings in America.

Judged by the aesthetic standards of the twentieth century, it may seem that the builders of Christ Church tried to introduce too many details in too small a space, with the result that the effect appears cramped and heavy to some. Of course this same observation might also be made of the more pretentious houses of the period, such as Mount Pleasant (Fig. 16) or Cliveden (Fig. 17), as well as of much of the furniture produced in the Philadelphia shops of such master cabinet makers as William Savery or Benjamin Randolph. But judgments of this sort are largely personal, and even those who prefer the simpler lines of such a Boston church as Old North (1723), Old South (1729), or the handsome King's Chapel designed by the Newport architect Peter Harrison in 1749, will agree that for its place and time Christ Church was a remarkable achievement.

No one has as yet succeeded in tracing the exact origin of the design for Christ Church, if indeed it had a single source, or in identifying with certainty the man responsible for it. The tradition that assigns this role to John Kearsley, a physician and communicant of the parish, seems credible when it is recalled that in the eighteenth century some acquaintance with architecture was considered part of a gentleman's education. Jefferson is the best-known example of an American who achieved distinction as an amateur architect, but the history of the colonial period offers many other examples of men in a variety of professions whose knowledge of architecture was sufficient to enable them to make tasteful adaptations and combinations of details found in American and European books. On Oct. 23, 1744, the committee appointed to review and settle the building accounts of Christ Church expressed "the Opinion that the Uniformity and Beauty of the Structure so far as it appears now Finished is greatly Owing to the Care, Pains and Labour of him the said Dr. Kearsley."

The role of the gentleman-architect was usually limited to the selection of the general design, however, and the preparation of the final drawings as well as the day-by-day supervision of the work must have been left in the more experienced hands of a trained carpenter-builder. In the minutes of Christ Church, Kearsley is spoken of as Trustee, Overseer, Principal Inspector, and Supervisor, but never specifically as the designer. The only mention of drawings that has come to light in this connection is found in the minutes of the vestry meeting of June 2, 1746, in which it is recorded that after several drafts of the tower and spire had been considered, "it was agreed and concluded upon that in the Erecting of the Spire the Draft which Mr. Harrison drew should be followed." The "Mr. Harrison" mentioned in the minutes has so far eluded more exact identification although Joseph Jackson has advanced the claim of John Harrison, one of the founders of the Carpenters' Company, who may have worked upon Old Swedes' Church and who was certainly employed as a carpenter on the State House. Nor is it known to what extent Harrison's drawing was followed by the carpenters Robert Smith and John Armstrong, who with John Palmer, the mason, constructed the tower of Christ Church between 1751 and 1754. Presumably this was the same Smith and Palmer who are recorded as having previously worked together on the construction of the Second Presbyterian Church on Arch Street, mentioned earlier for the height of its spire. Through these years Dr. Kearsley also continued to serve as one of the three "Supervisors for carrying on the Steeple" of Christ Church.

Although at the Second Presbyterian Church, at the Academy, and at Christ Church, Robert Smith is mentioned simply as a "carpenter," by about 1760 he begins to emerge from the ranks of the skilled craftsmen and assume something of the status of a designer and builder. More payments were made to him than to any of the others who worked on the steeple of Christ Church, and a few years later we meet him in the role of architect of the second Episcopal church erected in Philadelphia. This was St. Peter's (Fig. 12), begun in 1758 at Third and Pine streets as a "chapel of ease" for Christ Church, which was proving too small for the growing congregation and too inconveniently located for parishioners who had to travel more than a few blocks over unpaved streets. Even in this case, however, Dr. Kearsley served as chairman of the building committee, and the list of specifications that he and his associates drew up left very little to the discretion of the designer.

As befitted a chapel, the Georgian exterior of St. Peter's is much plainer than that of the parent church, but of all the Episcopal churches in Philadelphia, it alone retains the original high-backed box pews designed to reduce drafts and provide a measure of privacy for their occupants. The unusual location of the pulpit at the west end of the nave, opposite the altar, is also without parallel in other colonial churches of the city. Above the altar may still be seen the beautiful organ case which, like the pulpit and pews, is part of the Georgian furnishings of the church. Fortunately this was preserved when the musical parts of the instrument were renewed and enlarged in 1932. St. Peter's at first had only the small belfry seen in Figure 12; the present square tower that seems somewhat out of scale with the rest of the church was added in 1842 by the Philadelphia architect William Strickland. The gilded cross that still crowns Strickland's spire may well be the first use of such a symbol on an American Protestant church, antedating that of Richard Upjohn's Trinity Church (1845) in New York by several years. Heretofore a cross had been considered "popish" (Christ Church has a bishop's miter).

In 1760 a group of dissenters, led by the Rev. William McClenachan, broke away from Christ Church to found a new parish and to erect St. Paul's about 1761 on the east side of Third Street below Walnut. The identity of the architect of the third Episcopal church in the city is not known, but it may well have been Robert Smith. In 1830 William

Strickland made extensive alterations to the interior in order to provide additional space for the vestry and the Sunday school. Always the plainest of the early Episcopal churches, St. Paul's today serves as the headquarters of the Episcopal Community Services of the Diocese of Pennsylvania.

The foregoing description of the skyline of Philadelphia is evidence not only of the architectural changes that had taken place by mid-century but also of the presence in the city of a variety of religious groups other than the Society of Friends. By the Charter of Privileges, granted in 1701, Penn reserved the public offices of Pennsylvania for Christians, but he also guaranteed that any colonist who acknowledged *"One* almighty God" should be permitted to worship in accordance with his own conscience. Philadelphians were quick to exercise the religious freedom promised them; in addition to the churches of the German Calvinists and of the Presbyterians and Episcopalians noted earlier, a considerable number of other buildings were erected in the course of the eighteenth century by religious groups distinguished by widely varying beliefs and practices.

Mass was certainly said in Philadelphia as early as 1708, and in 1733-34 the Roman Catholic community built first a small chapel and in 1757, when the parish had increased in size, a larger church dedicated to St. Joseph. This was later demolished and replaced with the church that still stands between Walnut Street and Willing's Alley, just east of Fourth Street. In 1763 a second Roman Catholic church was founded as a mission of St. Joseph's. This was St. Mary's, located a short distance to the south of the parent church about midway between Spruce and Locust. Although portions of the original fabric exist within the present structure, the Georgian appearance of St. Mary's was altered completely by the Gothic additions of 1810. It was for the rebuilt church that William Rush carved the crucifix mentioned by Scharf and Westcott but apparently lost early in the twentieth century.

Also on Fourth Street at the southeast corner of New is St. George's, often referred to as the cradle of Methodism in America. Begun by the Presbyterians, who were unable to complete it for lack of funds, this simple brick structure was acquired by the Methodists in 1769. Plain to the point of severity, St. George's is valued more today for its association with such men as Joseph Pilmore and Francis Asbury than for its architectural character.

In 1743 the German Lutherans under the leadership of Dr. Henry Melchior Muhlenberg began the construction of St. Michael's Church at Fifth and Cherry streets, now known largely through Birch's engraving. Not even the ample dimensions of St. Michael's were adequate for its expanding congregation, however, and in the spring of 1766 the cornerstone was laid for Zion Church a block away on the corner of Fourth Street. Robert Smith was engaged as architect of the new building and although lack of funds delayed progress somewhat, construction was sufficiently far advanced by June, 1769, that the church could be consecrated. During the Revolutionary War this was one of a number of structures in Philadelphia seized by the British for use as a hospital.

In the winter of 1794 a serious fire destroyed the interior as well as the tower of Zion Church, but presumably the restorations carried out by William Colladay under the direction of a committee headed by Dr. Muhlenberg followed the lines of Robert Smith's earlier design. The rebuilt church was consecrated in November, 1796, and four years later pictured by William Birch in the first edition of his Philadelphia views (Fig. 13). To judge from the engraving, the spire of Zion Church had not been restored after the fire, but nevertheless it is easy to understand why Samuel Hazard considered this "the largest and handsomest [church] in North America." The richness of the exterior was matched within by "eight large columns of the Doric order which served for bases of the arches of the ceiling which was ornamented and finished in a most magnificent manner." Probably because it had one of the largest seating capacities in the city, it was at Zion Church that the Congress assembled for a memorial service on learning of the death of General Washington.

The same Dr. John Kearsley who played a prominent part in the construction of Christ Church was made a member of a committee of three formed in 1730 to consider an appropriate design for a new State House to be erected on the land that the Provincial Assembly had recently purchased on Chestnut Street between Fifth and Sixth. It was not Kearsley's design that the Assembly finally selected, however, but that "produced" by another member of the committee, the lawyer Andrew Hamilton, best known for his defense of John Peter Zenger, accused in 1734 of libeling the governing authorities of New York. Many difficulties delayed the completion of the State House until about 1748, but the pride with which Pennsylvania viewed the finished structure is reflected by its selection for representation on a number of the maps and panoramas of Philadelphia engraved from the designs of Scull and Heap, beginning about 1750 (Fig. 1).

As originally planned, the State House was a brick structure two stories in height and 100 feet in length. The first floor contained two large rooms, each about 40 feet square and separated by a central hall of approximately half that width. The chamber on the east, closed by a door for greater privacy, was intended for the Assembly; that on the west, entered from the hall through wide archways, housed the Supreme Court of the Province. On the second floor, a gallery, facing Chestnut Street and running the full length of the building, was used for public entertainment, and a room in the southeast corner served as a meeting place for the Provincial Council. To provide "for the greater security of the publick Papers" the Assembly also directed that office buildings be added at either end of the main block and joined to it by the arcades shown in the Scull and Heap view. These were nearing completion by 1736.

Contemporary documents make it clear that the plans "exhibited" by Andrew Hamilton were those adopted for the State House by the "House of Representatives" much to the annoyance of the other two members of the committee who seem to have had other ideas. This does not necessarily mean, of course, that Hamilton made the drawings from which the carpenters and masons worked. Probably his relationship to the State House was much the same as that of Dr. Kearsley to Christ Church. It is known, in fact, that in 1735 Edmund Woolley (d.1771) presented his bill for drawing "the Elivation of the Frount one End the Roof. . . . With the fronts and Plans of the Two offiscis And Piazzas Allso the Plans of the first and Second floors of the State House." This is not surprising, since Woolley is long known to have played a leading part in the erection of the State House, together with such other craftsmen as Ebenezer Tomlinson (carpenter), John Harrison (joiner), Thomas Boude (mason), Gustavus Hesselius (painter), and Thomas Godfrey (glazier). Benjamin Fairman and James Stoopes made the bricks.

In 1753 Woolley was similarly entrusted with the construction of the wooden steeple on the State House, which he may also have designed. This is the first steeple, shown in Figure 1, which stood until 1781 when rotting timbers forced its removal. For the next half century the brick tower was roofed only with the low pyramidal roof pictured by Birch and other early engravers. The present steeple was added in 1828 by William Strickland who, in his attempt to restore the State House to its original form, emerges as a kind of forerunner of the Georgian Revival that was to become popular in the twentieth century.

In the quality of its Palladian design, the State House stands in much the same relationship to the civic buildings of the Georgian period as Christ Church does to the ecclesiastic. Nowhere in the Colonies was a more ambitious project successfully carried out for the benefit of a provincial legislature at so early a date. Its only rivals for this distinction would appear to be the Capitol at Williamsburg (1701-5), now known in reconstructed form, and the dignified Colony House at Newport, Rhode Island (1739-41), and not even these share with the State House the full five-part plan (i.e., center block linked to flanking dependencies by passages or arcades) especially favored by Palladio. As befits a civic structure, the architectural lines of the State House are simpler than those of Christ Church which, as noted earlier, have a Baroque quality more appropriate to the traditional Catholic orientation of the Anglican Communion. Yet, except for such features as the decorative stone panels under the windows and the stone quoins at the corners of the State House, which take the place of the pilasters on Christ Church, both buildings are essentially similar in the manner in which they employ the developed Palladian forms of the Middle Georgian Period. The State House, even more than the church, was the later scene of stirring events: here between 1775 and 1783 the Continental Congress met; here in July, 1776, the independence of the Colonies was declared, and here in 1787 the Federal Constitution was written.

The growing prosperity of the community and the attendant skill attained by the Philadelphia craftsman were inevitably reflected in the city house of the middle of the eighteenth century. The simple two-room plan, noted earlier, was capable of further expansion in a variety of smaller rooms strung along one side of the lot to the rear and lighted by windows facing the narrow court thus formed. This is the type of city house found in the much-publicized Elfreth's Alley and on a larger scale, and embellished with fine examples of the art of the Philadelphia wood carver, in such notable houses as that built in 1765 by Charles Stedman on Third Street near Spruce (known today by the name of its second owner, Samuel Powel). Occasionally the basic plan might be further enlarged through the use of a double lot, which permitted a central hall, as in the case of the Reynolds-Morris House (1784-86) at 225 South Eighth Street.

To this roster of distinguished Philadelphia houses of the eighteenth century, one or more of which are illustrated in nearly every book on colonial architecture, additional research is gradually adding other examples scarcely less important. Illustrated here (Fig. 14) are two such houses built about 1759 on Second Street north of Spruce. The four

33

and one-half stories of the Abercrombie House were unusual for Philadelphia in the eighteenth century and no doubt support its right to be considered the tallest Georgian dwelling in the city.

The location of a city house on the corner, and hence at the end of the row, also permitted an entrance on the side and the elimination of the long hall leading from the front door to the stairs, as in the case of the Shippen-Wistar House (c.1750) at Fourth and Locust streets. Although English models must have been the ultimate source of most of their ideas, the builders of Philadelphia houses evolved a distinctive plan that made skillful use of the narrow city lot. With minor modifications it has continued in use down to the twentieth century and has understandably come to be regarded as an architectural symbol of the city where it first achieved prominence and where it was developed in the eighteenth century to a point of sophistication and elegance unknown in Boston, Baltimore, or New York.

Not all Philadelphia houses were built directly on the street, of course; some were located in the "courts" that gradually developed within a number of the large blocks originally laid out by Thomas Holme. Benjamin Franklin is probably the best-known Philadelphian who lived "up a courtyard at some distance from the street." No contemporary views of Franklin Court are known, but the drawing reproduced here as Figure 15, although necessarily conjectural in some respects, is based upon the considerable amount of information that historical research has thus far brought to light. Through the archway can be seen the entrance to Franklin's house, which he had built in 1764 while he was in England as agent for the Province of Pennsylvania. At that time three houses that antedated those in the drawing stood on the lots now numbered 316 and 318, and access to Franklin's house was through lot 322, then vacant. Franklin had acquired these three properties through his father-in-law, John Read, but he was never able to secure title to 320. Since he was almost constantly abroad in the service of his country, Franklin could not have spent a total of more than a year or two in his house on Market Street in the twenty years following its construction. But his wife Deborah lived there, and from her letters to her husband comes much of our information concerning the appearance of their new home. Shortly after his return from France in 1785, Franklin determined to build on his three lots the houses shown in the drawing, providing thereby a new approach to his own house through an archway leading from Market Street. Tradition has it that during the last years of his life Franklin spent many hours in his garden conversing with his friends in the shade of a mulberry tree. Through the archway still to be seen on Market Street must have passed nearly every figure of importance in the early years of the nation on his way to visit the sage of Philadelphia.

Although the handsome interiors of the Philadelphia houses might be eagerly sought by museums (rooms from the Powel House are in the Metropolitan and the Philadelphia Museum of Art; the parlor of the Stamper-Blackwell House, from 224 Pine Street, is in the Henry Francis duPont Winterthur Museum) their exteriors were usually plain, and the plan was necessarily restricted by the limited dimensions of even the larger city lots. To find a house that could more easily be considered the domestic counterpart of Christ Church and the State House it is necessary to go outside the city proper to the area known

34

in the eighteenth century as the Northern Liberties, now a part of Fairmount Park. Here the mansion called Mount Pleasant (Fig. 16) built for Capt. John MacPherson shortly after 1761, exhibits the basic elements of the Palladian five-part plan, except that for some reason the builder has omitted the passageways that often link the outbuildings to the main house, as we find them, for example, at Mount Vernon or Mount Airy in Virginia. This plan is common enough in the South, and it may be that MacPherson's desire for such a house was inspired by what he had seen on his trips through that region. In the case of Mount Pleasant, the pavilion on the south was probably intended as a kitchen and that on the north as an office for the estate. Originally the appearance of the ensemble must have been even more impressive when stables (now destroyed) also flanked the extant dependencies at either side.

The fact that MacPherson had two unmarried daughters should not be overlooked in judging the merits of Mount Pleasant, but it would be easier to suspect him of building the most elaborate mansion in the Middle Colonies in the hope of breaking into Philadelphia society were it not for the fact that most of the architectural features displayed by Mount Pleasant are also shared by other contemporary structures such as Christ Church and Cliveden, the home of the Chew family in Germantown. The simple fact seems to be that in Philadelphia the Georgian style in America received its most ornate expression; a profusion of quoins, pediments, pilasters, and cornices are included wherever the space will allow. The characteristic Renaissance lack of interest in materials is well illustrated by the exterior walls of Mount Pleasant, which are of rubble covered with stucco scored to imitate ashlar masonry. Symmetry was, of course, the guiding principle of all classic design, but at Mount Pleasant it seems to receive particular attention, especially in the main parlor where blind doors are placed at either side of the fireplace apparently for no better reason than to balance the opposite pair of doors leading into the central hall.

Second only to Mount Pleasant as an example of the Middle Georgian Period are Woodford, the house in Fairmount Park remodeled for the jurist William Coleman in 1756, and Cliveden, the Germantown mansion built in 1763-64 for Benjamin Chew, Chief Justice of Pennsylvania, and still owned by his descendants (Fig. 17). Both Woodford and Cliveden have in common with Mount Pleasant a façade on which the central bay is brought forward and crowned with a classic pediment. But Cliveden differs from the other two houses in having a façade of the finely dressed gray stone characteristic of the Germantown area, as well as in the very large stone urns mounted on the four corners of the roof and the apex of the central pediment. The most notable feature of the Chew mansion, however, is the spacious front hall, which measures 16 by 20 feet and is separated from the rear stair hall by a screen of fluted Tuscan columns (Fig. 18). At Mount Pleasant, in contrast, the stairs are in a separate hall to one side in order not to interrupt the sweep of the central axis begun by the drive at the front of the mansion and continued on the other side by the formal gardens, which originally must have descended in a series of terraces from the house to the Schuylkill River below. The Doric entablature that contributes greatly to the dignity of the hall at Cliveden is sufficiently close to similar features at Mount Pleasant and Port Royal, the house built about 1762 in Frankford (portions of

35

which are now in the Henry Francis duPont Winterthur Museum), to suggest some connection between the builders whose names still await identification.

The changes taking place in architectural style in the third quarter of the eighteenth century are emphasized when Mount Pleasant is compared with Stenton, the country mansion built in Germantown in 1728 for the prominent lawyer James Logan, here illustrated by a water color showing the house before it was repaired and opened to the public, after its purchase by the city in 1910 (Fig. 19). Those who occasionally find the developed Georgian style in Philadelphia too rich for their taste will admire the restrained lines of Stenton. A few such features as the symmetry of the façade (abandoned on the sides and rear), the slight elevation of the first floor above ground level, the sash windows with their segmental arches of rubbed and gauged brick, and the plain doorway with its simple rectangular transom are all that reflect the new Renaissance approach to architectural design. Only a hint of later Georgian forms may be seen in the hipped roof, crude brick pilasters —little more than strips—that mark the corners and center section of the façade, and the simple cornice on which oblong blocks are substituted for graceful Roman modillions. All things considered, Stenton is probably the finest example of a type of dwelling frequently identified as "Early Georgian" or, perhaps more appropriately, as "Queen Anne," which includes the Wythe House in Williamsburg (c.1755), the Trent House at Trenton (1719), and Hope Lodge at Whitemarsh (1723).

Fine architecture requires skilled craftsmen. The master builders who constructed and in many cases probably also designed important Georgian buildings such as Stenton or Mount Pleasant were doubtless members of the Carpenters' Company of the City and County of Philadelphia, established about 1724 for the aid and training of its members and the care and relief of their families. In this, as in nearly everything they did, the Philadelphians who founded what was certainly one of the earliest builders' organizations in the Colonies had in mind English precedent, specifically the Worshipful Company of Carpenters of London, chartered in 1477.

Although within a few years of its founding the Carpenters' Company seems to have become the richest and most powerful of several organizations of its kind in the Philadelphia area, it was nearly half a century later, and then only after lengthy debate, that the members finally decided to build as their headquarters the hall that still stands off the south side of Chestnut, between Third and Fourth. Since it is known that Robert Smith submitted at least one plan for the projected building, it has generally been assumed that he was also responsible for its final design. The view of the north elevation, published in the Company's Rule Book of 1786, shows Carpenters' Hall essentially as it appears today, except for the large urns which in the engraving decorate the roof after the fashion of Cliveden. Inasmuch as the minutes of the Carpenters' Company reveal its early members to have had a practical and frugal turn of mind, it was presumably decided that decorative details of this kind could well be dispensed with in the interest of greater economy.

In the treatment of cupola, cornice, windows, and doorway the design of Carpenters' Hall conforms to the somewhat heavy interpretation of the Georgian style characteristic of Philadelphia architecture of the middle of the eighteenth century. Much rarer in the

Colonies at this period is a plan in the form of a Greek cross. Although, from the time of Alberti on, Renaissance architects had favored the central plan for its balance and monumentality, the practical difficulty of adapting so rigidly symmetrical a shape to the specific function of a building frequently prevented its use, as in the case of St. Peter's in Rome or St. Paul's in London. The selection of a Greek cross for the plan of Carpenters' Hall suggests that the designer was not only aware of the most advanced Renaissance practice but also that he may have expected that his building would appear to equal advantage from any of its sides. If the latter consideration was indeed a factor in determining the plan of the new hall, it was soon disregarded, for as early at 1775 the carpenters had begun to sell off the frontage of their lot facing Chestnut Street. Later maps of the city all show Carpenters' Hall standing in a small court surrounded by other buildings and approached through a narrow alley as it existed until recent years and as the artist has pictured it in Figure 20.

Even before it was completed, the first floor of the carpenters' new hall had been rented to the Library Company in 1772, and throughout the first half of the nineteenth century portions of the building continued to be leased to a variety of tenants that included, among others, the Bank of the United States (which rented the whole building), the Bank of Pennsylvania, the Customs Office for the Port of Philadelphia, and the Musical Fund Society. The most famous tenant, however, was the First Continental Congress, which met in 1774 in Carpenters' Hall before it was feasible to move to quarters in the nearby State House.

In January of the same year that the Colonies declared their freedom from Great Britain, the first part of the new jail on Walnut Street directly behind the State House was completed (Fig. 21). Even though expression of function had never been a major concern of the designers of Renaissance buildings, it still comes as something of a surprise to discover that Robert Smith did not think it necessary to distinguish in any important way between the front elevation that he submitted for Philadelphia's gaol and the one he had used in 1754 for Nassau Hall at the College of New Jersey (now Princeton). Judged by later standards, the facilities of the new prison were extremely modest; the main building fronting on Walnut was of rough-hewn stone, two stories in height, and entered by a single central portal closed by two iron-grated doors. The sixteen cells facing the State House were each lit by two windows, and in each of the two wings that extended to the south, ten cells looked out onto the central courtyard. At first, additional space for prisoners was provided by dungeons in the basement, but these were later converted to storerooms. In the center of the roof was a cupola surmounted by a gilded weather vane, which appropriately took the form of the large key still preserved in the collections of the Atwater Kent Museum. On the south, the prison lot extended to the small building erected on Prune Street (now Locust) in 1785 as a workhouse and later set aside for those persons imprisoned for debt.

The Walnut Street Jail has been called "the first penitentiary in the world," but that title refers not as much to the main building as to the small rectangular structure in the rear, added in 1791. Built of brick in two stories and supported on arches to insure that the rooms would be dry and that the prisoners could not tunnel out, this was the "penitentiary house" in which were the sixteen cells, 6 feet by 8 feet by 9 feet high, intended for prisoners whose sentences called for solitary confinement. The practice of using imprisonment as punishment for crime has become so common that it is difficult to realize how novel it was in the eighteenth century. Heretofore a jail had usually been thought of as a place of temporary confinement for a prisoner who after his trial would be set free, fined, punished (by flogging, branding, the stocks, etc.), or executed. While awaiting trial persons who were financially able were expected to meet most of their own expenses, and the only pay the jailer received was the revenue he could extract in one way or another from his prisoners.

Quakers as a group opposed the harsh punishments of the day, which they regarded as unnecessarily degrading. Thus the penal code introduced by Penn was far more humane than most then in force in the other colonies; in contrast to the many capital crimes generally recognized, in Pennsylvania only treason and murder were punishable by death. It was against this background and at the urging of the Philadelphia Society for Alleviating the Miseries of Public Prisons that it was determined to send to the Walnut Street Jail the more serious offenders from all parts of the Commonwealth and to institute there changes designed to correct some of the worst aspects of the prevailing prison system. Henceforth, the jailers were to be paid from public funds, all prisoners were to receive the same treatment as directed by the court, regardless of wealth or position, and, perhaps most important, the conduct of the prison was to be under the constant surveillance of a Board of Inspectors, at least one of whom visited the premises every day. Those convicted of the more serious offenses, in other circumstances punishable by death, were to be subjected to "unremitting solitude at hard labor" for a period to be fixed by the court. Thus began the famous "Pennsylvania System," founded on the hope (false, as it turned out) that solitary confinement would force the contemplation of past faults, thus inducing repentance and, eventually, spiritual regeneration.

Probably the number of prisoners who were required to serve a part of their sentence in the "penitentiary house" is easily exaggerated. There is no denying, however, that during the last decade of the eighteenth century the Walnut Street Jail attracted the interest and admiration of many persons in Europe and America who were concerned with penal reform, or that from it the Pennsylvania system of solitary confinement spread throughout the world. But by 1800 the best days of the now famous Philadelphia prison were past; overcrowding of facilities that were no more than adequate in the first place probably contributed to the gradual breakdown of discipline. In 1835 the last prisoners were removed from the cells on Walnut Street to new quarters in the recently erected Philadelphia County Prison (Figs. 78 and 79) and the Eastern State Penitentiary (Fig. 77).

THE FEDERAL PERIOD
(c. 1775~c. 1810)

FROM 1790 UNTIL 1800 PHILADELPHIA WAS THE SEAT OF THE FEDERAL GOVERNMENT OF THE United States as well as the capital of the new state of Pennsylvania. The City Hall, which in 1790 had been built on the east side of the State House to supplant the earlier building on Market Street (Fig. 8) was now made the temporary home of the Supreme Court, and a place for the Congress to meet was provided by remodeling the County Court Building, which between 1787 and 1789 had been erected on the west side of the State House. Old prints such as that made by William Birch about 1803 (Fig. 22) suggest that these new additions to Independence Square look today very much as they did when first built. Only a few details such as the absence of quoins and the round-topped door and windows distinguish the style of the new buildings from that of the adjacent State House and indicate thereby a date of construction following the Revolution. When the federal government moved to the new city of Washington in 1800, the Supreme Court Building and Congress Hall, as these buildings continued to be called, reverted to the purposes for which they had been intended and for which they continued to be used by the City and County of Philadelphia until the completion of John McArthur's new building in Center Square, late in the nineteenth century.

Except possibly for the suppression of decorative details and a growing emphasis on flat surfaces, many of the buildings erected in Philadelphia shortly after the Revolution do not differ greatly from those built earlier in the century. One major change, however, was the appearance of the classic temple façade with massive free-standing columns, the so-called giant portico. Although this architectural form had been favored by Palladio and was often used by his English imitators, its appearance on public buildings in the Colonies prior to the Revolution was limited to a very few examples such as St. Philip's Church, Charleston (begun 1710; burned 1835), Peter Harrison's Redwood Library, Newport (1748), or St. Michael's Church, Charleston (1752). Had Christ Church been built a decade or two later, its design might well have included a pediment supported by classic columns in the manner of Wren or Gibbs. As it was, to Charleston goes the distinction of having in St. Philip's the first giant portico on an American colonial church. New York was fifty years behind with St. Paul's Chapel, designed by Thomas McBean perhaps as early as 1764, although the portico and spire were not actually constructed until 1794-96.

The first public building in Philadelphia to employ the giant order seems to have been the Presbyterian church which stood opposite the market sheds on the south side of High (Market) Street at the corner of Bank. Established on that site as early as 1704, "Old Buttonwood," as it was known to Philadelphians, had been enlarged at least twice in the 50's and 60's before it was entirely rebuilt in 1793-94. Although it was torn down many years ago, a view of the new façade with its imposing portico is provided by one of the Birches' best-known prints (Fig. 23); large Corinthian columns, unfluted in the Roman manner, rise from a high base to support a pediment adorned with the customary classic moldings and modillions. Perhaps the "Mr. Trumbul" mentioned by *Stephens's Philadelphia Directory, 1796* as the author of these innovations should be identified as John Trumbull, the painter of historical American subjects, who is known to have dabbled in architecture and who seems to have been in Philadelphia about 1792. But whatever the architect's identity, various details such as the giant pilasters, the enframement of the windows, and the urns on the corners of the roof suggest that the designer of one of Philadelphia's most impressive façades was still viewing his classic models through the eyes of his Renaissance predecessors.

The use of the giant order also characterizes the building that once housed the [First] Bank of the United States (Fig. 59) and still stands on Third at the head of Dock Street on the site of the gardens of Clarke Hall. After its incorporation was approved by Congress in 1791, the Bank of the United States had rented Carpenters' Hall until 1797, when it moved to its impressive new quarters designed by Samuel Blodgett, Jr., a talented businessman turned amateur architect. Copper sheets were sent over from England for the roof of Blodgett's bank, but the carving of the Corinthian capitals and such other architectural details as the acanthus-leaf modillions and the great mahogany eagle in the pediment was left to Claudius F. Le Grand, a French sculptor who from 1795 to 1801 maintained a yard at Tenth and Market streets in Philadelphia. Had the architect's plans been followed, the Bank of the United States would have been one of the first important buildings in America constructed entirely of marble. As it turned out, considerations of economy led the directors to specify brick for the sides and back—a decision for which there was ample precedent in Palladio—and even then, before it was finally finished in 1800, the bank had cost over $110,000, a very large sum for that time. The fact that Blodgett's design looks much like any large mansion of the period is consistent with Renaissance practice as well as a reminder that when today financial institutions are sometimes spoken of as banking "houses" it is because their predecessors had begun their existence in structures that were designed for or resembled private residences.

Earlier by five years than the design for the rebuilding of the First Presbyterian Church is the giant portico which in 1788 William Hamilton added to his mansion in West Philadelphia (Fig. 24). The Woodlands had been built about 1742 by Andrew Hamilton, named for his father mentioned earlier as the lawyer in part responsible for the design of the State House. Through marriage and their extensive shipping interests the Hamiltons increased the family fortune until on the eve of the Revolution, William Hamilton, second son of Andrew Hamilton II, was one of the richest men in Philadelphia. For a time after the Colonies had declared their independence it looked as though The Woodlands might be confiscated because of its owner's supposed Tory sympathies. The charge that William Hamilton had given aid to the enemy was never proved, but his fondness for things British is clearly revealed by his ideas on gardening and the other arts, especially architecture. In fact, it was shortly after his return from a trip to England that

Hamilton ordered the extensive changes made in The Woodlands that were designed to bring its appearance into harmony with more advanced European taste. The result was Philadelphia's first giant portico and one of the rare instances of that form employed for a private residence north of the Mason-Dixon Line prior to the nineteenth century.

Except for a few scattered examples such as Whitehall in Maryland (1764-65) and the Jumel Mansion in New York City (1765), colonial builders do not seem to have used the giant portico any more frequently for private residences than for public buildings. They did, however, favor the portico in two stories, a form also popular with Palladio. Before its later alteration, Jefferson's Monticello had such a feature, and other well-known examples include Drayton Hall in Charleston County (*c.*1740), the Miles Brewton House in Charleston (*c.*1765), and Shirley in Charles City County, Virginia (*c.*1769). As in the case of the five-part plan mentioned earlier for its connection with Mount Pleasant, the double portico is most frequently associated with the South where it doubtless afforded some relief from the heat. Never common farther north, in the Philadelphia area it existed, nonetheless, in one superb example. This was Lansdowne, the mansion on the Schuylkill built about 1773 for John Penn, twice governor of Pennsylvania and grandson of the founder (Fig. 25).

At Lansdowne the classic orders of the portico are superimposed, Ionic above Tuscan, in the manner prescribed by Palladio, following Vitruvius. In this, as in the quoins that accent the corners and the balustrade ornamenting the apex of the roof between the symmetrically spaced chimneys, the design conforms to what one would expect of a Middle Georgian house built shortly before the Revolution. In other elements, however, there is at least a hint of the style associated with the first decades of the new republic. Especially is this true of the polygonal bays, the elongated windows of the first floor, and perhaps an increasing emphasis on the flat surfaces of the walls.

The Late Georgian features that are only suggested at Lansdowne are far more explicit in the design of The Woodlands. Here, as elsewhere in this period, the flatness of the walls is unrelieved by belt course, quoin, or keystone. Round, oval, and semicircular shapes are extensively employed in both plan and elevation for bays, fanlights, niches, and especially the shallow recesses into which are set the round-topped windows that do much to impart to this post-Revolutionary style its distinctive flavor. But probably the most interesting part of the design of The Woodlands is the group of six large, but flat, pilasters that ornament the center of the north façade. The giant portico, after all, had been used by Palladio and his followers for two hundred years, whereas the giant pilaster, although derived ultimately from Alberti, was here employed in a way indicative of more recent English fashion, especially the work of Robert Adam (1728-1792). Presumably it was a building like Adam's Kenwood that William Hamilton had seen abroad and which on his return in 1788 he sought to imitate in the remodeling of his Philadelphia mansion.

Since the view of The Woodlands reproduced here is from the south, the giant pilasters are not visible, but similar ones may be seen on the new building erected about a year later by the Library Company (Fig. 26). Founded in 1731 as the earliest circulating library in America, the Library Company for the first sixty years of its life occupied rented quarters, which included the west wing of the State House (1740-73) and Carpenters' Hall (1773-90). To provide safe storage for their growing collections, by the end of the eighteenth century among the most extensive in the country, the directors in 1789 purchased a lot opposite the State House and advertised for the design of a new building that would be "as elegant as the unavoidable frugality of the plan will admit." The winner of this somewhat informal competition was Dr. William Thornton, a young physician who had only recently arrived in the city from the West Indies. Concerning his design for Library Hall, Thornton later recalled: "When I travelled, I never thought of architecture, but I got some books and worked a few days, then gave a plan in the ancient Ionic order, which carried the day." No specific titles or authors are mentioned, but the collections of the Library Company and the Carpenters' Company contained enough English architectural publications to supply all the help that an intelligent amateur needed. And Thornton soon proved to be both intelligent and resourceful. Of the books known to have been available in Philadelphia, Abraham Swan's *Collection of Designs in Architecture* (London, 1757) seems the most probable source for at least the façade of Library Hall. It may be assumed, also, that many of the architectural details were left to the discretion of the carpenter-builders, after the custom of the period.

Emboldened by his success in Philadelphia, in 1792 Thornton entered and won the competition for the national capitol, thereby determining the course of his future career. He never resumed the practice of medicine or returned to Philadelphia to live, preferring to remain in Washington, first as architect of the Capitol and later as head of the United States Patent Office. Among the most important residences that he designed during these years are Woodlawn (below Alexandria), Brentwood (in the District of Columbia), Tudor Place (in Georgetown) and the Octagon House (in the District). Built for John Tayloe about 1800 and used by the Madisons after the White House was damaged by the British, the Octagon House is today the national headquarters of the American Institute of Architects.

The statue of Dr. Franklin in the niche above the entrance of Library Hall was the gift of Senator William Bingham, the immensely rich Philadelphia banker, who had married the beautiful Ann Willing. The Binghams admired elegance and were not ashamed to show it. In 1790 they had leased Lansdowne from John Penn as their summer home, although only a year or two before—at about the same time that William Hamilton was remodeling The Woodlands—they had built on Third Street, just above Spruce, the finest city house Philadelphia had yet seen (Fig. 27). Set well back from the street amid extensive formal gardens, Bingham's town house was said to have been patterned after that of the Duke of Manchester in London, and such a source seems entirely credible. Visitors to the city, although not always approving of the magnificent style affected by the Binghams, described with more than a trace of envy the marble stair, which gave the front hall so "Roman" an air, and the mirrored parlors decorated throughout with the latest European furnishings. During such a visit to Philadelphia in 1789, Charles Bulfinch wrote his parents that he found the Bingham's town house "in a stile [*sic*] which would be esteemed splendid even in the most luxurious parts of Europe. Elegance of construction, white marble staircase, valuable paintings, the richest furniture and the utmost magnificence of decoration make it a palace . . . far too rich for any man in this country."

The Federal style, only suggested at Lansdowne and combined with the more massive forms of the Palladian at The Woodlands, is consistently expressed in nearly every part of the Bingham mansion. The lightest of cornices marks the roof line, and the quoins, stone lintels above the windows, and other boldly projecting elements characteristic of the Middle Georgian style are now considerably flattened or omitted altogether. Palladian balustrades crown the flat roofs of the two wings, but on the central block lighter railings, presumably of iron, guard the bottoms of the long windows extending almost to the floor of what must have been the principal parlors. Slender windows at either side enhance the graceful proportions of the doorway above which is the characteristic fanlight, larger and more elliptical in shape than at Lansdowne or The Woodlands, and here repeated with particular emphasis in the center of the façade at the third story. The footway posts lining the street in the Birch engraving were intended to keep wagons and horses from encroaching on the brick walks provided for pedestrians.

One other building in the old part of the city deserves mention in any discussion of the Federal style in Philadelphia. This was the structure erected at Third and Market streets about 1792 by Joseph Cooke, the goldsmith and jeweler (Fig. 28). Birch thought this sufficiently remarkable to include among his twenty-seven views of the city, and his opinion was apparently shared by most of his contemporaries. In the pursuit of his aim to create a block of shops and dwellings that would rival anything in London or Paris, Cooke had insisted on including all the latest architectural motifs wherever there was room and in some places where there was not. The upper three floors of "Cooke's building" were intended for elegant apartments, and the ground floor was given over to jeweler's shops so filled with "a grand display of mirrors, etc.," that they were invariably surrounded by crowds of curious spectators. The owner's shop was on the corner. This scheme sounds as though it should have succeeded, but as so often happens in such cases, Cooke soon found that his ideas were larger than his financial resources. An attempt to raffle off his building as part of a lottery failed, and one by one his tenants found other quarters. By the time "Cooke's Folly" was finally torn down about 1838 its fine apartments had been turned into workshops, its carved woodwork had long gone unpainted and "old hats and rags occupied the place of glass" in most of the windows.

Among the summer homes built by Philadelphians on the outskirts of the city, the finest example of the Federal style is the house designed for Robert Morris about 1770 and called by him The Hills. Here in the summer of 1797 the financier took refuge from his creditors, and from it the following winter he left for the debtor's prison on Prune Street. At the sheriff's sale a year later a portion of the estate was bought by Henry Pratt, who gave it the name of Lemon Hill by which it is known today. Opinions differ concerning the date of the present house, but its Federal lines clearly indicate a time after the Revolution when it must have been rebuilt or very extensively remodeled.

The front hall at Lemon Hill is lighted by slender windows beside the door as well as by an unusually large fanlight with delicate muntins, recalling the similar feature used

43

to light the hall of the Bingham mansion from the level of the third story. The large curved bay that sets Lemon Hill apart from such earlier mansions as Mount Pleasant and Cliveden is the exterior expression of the graceful oval parlor and dining room. Probably of French origin, the oval shape is found in the plans of numerous European buildings of the late eighteenth century. In America Hoban used it for the President's House in Washington, and it was so popular with New England builders that it has come to be regarded as a distinguishing mark of the Federal style. To such rooms as these Lemon Hill owes its place as one of the most delightful creations of a period known for the refinement and elegance of its architecture. Characteristic also are the stucco walls, especially valued by the Federal builders for their smooth unbroken surfaces.

In 1844 Lemon Hill was purchased by the city as a means of safeguarding the purity of the Schuylkill River, the source of the municipal water supply, and the following year the grounds were opened to the public. The drawing made by B. Ridgway Evans a few years later (Fig. 29) shows the house covered with signs and surrounded by picnickers, glad to escape the heat of the city for a few hours in the grounds of Robert Morris' old home. There, in addition to lager beer, could doubtless be bought a relatively new delicacy called "ice cream," said to have originated in Philadelphia about 1820. Most good prints of Lemon Hill date from the latter half of the nineteenth century and show the mansion surrounded by cast-iron verandas and crowned with one of the heavy bracketed cornices characteristic of the Victorian Period. The removal of these features and the restoration of the mansion to its present appearance about 1934 was predicated upon the evidence of old views like that reproduced here.

Speculation in western land was the principal cause of Robert Morris' financial ruin, but a contributing factor was the mansion which in 1794 he commissioned Pierre Charles L'Enfant to build for him on the south side of Chestnut between Seventh and Eighth (Fig. 30). L'Enfant was a French engineer who during the Revolution had been advanced to the rank of major in the Colonial army in recognition of his services at the siege of Savannah. When independence had been won and the representatives of the new republic assembled in New York City, it was L'Enfant who in 1788 remodeled the old City Hall for use by the Congress. As the first attempt at the creation of a national style, Federal Hall is of considerable importance in the history of American architecture. Its designer is principally remembered, however, as the author of the plan for the capital city which in 1790, after long debate, the Congress finally decided to locate on the banks of the Potomac. The basic plan of Washington as it exists today was proposed by L'Enfant, but unfortunately the temperamental French engineer proved so jealous and irascible that in February, 1792, the President felt obliged to end his federal service. From Washington L'Enfant went to New Jersey where he was engaged to lay out the town of Paterson as a center for cotton mills and related industries. His plans for this project included a masonry aqueduct supported on massive stone arches, the cost of which so alarmed his employers that the following year L'Enfant again found himself without regular employment. This meant that by 1794 he was free to devote his time and very considerable talents to designing a brick and marble palace for Robert Morris.

44

THE FEDERAL PERIOD (*c*.1775-*c*.1810)

Unfortunately L'Enfant does not seem to have profited from his previous experiences; his behavior in Philadelphia was much as it had been in Washington and New Jersey, and with much the same results. Two years after ground had been broken for his new mansion, Morris was still complaining to his architect that "the delay and accumulation of Expense [had become] intolerable," and L'Enfant was treating the matter in the same high-handed fashion that had characterized his relationship with his earlier clients. Inevitably the empty brick shell on Chestnut Street came to be known as "Morris' Folly." It was never finished and, except for the women prisoners from the Walnut Street Jail who were quartered there during the yellow fever epidemic of 1798, never occupied. Eventually it was dismantled and the expensive materials sold to satisfy Morris' creditors, leaving only the Birches' print as a record of what one English visitor referred to as "this superb mansion" that "bids defiance to simplicity and elegance."

In spite of such Federal features as the long windows and the rounded corners given to the bays projecting at either end of the façade, Morris' mansion brings to mind the Hôtel Biron in Paris and throughout has a French flavor that sets it apart from contemporary buildings in Philadelphia. Especially is this true of the mansard roof, surely the earliest American example of this characteristically French form that did not become popular on this side of the Atlantic until the 1860's. In addition to the door at either end, the main entrance was to have been in the center of the façade at the place marked in the drawing only by rotting boards and the two columns which were all of the impressive portico ever built. The small wooden structure at the left of the Birches' view is one of many set up at street corners as shelters for the watchmen who patrolled the streets at night, looking for signs of fire and crying the hour and the weather. Watchboxes like this one continued in use until fairly late in the nineteenth century, and one example is still preserved in the yard of the Friends' Meeting House at Fourth and Arch streets.

The magnificence of Morris' town house was rivaled in Philadelphia only by the the residence for the President of the United States, which in February, 1791, the Pennsylvania General Assembly had authorized be constructed at the southwest corner of Ninth and Market streets (Fig. 31). By this act of munificence the Assembly undoubtedly hoped to enhance the attractiveness of Philadelphia as the permanent capital of the country. L'Enfant is known to have been consulted about the presidential mansion, but there is no evidence that the building as finally erected was from his designs. Certainly it bears little similarity to the house a block away that he designed three years later for Robert Morris. Nor do the words "a private gentleman resident in the neighborhood of Philadelphia," used in 1795 by an English visitor to describe the architect of the presidential mansion, seem to fit the French engineer. They might better apply to Dr. William Thornton who had recently designed Library Hall, were it not for the fact that he seems to have been in the West Indies at the time when the drawings would have had to be prepared and approved. The cornerstone of the President's House was laid May 10, 1792, and Thornton did not return to Philadelphia until the following November. But the similarities between the design of the President's House and that with which Thornton won the competition for the national capitol seem too close to be entirely coincidental. If Thornton did not

45

design the former, he may at least have found there some of the architectural ideas that he embodied in the latter. Of those who are known to have been most closely connected with the President's House, the carpenter-builder Col. William Williams, a native of Philadelphia who had received some of his training in London, appears to have been the most competent and the most important. On at least one voucher Williams signed himself as "architect" of the President's House, and probably until proof to the contrary is discovered, we may so regard him.

After many delays and the expenditure of nearly $100,000, the mansion in Philadelphia was finally finished and in 1797 offered to President-elect John Adams, who declined it on constitutional grounds. Since it was now evident that it was not going to serve the purpose for which it had been built, the President's House was sold the following year to the University of Pennsylvania, which shortly thereafter employed Benjamin Henry Latrobe to make a study of the necessary alterations. The attractive building with the low dome that appears at the left of Strickland's drawing was added by Latrobe in 1805 for use by the Medical School.

To the extent that they reflect the more recent changes in European taste, the great houses built by the Hamiltons, Binghams, and Morrises cannot, of course, be considered typical of Philadelphia architecture in the Federal Period. Their owners, who must have had a deciding voice in determining the designs, were much more widely read and traveled than most Americans. Nor was it only a coincidence that at this time other important buildings in Philadelphia were frequently designed by persons of foreign birth; the engineer L'Enfant was a Frenchman, and Thornton was a native of the West Indies who had been educated at Edinburgh. Under the restraining influence of the conservative Carpenters' Company the majority of Philadelphia builders were slow to abandon the architectural forms of the Middle Georgian Period. Only a few details like the enlarged fanlights betray the later date of such a structure as the headhouse, which still stands on Second below Pine Street (Fig. 32). The first market sheds had been erected in this area as early as 1745 when the older market in High Street proved too inconvenient for the residents of Society Hill. Not until 1804, however, did the city Councils provided for the erection, at the northern end of the shambles, of the pleasant Late Georgian structure pictured in Evans' drawing. It was planned that the new headhouse should resemble in finish that at the southern end of the market and like it provide space on the ground floor for several fire engines. The room on the second floor was to be fitted with such "closets" as would make it convenient as a meeting place for fire companies "and for other purposes." Both the clock in the northern gable and the "alarm bell" in the cupola on the roof were the gifts of the citizens of the "lower district of the City." Although the headhouse at the Cedar Street end of the New Market was torn down in the middle of the nineteenth century, that at the Pine Street end still stands and is being restored by the city as part of the general rehabilitation of Society Hill.

Many of the meeting houses that had been established earlier continued to serve the Society of Friends in the period after the Revolution. The few that were built, such as that which still stands on the old Friends' Burial Ground at Fourth and Arch (c. 1804), continued

46

the plain style that had marked their predecessors. Mention should here be made, however, of the Quakers who, when they were disowned by their brethren for taking up arms in the American cause, built the meeting house on the southwest corner of Fifth and Arch. As if to underscore their patriotism, the Free Quakers, as they were called, recorded on the date stone of their new building that its construction had been accomplished 1,783 years after the birth of Christ and eight years after the establishment of the American "Empire."

The traditional design of most of the row houses built about the turn of the century is illustrated by the plans of Thomas Carstairs for twenty-two dwellings built shortly after 1800 on the south side of Sansom Street between Seventh and Eighth (Fig. 33). The doorway with its Tuscan columns and small fanlight will be recognized as a simplified version of a type met earlier at Mount Pleasant and frequently used by Philadelphia builders in the third quarter of the eighteenth century. Three and a half stories in height, with two rooms to a floor, the scheme of the Sansom Street houses has also been met before (p. 24) when it was described as having made its appearance early in the history of the city. Characteristic of this plan is the front parlor, which is smaller than the one in back by reason of the narrow hall leading from the front door to an open stairway in the center of the house. The only exceptions are the houses at either end of the row which, because of their location, can make use of side entrances, thereby saving the space of the entrance hall. Each room shown on the plan is heated by a fireplace opening into a chimney shared with the house adjacent.

Carstairs' houses were built on a portion of the lot formerly occupied by "Morris' Folly" (Fig. 30) and acquired at the sheriff's sale the year before by William Sansom, the prominent real estate promoter. About this same time Sansom also engaged Benjamin Henry Latrobe to design a block of houses, similar to those of Carstairs, but facing Walnut Street. Back to back, the two rows of houses thus formed a hollow square, and to preserve the character of this garden area, Sansom entered a deed restriction limiting the height of future back-buildings to ten feet. This was necessary because he hoped to sell the houses outright or under a mortgage-loan agreement. For some time after they were finished, however, many of the dwellings were leased at a yearly rental of $200. At this figure tenants were not plentiful who were willing to live so far from the business district, especially since Walnut Street was then paved only as far as Sixth. To help attract tenants and buyers, Sansom paved at his own expense the short street between Seventh and Eighth that he cut through and that still bears his name. He also offered to advance the money if the city Councils would extend the paving of Walnut Street for an additional two blocks.

Contiguous houses had long been the rule in Philadelphia, and earlier examples of groups of identical dwellings are certainly not unknown, but the Sansom and Walnut Street rows seem to have been the first examples in the city of the large-scale speculative development that became common in the nineteenth century. Although the idea of designing whole blocks as a unit can be traced back to the squares and terraces of Bath, London, and Dublin, the Sansom and Walnut Street rows are rightly recognized as an important step in the development of the Philadelphia house. Willis P. Hazard, in his supplement to

Watson's *Annals,* calls the Sansom Row "a novelty for that time," and Oberholtzer, quoting Mease, notes that when Sansom planned his rows "there was objection to houses built according to a uniform plan, which was a new idea in Philadelphia." Subsequent alterations have obscured Latrobe's and Carstairs' designs, but enough remains, especially on Walnut Street, to form some idea of the original appearance of what must have been an exceptionally attractive block of residences.

The Conestoga wagons that Evans included in his view of the New Market (Fig. 32) had doubtless brought garden produce from the fertile farms that lay to the west of the city. For anyone in Philadelphia to reach the western counties over the Lancaster turnpike it was of course necessary to cross the Schuylkill. Throughout the eighteenth century this had been accomplished by means of floating bridges. Washington's army used such a bridge in 1777 when it entered the city by way of Market Street, and today the designation Gray's Ferry, applied to a bridge and the avenue that crosses it, recalls the name of George Gray, one of the masters of the important Lower Ferry that lay on the route to the southern colonies.

As if to herald the economic promise of the nineteenth century, on Oct. 18, 1800, the cornerstone was laid for a new bridge at the Market Street crossing of the Schuylkill, called the Middle Ferry (Fig. 34). Because, unlike its floating predecessors, the Market Street Bridge was supported on two masonry piers sunk to bedrock forty-two feet below tidewater (a record at the time), it soon came to be known in Philadelphia as "The Permanent Bridge." William Weston of Gainsborough, England, drew plans for the caissons, but since he could not be in the United States while the bridge was under construction, Judge Richard Peters, President of the Schuylkill Bridge Company, undertook to supervise their execution, "there being no general engineer." The American designer of the wooden superstructure was Timothy Palmer of Newburyport, Massachusetts, who also brought with him from New England his assistant, a Mr. Samuel Carr, and four skilled workmen. Palmer's earlier training included experience with bridges over the Merrimac and Piscataqua rivers, and more recently he had built the bridge across the Potomac at Georgetown.

On Jan. 1, 1805, the Permanent Bridge was opened for traffic, and the following year the wooden cover was completed. In his account of the Schuylkill Bridge Company, Judge Peters takes full credit for the general concept and design of the protective covering, which in his view made the Market Street Bridge the only example of its kind in the world, an inferior covered bridge in northern Europe excepted. Such a claim probably fails to give due credit to foreign prototypes, but Peters does seem to have been correct in considering his the first covered bridge in America. In "delineating" his sketch for the cover Peters acknowledged the assistance of Adam Traquair and the benefit of the suggestions of John Dorsey, a director of the bridge company who later became its treasurer. Traquair was a skilled draftsman, the son of the Philadelphia sculptor, James Traquair, and we shall meet Dorsey again as one of the most interesting and imaginative amateur architects active in Philadelphia in the first quarter of the nineteenth century. Although later notices credit Dorsey with having designed the cover of the Permanent Bridge, there is nothing in Peters' account to indicate that he played any very significant part in its evolution. Of greater im-

48

portance was the contribution of Owen Biddle, who executed the design for the cover, and whom Peters mentions as "an ingenious carpenter and architect of Philadelphia, who made additions to the design." Biddle is generally considered to have been the builder of the Arch Street Meeting House and is remembered also as the author of *The Young Carpenter's Assistant,* a builder's guide that he brought out in 1805. To judge from his writings, Biddle's professional views were rather conservative, but he deserves mention as being among the first to suggest that there is, or ought to be, "a system of architecture adapted to the style of building in the United States." These words, which serve as the subtitle of Biddle's book, were echoed the following year by his New England contemporary, Asher Benjamin, in the full title he gave his *American Builder's Companion.* Both authors were native-born Americans who sought to capitalize on the growing awareness of the national identity.

Although none of the prints shows them, it is known that about 1812 William Rush carved for the Permanent Bridge the wooden statues of Commerce and Agriculture that had been "contemplated in the original design." Beyond the fact that these were described as "recumbent" figures, which might therefore appropriately have adorned the pediments at either end of the bridge, it is not known where Rush's figures were placed. Passage over the Market Street Bridge was made free of toll when it was bought by the city in 1840, and ten years later it was rebuilt to allow the tracks of the City Railroad to connect with those of the Columbia and Pennsylvania line. Rush's statues appear to have been still on the bridge when it burned Nov. 20, 1875.

In describing the major buildings erected in Philadelphia between the Revolution and the War of 1812, attention has been called to the elegance and sophistication with which many of the designers handled the classical forms inherited from their predecessors. Historians who seek to emphasize the continuity of the Renaissance tradition would doubtless prefer to speak of the taste of this period as "Late Georgian." Others would consider that the architectural forms most favored, the curving bays, flatter roofs, long windows, slender muntins, elliptical fanlights, and plain walls, when taken together constitute a distinctive style which, corresponding as it does to the first decades of the new republic, deserves the name of "Federal." Both terms are correct, and both could be considered somewhat misleading: Georgian because it might seem to give too little weight to the national qualities of the style; Federal because it might imply the absence of European influences.

Although domestic buildings such as the Bingham mansion or Lemon Hill have a distinctly American flavor, the original inspiration for their style is no less unmistakably European. In France a fondness for simple geometric shapes and plain surfaces also distinguishes the style of Louis XVI from the curvilinear forms of the Rococo, associated with his predecessor. Similarly in England a more graceful interpretation of classical decorative motifs appears about 1760 in the work of the brothers Robert and James Adam, noted earlier for their probable influence on the design of The Woodlands. Nor is evidence of direct contact between Europe and America wanting. Thornton and L'Enfant have already been mentioned for the part they played in the history of Philadelphia architecture, but the names of other European architects active in America come no less readily to mind:

49

in Baltimore the unhappy Maximilian Godefroy, who gave America its first Gothic church and first Egyptoid public monument; in New York Joseph-François Mangin who, with native-born John McComb, built the City Hall, one of the few distinguished buildings erected in Manhattan before the second quarter of the nineteenth century; in Washington Etienne Hallet who, but for Thornton, would have been the designer of the Capitol, and James Hoban the Dublin-trained architect of the White House, who practiced briefly in Philadelphia about 1785. And this list could easily be doubled. Of the major eastern states only those of New England seem to have preferred to find their architects among native sons.

But whether transmitted to America via France or England, the principal source of the new attitude toward classical architecture was the archaeological discoveries that had been taking place in Italy since the middle of the eighteenth century. Excavations at the buried city of Herculaneum began in 1738, and even richer treasures were yielded by the ashes of Pompeii, uncovered a decade later. As a result, many Europeans now for the first time became aware of the light and playful character of late Roman wall decoration. To be sure, Raphael and his contemporaries had admired and used such motifs in their designs for the interiors of Renaissance palaces and villas, but this fact had been largely overlooked or forgotten, so universal was the admiration for the heavier forms of Palladio.

The excavations at Herculaneum and Pompeii were followed by the exploration of other ancient sites, not only in Italy but in Greece and the Near East as well. Soon books about these new archaeological discoveries began to supplant Palladio and his translators and imitators as a source for architectural designs: the Italian artist Giovanni Battista Piranesi (d.1778) dramatized the civilization of Rome in his etchings; the German scholar Johann Joachim Winckelmann (1717-1768) fostered an interest in Greek sculpture through his writings; the French antiquarian Charles-Louis Clérisseau called attention to the classic monuments of his country in his *Antiquités de la France* (1774). Among the first of many Englishmen to become interested in the study of ancient art was Robert Adam who spent the years 1754 to 1757 in Italy and Dalmatia studying Roman villas and sharing the enthusiasm for antiquity of his friends Winckelmann and Piranesi.

When he returned to England, Adam eventually published the *Ruins of the Emperor Diocletian at Spalatro, in Dalmatia* (1764), but his fame rests principally upon his skill as a designer of interiors in the neoclassic manner. Based on what he had seen in Italy, Adam recognized that the massive classical orders made popular by the Palladian school had been used by the Romans for public buildings rather than for private residences. With his new awareness of Roman decoration for his inspiration, in the interiors of important English houses such as Syon (1763), No. 20 St. James's Square (1772), and Lansdowne (1762, the drawing room of which is now in the Philadelphia Museum of Art) Adam demonstrated how effectively slender colonnettes might be interspersed with arabesques of the greatest delicacy to form a tasteful background for contemporary British life. Such motifs as the fan, urn, and medallion, which he used with particular finesse, were also carried into the furnishings required to complete the spacious effect of rooms decorated in the new style. The result of the fresh view of antiquity afforded by archaeological discovery and popular-

50

ized by the Adam brothers was little short of a revolution in English taste. Its effects are visible in the furniture of George Hepplewhite (d.1786) and Thomas Sheraton (1751-1806), the pottery of Josiah Wedgwood (1730-1795), the painting of Angelica Kauffmann (1741-1807), and the sculpture of John Flaxman (1755-1826). With modifications it carried over into the period of the Regency, when during the incapacity of George III (1738-1820) the royal authority was vested in the Prince of Wales, later George IV (1762-1830).

In America the Adamesque style is most closely identified with the graceful and delicate details that characterize much of the architecture of New England. The essential spirit of the Gardner-White-Pingree House in Salem (1810) or the Gore Mansion (1806) at Waltham, Massachusetts, for example, is not unlike somewhat earlier work in England, except that American builders often used for doorways and cornices delicate motifs which in Europe had usually (though not exclusively) been reserved for the drawing room or boudoir. It should be pointed out, however, that for the most part the New England houses are considerably later than Philadelphia examples such as The Woodlands or the Bingham mansion. It may be doubted, also, whether even the finest products of the skill of Samuel McIntire (1757-1811) or Charles Bulfinch (1763-1844) surpass in architectural distinction the central pavilion that was added to the Pennsylvania Hospital between 1794 and 1805 (Fig. 35). In place of the low Roman dome originally planned, a circular balustrade crowns the roof, marking the site of the skylight of the surgical amphitheater below. This unusual feature, the first of its kind in an American building, attracted favorable attention, including that of Charles Bulfinch, who visited Philadelphia in preparation for the task of designing the Massachusetts General Hospital at Boston. From the graceful doorway, with its sidelights and embracing fan, through the shallow pilasters, which give unity and monumentality to the façade, to the pediment, with its oval window and light cornice decorated with rosettes, the Center House of the Pennsylvania Hospital is a nearly perfect example of a style that has itself been called "one of the most . . . nearly perfect of American architectural achievements."

The appearance of the Philadelphia skyline in the first decade of the nineteenth century is suggested by the water color (Fig. 36) that Boqueta De Woiseri made about 1810 from a point on the Jersey short not far from that taken sixty years earlier by George Heap for his "East Prospect" (end papers). Independence Hall, the old Town Hall, and Christ Church are still prominent landmarks, as they had been for more than half a century, but the spire built on Arch Street by the Presbyterians and that erected on Race Street by the Dutch Calvinists are now gone. The tall structure looming above Southwark on the left is one of the earliest shot towers in the country, erected about 1807 by Bishop & Sparks and still standing on the north side of Carpenter (John) Street, west of Front. Both this and the contemporary tower built by Paul Beck on the other side of town were the direct result of the embargo on British exports that preceded the War of 1812. When war was finally declared and the firm of Bishop & Sparks was asked to divert its product from the use of sportsmen to the support of the American armies, Bishop, being a Friend, withdrew from the partnership.

Presumably the people standing on the wharf, like those approaching it in Boqueta De

Woiseri's painting, are waiting for a boat to take them to Philadelphia. Although it appears that they may have to depend upon oars to reach the other side, in the early years of the nineteenth century steam began to be used for the ferries that in one form or another had plied between the New Jersey and Pennsylvania shores almost from the founding of Penn's great town.

ROMANTIC ECLECTICISM
(c. 1810 - c. 1860)

THE NEW ARCHAEOLOGICAL DISCOVERIES OF THE EIGHTEENTH CENTURY HELPED TO ESTABLISH the modern concept of history. Gradually style came to be recognized as the imprint on artistic form of the point of view of the culture that produced it. So widely is this principle accepted today that it is difficult to realize what an exciting discovery it appeared to a generation that had heretofore believed that the world was not more than about four thousand years old and which, when Charles Willson Peale exhumed his mastodon, was reluctant to accept it on the grounds that the Creator would never permit any of his creatures to become extinct. Undoubtedly the most important factor in the history of nineteenth-century architecture is the fact that the nineteenth-century architect himself discovered history.

For Americans a century and a half ago the contemplation of the past became an exhilarating experience. A glimpse of the architectural style associated with a former civilization was all that was required to give rise to the most pleasurable associations in the mind of the historically oriented spectator. One of the results of this new awareness of history was a change in the basis of artistic judgment. Time itself became endowed with aesthetic possibilities. From the Renaissance qualities of proportion, balance, and symmetry inherent in the object, emphasis now shifted to the reactions evoked in the observer by the work of art. Greatness in the realm of art came more and more to be identified with the number and sublimity of the ideas and emotions experienced by the critic. For the nineteenth century beauty was indeed in the eye of the beholder, and if many of the buildings of that period no longer have the power to evoke in us the same enthusiastic response as they did a century or more ago, it is not so much that age has changed the work of art as that we no longer view it with the same sympathetic eye.

This more subjective approach to art is usually described by the word "Romantic" and in America is identified most closely with the period from the War of 1812 to that between the States. Used in this context, the term does not necessarily imply the wavering grasp of reality that is often supposed. On the contrary, writers of the period are apt to put fully as much emphasis on the useful and the practical as upon the Beautiful and the Picturesque. Scratch the surface of the most Romantic aesthete and you will frequently find a scientist underneath. Robert Fulton and Samuel F. B. Morse are only the best known of a considerable number of nineteenth-century artists whose scientific contributions overshadowed their artistic achievements. It is true, of course, that the romantic spirit is usually discontented with its own environment and seeks escape by excursions into the world of memory and imagination. For such flights into the past in time and to the distant in place, the new understanding of history supplied the ideal vehicle.

Principally because of the emphasis given to the classical revivals in the nineteenth century, some historians prefer to consider what has here been called the Romantic Era as essentially the culmination of the Renaissance interest in the past. Although not without foundation, since every age is in some degree the product of what preceded it, this view seems inadequate in that it equates similarity of motivation with similarity of result. The Roman architectural forms characteristic of the eighteenth century may occasionally resemble those found in the nineteenth, but in most cases the reasons that lay behind their selection were distinctly different. The Renaissance architect regularly used variants of classical motifs because they were all he knew; the Romantic architect occasionally chose Greek or Roman models from among the many styles available to him because of the way he *felt* about them. And there, of course, is the crux of the matter. Renaissance architecture appeals fundamentally to the human reason; that of the nineteenth century to the emotions. This is the usual definition of "Classic" and "Romantic" which, so defined, appear as the antithesis of each other. But in the period here under discussion the traditional meaning of these words tends to become somewhat blurred. In the sense that the Greek and Roman are among the many styles favored for their emotional impact, Classicism becomes for a time a phase of Romanticism. This is one of the reasons why the nineteenth century is sometimes difficult to understand—and also why it is of such unusual interest.

Of the other implications for architecture of the Romantic view of life, only one or two need be mentioned here. The observation that artistic style is the expression of culture led to value judgments concerning the moral worth of the civilizations of the past. Favorable opinion of a work of art came more and more to be predicated upon acceptance of the supposed ethical and religious beliefs of those who had created it. In this way the Beautiful became somehow confused with the Good and the True, and judgments concerning art turned out to be based upon nonartistic criteria. However fallacious, this attitude proved to have remarkable vitality. Even in the twentieth century architectural critics who prided themselves on their contemporary view of art would continue to reveal their nineteenth-century heritage by favoring architecture that was "clean," "honest," and "truthful."

Of more artistic validity than the moral bias of Romanticism was the practice of nineteenth-century architects of using the memories and emotions engendered by a historic style to suggest the purpose of their buildings. Expression of function was not, as we have seen, a part of the architectural theory of the Renaissance. Together with a new concern for the site, for the materials of construction, and for the individuality of the client, this interest in the expression of function is among the more specifically architectural contributions of the Romantic Era.

THE ROMAN REVIVAL

Since Pompeii and Herculaneum were the first of the ancient sites to be excavated, it was to be expected that one of the earliest fruits of the new archaeological approach to the past would be a revived interest in Roman antiquities. The name "Pantheon" popularly applied by Parisians to the Church of Sainte Geneviève is evidence of the Roman source to which the French architect Jacques Germain Soufflot (1709-1780) had turned as early as the 1750's for the design of his free-standing portico. But it was not as much the artistic talents of the Romans as their supposed moral virtues that attracted Napoleon and his court to the classical paintings of Jacques Louis David (1748-1825) and the sculpture of Antonio Canova (1757-1822). Fortunately for the classicists, Rome had been both a republic and an empire, so there was no need to search for new models when the imperial ambitions of Napoleon got the better of his earlier democratic sentiments. Thus the Roman Revival and Romantic notions of the moral basis of art underlie the Empire style, whether in costume, furniture, or such architectural examples as the Vendôme Column and the Arc du Carrousel.

But if the Roman Revival appears early and most clearly in France, it was certainly not confined to that country. In England about 1805 Sir John Soane used the order of the so-called Temple of Vesta at Tivoli as a part of the additions he made to the Bank of England. Nor was America unaware of the implications of the new discoveries. There at least as early as 1785 Thomas Jefferson had conceived of a capitol for Virginia modeled after the best-preserved of all Roman temples, the Maison Carrée at Nîmes. Mindful of the difficulty of carving the complicated Corinthian capitals, Jefferson agreed to substitute for those of the original "the modern [Ionic] order of Scamozzi," a pupil and follower of Palladio. Although he took this step with evident reluctance, Jefferson did not mean to abandon his admiration for Renaissance architecture. On the contrary, he continued to use Palladian motifs at Monticello and even went as far as to propose a design for the official residence of the President of the United States based on Palladio's Villa Rotonda at Vicenza. Jefferson's attitude toward classic models points up the difficulty of separating those architectural forms that stem directly out of a new interest in archaeology from those that had descended indirectly through Vitruvius and the Italian Renaissance. The source was Roman architecture in both cases, and since the fourth part of Palladio's *I Quattro Libri dell' architettura* deals with specific ancient temples, which he describes and illustrates in some detail, this may on closer examination prove to be a distinction without much of a difference.

Perhaps for this reason it is difficult to point to buildings in Philadelphia that may be cited as unqualified examples of the Roman Revival. Some historians would see the more archaeological approach to antiquity in the use of the temple portico for the First Presbyterian Church (Fig. 23), Blodgett's Bank (Fig. 59), and The Woodlands (Fig. 24). Yet there seems no obligation to seek the origin of this feature beyond the revived interest in Palladio associated in England with the Earl of Burlington (1695-1753) and his protégés, William Kent (d.1748) and Colin Campbell (d.1729), and in America with the work of Thomas Jefferson. Especially is this true when, as in this case, the Roman forms are combined with architectural elements of unmistakable Renaissance origin.

To the extent that the Adamesque was derived from a study of the decoration of Roman houses and villas, the Federal style discussed in the preceding section may also be regarded as one aspect of the Roman Revival. As described here, however, the distinctive qualities of the art of the Adam brothers are best exemplified by their interior designs.

55

For the exteriors of their buildings more massive forms were regularly employed, and it may well be that the increased monumentality apparent in American architecture after the turn of the century also owes something to the newer archaeological approach to art.

In this category of later Federal structures is the first home of the Pennsylvania Academy of the Fine Arts (Fig. 37). This was erected in 1805 from the plans of the same John Dorsey mentioned earlier for his connection with the design of the wooden cover of the Permanent Bridge, with which the new building for the Academy is contemporary. Between about 1785 and his death in 1821 Dorsey appears variously as a grocer, sugar refiner, state senator (1805-9), auctioneer, and "keeper of the standard of weights and measures." The extent of his activities as an amateur architect is indicated by a letter written in 1806 by Benjamin Henry Latrobe to his father-in-law Isaac Hazlehurst: "As to private business, I shall get none . . . ," wrote Latrobe bitterly, "John Dorsey has now no less than 15 plans now in progress of execution, because he charges nothing for them." Since it preceded Robert Cary Long's Peale Museum in Baltimore by at least eight years, Dorsey's Academy ranks as the first art museum in America. It may, in fact, be one of the first buildings in the world erected specifically for that purpose, inasmuch as most European museums were like the Louvre originally designed as palaces.

In the flatness of the walls and the use of round-topped windows the Academy conforms to the Federal manner, described earlier, but the low dome and deep porch with the two Ionic columns *in antis* might also be considered as showing the influence of the Roman Revival. Evidence of the new archaeological interest in antiquity should certainly be seen in the emphasis placed on sculpture in Dorsey's design. On the interior the central rotunda beneath the dome served as a gallery for the display of plaster casts of classical statues. These had been made in Paris at the Musée Napoleon through the good offices of the youthful Nicholas Biddle, then Secretary of the American Legation, but when set up at the Academy their nudity made it seem desirable to set Mondays aside "with tender gallantry for ladies exclusively." On the exterior, sphinxes—unusual for this time and place—decorated the parapets at either side of the stairs, and above the entrance an eagle clutched in his talons an artist's palette and brushes to indicate the purpose of the building.

Early in the Federal Period American eagles like that on the Academy had become extremely popular as the symbol of the new republic. William Rush, among others, is known to have carved this subject in a number of poses for a variety of clients. For this reason, and because there seem to have been in the city at that time few, if any, other sculptors capable of handling figures of such size and complexity, we are probably justified in adding these pieces of sculpture to the list of works attributed to this Philadelphia wood carver who has been called "the first native-born American sculptor." Such an attribution is further supported by the fact that Rush was on the building committee, which also numbered among its five members John Dorsey, architect of the new home of the Academy.

In the spring of 1845 a serious fire at the Academy left standing only the walls of Dorsey's rotunda. Such important Philadelphia architects as John Notman and John Haviland are known to have submitted designs for the rebuilding, but in the end the commission went to Richard A. Gilpin, a man otherwise unknown, whose chief qualification may have been a brother on the building committee of the Board. Sartain's engraving (Fig. 38) shows that to Dorsey's rotunda Gilpin added a more monumental entrance, still with two Ionic columns *in antis* but now much enlarged and supporting a classic pediment. The low hipped roofs of the lateral extensions provide for skylights that furnish the illumination for the pictures hung on the windowless walls below. The Academy continued to occupy the building on Chestnut Street until 1870, when it was sold in preparation for the move to the present location at Broad and Cherry streets.

Many of the qualities of Dorsey's design for the Academy are also shared by the Orphan Asylum erected in 1817 on the northeast corner of Cherry and Eighteenth streets (Fig. 39). Such features as the flatness of the walls, the fondness for the fan motif, and the large inset arch in the center of the façade bear witness to the persistence of the Federal style in Philadelphia. But at the same time the emphasis given the Tuscan columns of the porch suggests the neoclassic, as do the small figures resting on the entablature above. For this last feature the unknown designer of the orphanage seems to have had in mind the sculptural decoration frequently found in the pediments of classical temples. Here again the name of William Rush inevitably comes to mind. There are, in fact, a number of extant works by Rush that appear to be inspired by classic pedimental sculpture of a type not unlike that suggested in the view of the Asylum included here. This is especially true of the figures of Faith, Hope, and Charity now owned by the Grand Lodge, Free and Accepted Masons of Pennsylvania, and presumed once to have adorned the Masonic Hall designed by William Strickland (Fig. 74). Could these be related in some way to pieces of sculpture intended for the Orphanage on Cherry Street?

All in all, the architectural design of the Asylum seems too imaginative to be the work of the typical Philadelphia carpenter-builder and too naïve to be the product of a professional architect. Perhaps until a better candidate is found, we should suspect here the hand of John Dorsey. In 1822 the Asylum burned, and the short life of the building may help to account for its neglect by later historians.

THE GREEK REVIVAL

Although the view that the first building of the Pennsylvania Academy of the Fine Arts was the work of Benjamin Henry Latrobe has now been disproved, it seems altogether likely that John Dorsey was strongly influenced by Latrobe's earlier work in Philadelphia. This becomes apparent when the low dome and recessed portico of the Academy are compared with similar features of the Pump House, which Latrobe designed for Center Square about 1800 (Fig. 40).

In the late eighteenth century serious epidemics had proved to Philadelphians the undesirability of depending on shallow wells for drinking water. As an alternative, Latrobe proposed that steam pumps be used to draw water from the Schuylkill through a settling basin to a water tank in Center Square, whence it could be distributed by wooden pipes to all parts of the city. In spite of the opposition of those who hoped to profit from the construction of a gravity aqueduct and the general reluctance of the public to rely on mechanical devices in any form, Latrobe was commissioned to begin the new waterworks in the spring of 1799. Unexpected delays followed, while costs mounted, but on the morning of Jan. 27, 1801, surprised Philadelphians awoke to find clear water flowing from open hydrants into the gutters of the streets.

An attractive water color by the Russian diplomat Pavel Petrovitch Svinin shows the Pump House set in a pleasant park (Fig. 41). Smoke from the steam pump built by the erratic inventor Nicholas Roosevelt of New York issues from an opening in the top of the dome, while in front of Latrobe's classic building a man spreads his arms wide in wonder at the sight of William Rush's fountain. Presumably the unknown spectator shares the astonishment of many Philadelphians at the boldness with which the sculptor has revealed the form of his female model, known in this case to have been a certain Nancy Vanuxem, the daughter of one of Rush's friends. Before the Pump House was torn down in 1827, Rush's "Nymph and Bittern" were moved to the site of the new waterworks on the bank of the Schuylkill, and when about 1850 the wood from which the figures were carved showed signs of deteriorating, the group was cast in bronze at the important Philadelphia foundries of Robert Wood & Co. Today the cast of Rush's "Nymph and Bittern" in the Philadelphia Museum of Art is all that remains of the delightful park in Center Square. It also serves as a reminder of the significant place occupied by sculpture in the classical designs of the early nineteenth century when Philadelphia was earning the title of "Athens of America."

In at least one important way the classical forms of Latrobe's Pump House differ from those of Dorsey's Academy. The columns of the portico of Latrobe's building are no longer Roman, but Greek. This is evident from the lack of bases, and, what is more, the overhang of the capitals marks them as derived from the somewhat archaic Greek models apparently favored by Latrobe in his earlier work.

It did not take long after the discovery of Pompeii and Herculaneum for interest to spread to Greek art, which gradually came to be recognized as earlier and in some respects superior to that of the Romans. Winckelmann, among others, directed attention to Greek antiquities, and in 1768 Thomas Major published reports of the important ruins at Paestum, a site to the south of Pompeii. But of all the books on Greek art none was as influential as the three-volume *Antiquities of Athens,* brought out in London by James Stuart and Nicholas Revett, beginning in 1762. Only Vitruvius and Palladio had greater influence on the history of Western architecture.

Although the Greek Revival cannot be said to have appeared first in America (K. G. Langhans, for example, had designed the Brandenburg Gate in Berlin c.1789) it seems to have been more popular there than in Europe. One explanation for this lay in the ideas then associated with the culture and institutions of the ancient Greeks. Much as the French had earlier considered the "republican" background of Roman art sufficient justification for its use to express the ideals of the French Revolution, Americans now found that the "democratic" qualities of Greek art made it an especially appropriate model for their new

58

nation. This belief was re-enforced by the War of Independence (1821-29) by which the Christian Greeks won their freedom from Moslem Turkey in a fashion that seemed to Americans to parallel their own struggle with Great Britain. As a result, the Greek Revival in America achieved something approaching the status of a national style. Scores of towns and cities were given such names as Corinth, Troy, and Syracuse. Hiram Powers' (1805-1873) "Greek Slave" was extravagantly praised on both sides of the Atlantic, and in Italy through the 1830's Horatio Greenough (1805-1852) labored to complete for the United States government his statue of George Washington, nude to the waist, in the guise of Olympian Zeus.

The first important American building to make use of one of the Greek orders is usually considered to have been the Bank of Pennsylvania erected between 1798 and 1801 from the designs of Benjamin Henry Latrobe (Fig. 42). In discussing earlier Philadelphia buildings the term "architect" has been used with some freedom, since most of the designers were, in fact, either talented amateurs as were Kearsley, Thornton, Blodgett, and Dorsey or such skilled craftsmen as Edmund Woolley, Owen Biddle, and Robert Smith who had been trained as carpenter-builders. Except possibly for one or two such men as L'Enfant or Hoban, neither of whom remained long in Philadelphia or made any lasting impression on the architecture of the city, Latrobe is the first person we have met who may be called an architect in the modern sense. Born in Yorkshire and educated in Germany, he had spent two years as chief draftsman in the London office of Samuel Pepys Cockerell, a conservative architect who adhered to the earlier Palladian tradition. While in London, Latrobe must have been attracted to the severe lines of the newer classicism of the younger Dance (1741-1825) and Sir John Soane (1753-1837) whose work his own mature style often resembles. Saddened by the death of his young wife, Latrobe came to the United States in 1795 seeking a new environment for his talents. There he settled first in Norfolk, Virginia.

The commission for the Bank of Pennsylvania was a milestone in Latrobe's life. It led him to establish his practice in Philadelphia where he made his architectural reputation and where he entered into a second marriage that continued a rare source of happiness in an otherwise tragic life. The Bank is also Latrobe's first public commission of importance. No other building is as central to an understanding of his career, and few are as significant for the history of American architecture.

At the core of the style of the Bank of Pennsylvania is the "stripped classic" manner associated in England with Dance and Soane and sometimes in America with a number of architects whose activity coincides with the beginning of the Greek Revival. To the plain surfaces and arched and inset windows of the late Federal style, Latrobe has added his favorite Roman dome and classic porticoes based on Greek models, elements that appear again in many of his later designs such as the competition drawings for the New York City Hall (1802), his suggested modifications for the national capitol (1803-12; 1815-17), the Baltimore Cathedral (1804-21), and the Baltimore Exchange (1816-20). A drawing now in the Maryland Historical Society shows that had the Bank been built as the architect had first intended, it would have adhered more closely to the canons of the classical

59

revivals. As executed, the stepped dome over the banking hall was suppressed on the exterior in favor of a cupola that must have given the building a somewhat Georgian cast. For the roof of the cupola, however, Latrobe retained a Roman dome like those he repeated on the four lodges at the corners of the lot.

The right of the Bank of Pennsylvania to be considered "the country's first Greek Revival structure" is based, of course, on the Ionic capitals of the two porticoes. These, like the rest of the building, Latrobe is sometimes said to have designed "out of his own head" without reference to books of any kind. Although this statement may be true of the bank as a whole, it can hardly apply to the Ionic order of the porches. A recently discovered drawing by Latrobe's assistant Frederick Graff (Fig. 43) leaves no doubt that the specific source of the capitals was, in fact, the much-admired north porch of the Erectheum at Athen as illustrated in the second volume of Stuart and Revett (Fig. 44). The cost of fluting the columns and of carving the anthemion (honeysuckle) band at the neck probably led to the abandonment of these details, but the form and treatment of the other moldings are too close to the Greek model to have been coincidental. The rectangular chimneys of the Bank we have also met before on the Pennsylvania Academy of the Fine Arts, additional evidence of Dorsey's dependence upon Latrobe for many of his architectural ideas.

On the whole, the residences that Latrobe designed in Philadelphia represent less of a departure from prevailing practice than do his public buildings. The row of houses on Walnut Street commissioned about 1800 by William Sansom was noted earlier. A few of these have survived, at least in part, but all the other Philadelphia examples of Latrobe's domestic style were destroyed many years ago. Because of his financial problems, William Waln, the China merchant, found it prudent to sell his house (built 1805-8) on the southeast corner of Chestnut and Seventh streets to Dr. William Swaim who had made a fortune from the sale of patent medicine. Swaim had the house converted into a public bath in 1828 and about 1848 his son had the bath torn down and replaced with "Silsbee's Atheneum and Museum," later leased by Phineas T. Barnum. A similar fate befell the Marcoe House (built 1808-10), also on Chestnut Street, which in spite of the latest appointments (including one of the first complete bathrooms in Philadelphia) was abandoned as a private residence and turned into a hotel within a few years after it was completed.

Talbot Hamlin has called the large house on Chestnut at Ninth Street, designed by Latrobe about 1801 for Edward Shippen Burd, "an almost arrogant challenge to the prevailing Philadelphia conservatism" (Fig. 45). Perhaps this was true of the plan and the severity of the lines, but the individual elements of the façade seem to offer little that is new. Especially noticeable by their absence are such features as the free-standing columns and domed rotundas used by Latrobe with such success in his earlier houses in Washington and Virginia. Here the prominence given to the inset arches is evidence of the architect's continuing reliance upon motifs of the Federal style not unlike those used earlier by the designer of the Bingham mansion (Fig. 27).

Not all Latrobe's work in Philadelphia was connected with the designs of new buildings. Several of his commissions were for alterations to existing structures. The Medical School added in 1805 to the President's House by the University of Pennsylvania was

60

illustrated in Figure 31. Another such commission was the remodeling of "Old Drury," the theater on Chestnut Street, built about 1793.

The role played by Philadelphia in the early development of the American theater is an interesting one. Although the prohibition of plays and players that Penn had included in the Great Law of 1682 was not formally repealed by the Assembly until 1789, we hear of an occasional play being produced in Philadelphia at least as early as 1749. In spite of protests from Quakers, Baptists, and Methodists, David Douglass was even permitted in 1766 to erect a permanent structure on South above Fourth Street to house his "American Company." Known as the Southwark Theater, this simple brick building continued to be used for plays until the early years of the nineteenth century, when it was turned into a liquor warehouse. Here was given in 1767 Thomas Godfrey's *The Prince of Parthia*, "the first play, written by an American, to be produced upon an American stage by a professional company." During the Revolution the Congress tried with indifferent success to discourage "exhibitions of shews, plays and other expensive diversions and entertainments," and after the war it became increasingly clear that Philadelphia would need a new theater more in keeping with its status as capital of the country.

The building that the comedian Thomas Wignell opened Feb. 17, 1794, on Chestnut above Sixth Street is said to have been copied from the Royal Theatre at Bath, England, but whatever the source of its design it was probably the most elaborate playhouse erected in the United States. And soon even this was outmoded. In 1801 Latrobe was engaged to improve the lobbies and withdrawing rooms and presumably to give the façade a more fashionable appearance. Although the exterior of the Chestnut Street Theater pictured in the second edition of Birch's engravings (Fig. 46) is sometimes cited as the work of Latrobe, earlier representations of the building on stock certificates and in the first edition of Birch's views make it clear that he was responsible principally for the Corinthian colonnade and the low wings at either end. Lack of funds made necessary wooden columns with capitals of papier mâché, but the faces of the wings were of marble and above the doorway in each can be distinguished one of the semicircular reliefs of the tragic and comic Muses originally carved by the Italian sculptor Giuseppe Jardella for "Morris' Folly" (Fig. 30).

William Birch made the drawing of the Chestnut Street Theater, but it was etched by the comedian Gilbert Fox, best known as having introduced the song "Hail Columbia" for which Joseph Hopkinson had composed the words. This was at the Chestnut Street Theater in April, 1798, when strong anti-French sentiment among the Federalists probably contributed more than the merits of the song to Fox's spectacular success. Sculpture in niches at either side of the large Palladian window had been included in the earliest design of the Chestnut Street Theater, but William Rush did not carve until about 1807 his lively figures of Comedy and Tragedy, now in the Pennsylvania Academy of the Fine Arts.

The stages of the early theaters had to be lit, first by candles, and later by oil lamps —raised to give the effect of night and lowered to produce the appearance of day—and from these and similar sources fire was an ever-present hazard. But the work of an incendiary or a spark from a torch was variously reputed to have been the cause of the blaze that totally destroyed the Chestnut Street Theater, on Apr. 3, 1820. Jardella's reliefs and Rush's statues must have survived the holocaust, however, for they appear again on the façade of the new theater designed the same year by William Strickland (Fig. 47).

In the rebuilding of the Chestnut Street Theater, Strickland raised the height of Latrobe's lateral wings and ran the Corinthian colonnade across the façade at the level of the second story. Below the colonnade five arches sheltered doorways through which it was claimed the auditorium could be emptied in less than three minutes, even when all 2,000 seats were filled. Contemporary accounts of Strickland's building mention "spacious lobbies, warmed by fireproof furnaces" and on the second floor a "splendid saloon and coffeerooms." Three rows of boxes surrounded the domed auditorium in a semicircle 46 feet in diameter. The façade was of marble, and the columns, unlike those of the earlier theater, were of the same material, carved in Italy. Before its demolition in the 1850's, the second Chestnut Street Theater had been the scene of many opening nights, including the presentation in 1845 of William Henry Fry's *Leonora*, often considered the first American opera worthy of the name. In 1863 still another theater was built at 1211-1215 Chestnut Street which, after being remodeled in 1875, stood until about 1917, when it was torn down to make way for an office building.

Strickland was also the architect of a new theater on Arch Street above Sixth (Fig. 48), opened Oct. 1, 1828. In both plan and elevation this conformed to the general pattern set by its predecessors on Chestnut Street. The Tuscan columns of the portico were Roman rather than Greek, but the large pediment with Gevelot's statue of Apollo in the tympanum helped to give the façade a more classical appearance in keeping with the prevailing taste of the period. Padded seats covered with calfskin contributed to the comfort of the audience, and supporting the tiers of boxes were columns made of iron, a relatively new use of a material especially favored by Strickland and presumably used here as a means of saving space. Of "the Arch" R. A. Smith wrote in 1852: "There is no place of amusement in this city where the public are better catered for, or where the amusements are more varied . . . novelties being produced in quick succession."

But if the Arch Street Theater offered the most lively entertainment, Smith considered the theater on Walnut Street (Fig. 49) the "most fashionable." Built in 1809 as a circus and known for a time as the "Olympic," the Walnut Street Theater was extensively remodeled in 1828 by the architect John Haviland. Here such well-known American actors as Mrs. John Drew and Edwin Forrest made their stage debuts, and on its billboards have appeared most of the other great names associated with the American stage. Of the three Philadelphia theaters of architectural importance in the nineteenth century, only the Walnut Street Theater remains standing today. In spite of political and financial crises it has never missed a season in 150 years, thereby earning the right to be considered "the oldest surviving theater in the English-speaking world." But the presence of three good theaters in Philadelphia contributed to the financial problems of each, and before the middle of the nineteenth century theatrical leadership had passed to New York City.

Ease of access to Philadelphia from the western counties, promoted earlier by the bridge at Market Street (Fig. 34), was further improved in 1812 by the opening at Fairmount of a second permanent span (Fig. 50). Sometimes called "The Colossus" because its single arch of 340 feet made it the longest single-arch bridge in the world, this remarkable structure was designed by Louis Wernwag, a self-taught engineer of German birth who had settled in Philadelphia while still a boy. Beneath the wooden cover, two carriageways and two footpaths were supported on five arches of laminated wood, each of seven plies. The history of architecture offers few structures bolder in concept or more graceful in form.

When Wernwag's bridge burned in 1838, it was replaced by a wire suspension bridge (Fig. 51) designed by Col. Charles Ellet, Jr., a native of Bucks County, who had studied briefly in Paris. Although the use of rope bridges is almost as old as man himself, the credit for having first used a level roadway suspended from chains or cables probably belongs to James Finley, an American. Finley's experiments date as early as 1801, but little was done in the United States to exploit his system until after the French and Swiss had developed methods of spinning wire cables in position. Even when viewed against this background, the Wire Bridge at Philadelphia may well have been, as is often claimed, the first of its kind "opened to general traffic in America." The length of Ellet's bridge across the Schuylkill was 343 feet between abutments, and six years later he achieved a world record with the 1,010-foot span over the Ohio River at Wheeling, West Virginia. In 1875 the Wire Bridge was replaced by the two-level Spring Garden Bridge, which today connects the West River Drive with that on the east.

Beside the Wire Bridge in George Lehman's lithograph may be seen the Fairmount Waterworks, built between 1812 and 1822 to replace Latrobe's pumping station in Center Square (Fig. 40), which within ten years of its completion was found to be no longer adequate for the needs of the growing city. The dam just visible at the extreme left was used to back up the Schuylkill for about six miles, thereby creating the necessary power to run the pumps capable of raising millions of gallons daily to the reservoir located at the top of "Faire Mount" (right of center in Lehman's view). In the lower left corner of the lithograph is the entrance to the canal, approximately 1,000 feet long and including two chamber locks by which river traffic bypassed the dam. On the east bank of the river are the stone mill houses, and behind them is the mill race (forebay), concealed from view in the lithograph. In the twentieth century when Fairmount ceased to be the source of the city's water supply, the mill houses were converted into the aquarium known to present-day Philadelphians, but originally they included space for up to eight double-action pumps run by water power. The large structure standing to the south of the mill houses was begun about 1812 to house the steam engines used to pump the water to the reservoir on Fairmount before the construction, between 1819 and 1822, of the dam and the mill race. An office for members of the Watering Committee and quarters for a caretaker were provided by the pavilions at either end of the mill houses. Tradition has it that these little classical temples were inspired by LeNôtre's "Temple d'Amour" at Chantilly; but whatever their source, they remain among the best examples of the Roman Revival in Philadelphia.

The roof above the pumps at Fairmount (Fig. 52) was paved to afford a promenade over 250 feet long from which the Schuylkill could be seen to advantage, and the grounds adjacent were pleasantly landscaped to provide one of the first parks in America to be established apart from the colonial common and the city square. To these walks and the gazebos erected beside the dam and part way up the slope of Fairmount the citizens of Philadelphia and their guests came in great numbers during the warmer seasons of the year. Riverboat excursions from Fairmount to Manayunk were also considered especially fashionable, and about 1835 rowing clubs like those pictured in the print began to hold races on the Schuylkill. "It would be considered as the absence of all taste, for a stranger to appear in Philadelphia, and not devote an hour to visit 'the Fairmount Water works,'" J. C. Wild wrote in the explanatory notes accompanying his *Views of Philadelphia* (1838). And the number of contemporary prints of Fairmount would seem to corroborate his statement; probably no scene in America was depicted more frequently or by a larger number of different artists. Even Charles Dickens, seldom enthusiastic about things American, had a good word to say for the waterworks at Philadelphia.

The engineer for the new water system was the same Frederick Graff who had been Latrobe's chief draftsman for the Center Square Pump House. In view of this earlier experience, there seems no good reason to suppose that Graff was not capable of serving the Watering Committee both as architect and engineer. Nevertheless, some modern historians have seen the influence of Robert Mills in the classic pavilions at Fairmount, and although without any documentary basis, such a possibility cannot be discounted entirely.

Mills is best known as the designer of the Treasury Building in Washington, D.C. (1836-42) and of the monuments to the first President erected in Baltimore (1815-29) and Washington (c.1833-84). Born in Charleston, South Carolina, in 1781, Mills studied there briefly with James Hoban, through whom he was later introduced to Thomas Jefferson. No doubt the two years he spent working at Monticello help to account for Mills's interest in Roman architecture, for of all the important architects active in Philadelphia in the first half of the nineteenth century, he remained most steadfast in his allegiance to the Classic Revival.

After a tour of the eastern seaboard, Mills settled in Philadelphia in 1803 as an assistant to Latrobe. When he opened his own architectural office five years later, one of his first important commissions was for the wooden cover of Wernwag's bridge (Fig. 50). The hand of the architect is clearly distinguishable in the classical entrances to the bridge, but since Mills was also a competent engineer, his contribution to the total design probably went beyond the addition of decorative details. About this same time Mills also designed two new wings with domed cupolas to replace the earlier arcades and dependencies at either side of Independence Hall (Figs. 1 and 22). These were taken down in the twentieth century as part of the program to restore the State House to its eighteenth-century appearance, but they are clearly visible in Poleni's view of 1876 (Fig. 108).

Another of Mills's early commissions in Philadelphia was Washington Hall (Fig. 53), designed perhaps as early as 1809, but not completed until 1816. The Washington Benevolent Society was chartered in 1813 to give aid and counsel to all who desired it, particular attention being paid to the ill, the old, the unemployed, and the destitute. As its first headquarters the Society purchased the Bingham mansion on Third Street (Fig. 27) which since the untimely death of Ann Bingham at the age of thirty-seven and that of her husband four years later had been operated as a hotel. When it appeared that the necessary alterations might endanger the structure of the old house, the Society decided to purchase the adjacent lot and erect there a new hall.

The use of the unusually large niche, 22 feet in diameter, with its screen of Ionic columns and capping half-dome sets Washington Hall apart from Mills's other buildings, which more frequently display professional competence than artistic imagination. Nor does this feature of the Hall seem to have been original with Mills. Its probable origin is the Hôtel Guimard in Paris designed by the French architect Claude-Nicolas Ledoux (1736-1806) and illustrated in his *L'Architecture considérée sous le rapport de l'Art des Moeurs et de la Législation* (1804). The work of Ledoux and E.-L. Boullée (1728-1799) is often mentioned as among the sources for the more severe classical style used by Latrobe and his contemporaries, but it is seldom that so specific an example of borrowing from French models can be cited.

In keeping with the conservative spirit of much of the domestic architecture of Philadelphia, the row of houses that Mills built on Ninth Street between Walnut and Locust was essentially Federal in style. One of these at 228 South Ninth Street remains, but the rest, like most of Mills's other work in Philadelphia, have been demolished. Not even a sketch has survived as evidence of the exterior appearance of the circular Baptist Church on Sansom Street, remarkable both for its 4,000 seats and for its acoustical properties, said to have been unrivaled in the country. On the basis of contemporary comments and a few drawings, the Octagon Unitarian Church (opened 1813) at Tenth and Locust streets appears also to have been among Mills's most interesting designs and one that may well have influenced his later Monumental Church, still standing at Richmond, Virginia.

Mills has been called America's first native-born architect regularly trained for the profession, but much this same claim might be made for his slightly younger contemporary, William Strickland. Strickland's name has already appeared in this account as the architect who remodeled St. Paul's Church, added a tower to St. Peter's, and restored the spire of Independence Hall. He will also be recalled as having rebuilt the theater on Chestnut Street (Fig. 47) and designed that on Arch (Fig. 48).

A native of New Jersey, Strickland was early apprenticed to Benjamin Henry Latrobe whom his father knew well by reason of having been the carpenter for the Bank of Pennsylvania (Fig. 42), which Latrobe had designed. After leaving Latrobe's office in the fall of 1805, Strickland's first important commission was the Masonic Hall on Chestnut Street (Fig. 74), to be discussed later for its Gothic design. But it was principally as a surveyor, artist, and designer of stage sets that he sought to support himself for the next ten years. To him we owe the painting of Christ Church reproduced as Figure 11, and a number of the most interesting engravings of the early nineteenth century are from his drawings (Figs. 7, 24) and those of George Strickland, his younger brother, who proved a better draftsman than architect (Fig. 53).

In 1818 Strickland won the competition for the new building of the Second Bank of the United States (Fig. 54), much to the disappointment of Latrobe who accused his former pupil of having stolen his ideas. The drawings submitted by Latrobe are preserved at the

Historical Society of Pennsylvania, and although it is possible that Strickland may have been influenced by the designs of his older and more experienced competitor, many elements shared by the two schemes seem most easily explained by the terms of the competition. In their advertisement in the *Philadelphia Gazette* the directors of the bank specified that their new building should be "a chaste imitation of Grecian Architecture" having "a portico on each front resting upon a basement or platform of such altitude as will combine convenience of ascent with due proportion and effect." Under these conditions a design like that proposed by both Latrobe and Strickland was natural, if not inevitable.

Strickland was fond of telling his pupils that there was no need for a competent architect to seek his models beyond the pages of Stuart and Revett, and for most of his important commissions he seems to have followed his own advice. The plate of the Parthenon from *The Antiquities of Athens* (Fig. 55) was unmistakably the source for the two porticoes of the Second Bank of the United States. But in adapting Greek forms to contemporary problems some modification was of course necessary; all sculptural decoration had to be omitted; windows were added, and the lateral colonnades were dispensed with in order to make efficient use of the lot and to provide enough light for the vaulted banking room and other offices.

For the most part, the Second Bank with Nicholas Biddle as its president was managed to the advantage of the nation. But to Andrew Jackson it seemed the embodiment of the monopolistic financial practices of the eastern bankers, which he feared and detested. In 1836 he vetoed the bill to renew the Bank's charter, and although rechartered by the state as the United States Bank of Pennsylvania, its days as a leading financial institution were numbered. Three years later Nicholas Biddle resigned as president, and in the panic of 1841 the "monster" closed its doors for the last time. The financial leadership of the country was passing from Philadelphia to New York. In 1844 the marble temple on Chestnut Street was sold to the federal government.

As the first public building to be based on the design of the Parthenon, the bank on Chestnut Street attracted wide attention in both Europe and America. Strickland was now established as one of the leading architects of the day, and other commissions soon followed. In 1826 he designed the U.S. Naval Asylum (now the Naval Home), which still stands on Gray's Ferry Road (Fig. 56). Public rooms, auditorium, dining rooms and officers' quarters were provided in the main block, and in the wings were dormitories for the men. The Ionic order of the stately portico was apparently based upon the engraving in Stuart and Revett of the Temple on the Ilissus, no longer extant, but the iron "piazzas" of the wings had nothing to do with classic precedent. They were the product of the nineteenth century's interest in the healthful effects of fresh air and the search for new materials that would be strong, economical and, above all, impervious to fire. Later experience, especially the Chicago Fire in 1871, would prove that exposed iron was not the fireproof material it had first appeared, but at the time it was built, the Naval Asylum represented the most advanced architectural thinking in this respect. In addition to providing a home for retired seamen, the building on Gray's Ferry Road also served as a naval training school prior to the establishment of the Academy at Annapolis in 1845.

66

Within ten years after the completion of Mills's Octagon Church, its Unitarian congregation under the effective leadership of Dr. William H. Furness was feeling the need for additional space. To replace the earlier building, Strickland in 1828 designed the rectangular marble church with a windowless façade that stood until 1885 at the corner of Tenth and Locust streets (Fig. 57). Some of the materials from the Octagon Church were reused for the new building, but the Doric columns of the classic portico came from Latrobe's Pump House (Fig. 40), demolished the same year.

By no means all Strickland's time was devoted to architecture in the narrower meaning of the word. In 1825 he visited England to study the transportation system of that country on behalf of the Pennsylvania Society for the Promotion of Internal Improvement, and the following year in his *Reports on Canals, Railways and Roads* he went against prevailing opinion in expressing the view that railroads held more promise for the future than did canals. From 1826 to 1827 he was engineer in charge of the Eastern Division of the Pennsylvania Mixed System (Philadelphia to Pittsburgh), a method of travel, as the name implies, involving an inconvenient combination of canals and railroads. As supervising engineer, Strickland was also responsible for the construction of the Delaware Breakwater, which still protects the Philadelphia harbor.

The year following the completion of the First Unitarian Church, Strickland was commissioned by the United States government to prepare the plans for a new Mint to be erected on the northwest corner of Chestnut and Juniper streets (Fig. 58). This replaced the modest building on North Seventh Street, notable as having been the first structure authorized by the U.S. Congress. Except for the use of a central court, the design of the Mint was not significantly different from that of most of Strickland's other buildings in the classical style. Six marble columns of the Greek Ionic order formed the portico facing Chestnut Street, and on the interior iron was again extensively used for stairways and piazzas. Subsequent commissions for branch mints in Charlotte, North Carolina (1835), and New Orleans (1835) were doubtless the result of the success of the earlier one on Chestnut Street. In 1901 the Philadelphia Mint moved to its present location on Spring Garden Street, and the following year Strickland's building was demolished except for its Ionic columns, which were given to the Jewish Hospital, now a part of the Albert Einstein Medical Center.

After long relying on taverns as convenient places in which to transact their business, early in the nineteenth century Philadelphia merchants began to think in terms of a special building devoted to the commerce of the city. In this they had in mind the exchanges known in Europe since at least the sixteenth century as well as the impressive structures that Godefroy and Latrobe provided for Baltimore in 1820 and Martin Thompson designed for New York in 1825. To promote this project the Philadelphia Exchange Company was formed about 1831, and shortly thereafter the Board of Managers commissioned Strickland to design a suitable building for the triangular site bounded by Third, Dock, and Walnut streets.

By way of publicity for the Exchange Company and its stock, Strickland made a wash drawing of his projected building, later engraved by John Sartain (Fig. 59). As finally constructed in 1834, the Philadelphia Exchange did not differ greatly from Strickland's drawing, except that a more orthodox weather vane was substituted for the classical Nereid on the apex of the cupola. In the choice of the Corinthian order Strickland may have been influenced by the style of Blodgett's bank, nearby, but for his specific model he again turned to the pages of Stuart and Revett. The Greek monument in this case was the so-called Choragic Monument of Lysicrates, on which are based the capitals of the semicircular colonnade and which appears in more complete form as the cupola of the Exchange. Although he used it again for the tower of the capitol at Nashville, Tennessee, Strickland was not alone in his admiration of this little structure erected in Athens in 334 B.C. as the base for the bronze tripod awarded to the winner of the choral contest for that year; together with the Temple on the Ilissus, mentioned earlier, the Monument of Lysicrates probably found its way into the design of more Classic Revival buildings than any other Greek structure of antiquity. On the interior of the Philadelphia Exchange, the principal feature was the circular Exchange Room with its frescoed dome. To the right of this was an "extensive reading room" open to subscribers only, and throughout the other parts of the building were quarters for the post office, the chamber of commerce, brokers, artists, and various banks and insurance companies. For half a century the Exchange served as the center of the commercial life of the city.

Italian sculptors are known to have carved the intricate and beautiful capitals of the Philadelphia Exchange, and perhaps they also had a part in the sumptuous new quarters for the Philadelphia Bank designed by Strickland in 1836. This is the marble building to the east of the Second Bank of the United States in Koellner's lithograph (Fig. 54). Shops occupied the ground floor, but the principal rooms of the second story, expressed on the exterior by the impressive Corinthian colonnade, were divided between the offices of the Philadelphia Bank and the Bank of the United States, which had shared the cost of construction. In the same year that the new bank on Chestnut Street was begun, Strickland was called to Providence, Rhode Island, to design the Athenaeum, which still stands, considerably altered, on Benefit Street. The building committee of the Athenaeum had first turned to the local architect Russell Warren (1792-1860) for the plans of their new building, but when these proved too expensive and Warren was not available to change them, Strickland was approached as an architect having "a reputation second to none . . . in his profession." At Providence Strickland showed how effectively Greek forms might be adapted to contemporary use at moderate cost; the rectangular shape of the classical temple was well suited to the needs of a library, and the simple wooden cornice and two Doric columns of the recessed porch offer a pleasing contrast to the granite walls.

The Corinthian was also the Greek order selected for the portico of the Merchants' Bank, now the Norwegian Seamen's Church, in Philadelphia. Erected in 1837, this modest structure, which still stands on the west side of Third Street between Market and Chestnut, was one of the last buildings designed by Strickland for a Philadelphia client. In 1844 he was called to prepare the plans for the new state capitol of Tennessee, and the following year he moved his office to Nashville where he continued to practice until his death in 1854.

Of Strickland it was said, as of Rome and the Emperor Augustus, that he found Philadelphia a city of brick and left it a city of marble. Better than any of his contemporaries, he exemplifies the archaeological phase of the Greek Revival. Only occasionally did he try his hand at the Gothic or the more exotic Egyptian, and even less frequently does his style reflect the earlier Federal manner. Probably his biographer is correct in suggesting that the late Georgian qualities apparent in the two buildings designed about 1829 for the University of Pennsylvania (Fig. 60) are attributable to the influence of the earlier President's House and Medical School (Fig. 31), which stood on the same site. Medical Hall, at the left of Wild's lithograph, contained facilities for the chemical and anatomical departments. Collegiate Hall, built second, was similar to Medical Hall on the exterior, but was planned to meet the needs of the Faculty of Arts.

Strickland and Mills were well launched on their professional careers and Latrobe was at work on the Capitol in Washington when John Haviland opened his architectural office in Philadelphia about 1816. Of English birth, Haviland had received his professional training under James Elmes, a London architect more often remembered for his writings than for his buildings. Although he is best known as the designer of the prisons that will be discussed under the heading of the Gothic and Egyptian styles, Haviland also deserves mention as one of those whose work contributed to Philadelphia's pre-eminence in the Greek Revival. His three-volume *Builder's Assistant,* brought out in Philadelphia between 1818 and 1821, was the first book published in America to contain the Greek orders.

No doubt *The Builder's Assistant* was helpful in bringing the professional qualifications of its author to the attention of prospective clients. When about 1820 the wooden columns of the First Presbyterian Church (Fig. 23) needed replacing, the congregation decided to abandon the old building and its site in the commercial section of the city in favor of a more fashionable location on Washington Square and a new building from the designs of John Haviland (Fig. 61). The ever-popular Temple on the Ilissus was the model for the portico of the new church, but the need for economy obliged the architect to use brick walls roughcast to resemble the marble of the original.

Contemporary accounts speak well of the Washington Square Presbyterian Church, and its favorable reception probably contributed to Haviland's selection as the architect of St. Andrew's Protestant Episcopal Church, built a block away on Eighth Street below Locust in 1822. In this case the Temple of Bacchus at Teos is said to have been the source for the Ionic colonnade which R. A. Smith in 1852 called "one of the most perfect specimens of the Grecian Ionic order" in the city. Smith also speaks of two of the columns on the interior "with their pilasters and entablatures" as being "copied from the Temple of Minerva Polius at Athens, and executed with all the enrichments, without the slightest deviation from the proportions given in 'Stewart's Athens.' " St. Andrew's was apparently Haviland's own parish. He speaks of it as "our church" in his notes (now in the Library of the University of Pennsylvania), and at his death in 1852 he was buried in a crypt under the floor. In 1921 the dedication was changed from St. Andrew to St. George when the church was acquired by the present Greek Orthodox congregation.

St. Andrew's and the Washington Square Presbyterian Church were among Haviland's earliest commissions in Philadelphia, as well as the most archaeological of all his work in the city. To be sure, the classic pediment and four Doric columns of the recessed porch mark the Asylum for the Deaf and Dumb (now the Philadelphia Museum College of Art) at Broad and Pine as belonging to the Greek Revival (Fig. 62). But the shallow inset arches on the two wings are derived from the earlier Federal style, and the plan is the product of the special requirements of the institution rather than of any attempt to imitate antique models. Haviland's papers indicate that he experimented with a number of different schemes over a period of several years before determining upon a U-shaped plan for the asylum. Originally the basement contained the dining facilities and workshops; parlors, offices, and chapel were on the first floor, with classrooms and quarters for the faculty on the second. Dormitories for the students were in the wings.

The building erected on South Seventh Street in 1825-27 for the Franklin Institute, and now the property of the Atwater Kent Museum, was clearly inspired by the no longer extant Choragic Monument of Thrasyllus in Athens, but other of Haviland's designs of this period seem to owe much less to specific antique models. This was especially true of the Philadelphia Arcade built in 1826 on Chestnut Street near Strickland's theater (Fig. 47) on the site formerly occupied by the Carpenter mansion (Fig. 3). In the eighteenth century such important merchants as Samuel Neave had been content to use the first floor of their houses as a place of business (Fig. 14), and it was pointed out previously that there was little but size to distinguish Blodgett's new Bank of the United States from any important mansion of the period (Fig. 59). Although earlier European examples like the Burlington Arcade in London probably influenced Haviland's thinking, the Philadelphia Arcade was one of the first American buildings to reflect clearly its commercial purposes in its plan.

George Lehman's lithograph (Fig. 63) was made to advertise the fancy and staple dry goods offered for sale by Joseph L. Moore at the store in the Arcade identified by his initials. Moore's shop was one of about eighty grouped in rows on either side of two avenues that ran the 150-foot length of the building from Chestnut Street to Carpenter (later Jayne). Large skylights provided illumination for the interior, and stairways at either end led to a second floor, similar in its arrangement to the first. The third floor contained the Philadelphia Museum of Charles Willson Peale, hitherto quartered in the long gallery on the second floor of Independence Hall, and for a number of years a popular restaurant occupied the basement. Both façades of the Arcade were of Pennsylvania marble, and the niches at either side of the entrances were intended to contain iron statues of Commerce and Navigation, never completed. Above the niches were carved in relief the arms of Philadelphia and Pennsylvania.

Through the extensive use of iron and stone Haviland sought to insulate the various shops and thereby reduce the hazard of fire. In this he appears to have been successful, but in spite of special features of this kind, the Arcade never produced the revenue that its promoters had expected. About 1850 the building was bought by Dr. David Jayne, the manufacturer of patent medicine, who first turned it into a hotel and then, ten years later, tore it down in order to erect three stores in its place. Jayne's marble buildings were landmarks on Chestnut Street for many years, until they, too, were demolished in 1959.

Among Haviland's most interesting commissions was a row of ten identical houses on the southwest corner of Fifteenth and Chestnut streets described by *Hazard's Register of Philadelphia* for 1832 as "one of the handsomest squares in Philadelphia" (Fig. 64). Built in 1830, these houses differed principally from the earlier rows of Latrobe and Carstairs (Fig. 33) in having piazzas supported by Ionic columns, a feature probably based upon English precedent but sufficiently novel in Philadelphia to make the name "Colonnade Row" a suitable identification for the block as a whole. Of brick roughcast to imitate stone, each house was four stories high and occupied a lot 20 feet by 140 feet—space enough for a small garden in the rear. Although originally built as a unit, by the time Hazard described them two years later most of the houses on Colonnade Row appear to have been owned individually by their occupants. In 1868 a portion of the row was remodeled to form the Colonnade Hotel, which remained in use until 1925 when it gave way to the Pennsylvania Building now standing in its place.

The promoters of Colonnade Row were George and Charles Blight, nephews of Peter Blight, a Philadelphia merchant who had made a fortune in the China trade. For the Blights Haviland had also designed in 1828 the classical mansion that formerly stood on the southeast corner of Chestnut and Sixteenth streets (Fig. 65). Called the East India House because of its Oriental furnishings, the Blight mansion must have been one of the most striking of the many elegant residences being built in what was then a fashionable part of the city. Between the slightly projecting wings of the 80-foot façade was a recessed porch, 12 feet deep, facing Chestnut Street. The statue of a female figure, suitably draped, stood in a central niche visible to passers-by between the paired Tuscan columns supporting the entablature. The plan of the mansion has not been found, but the two doors of the façade suggest that it was, in effect, a double house, reflecting its dual ownership by the Blight brothers. A large garden surrounded by a graceful iron fence mounted on a low wall extended through to Sansom (George) Street in the rear. As long as they stood, the Blight Mansion and Colonnade Row, together, made the block between Fifteenth and Sixteenth among the most interesting and impressive on Chestnut Street.

The classical forms of the Blight mansion belong more to the Federal Style or to the English Regency than to the more archaeological phase of the Greek Revival. Other clients, however, were not content with so general or restrained a reference to antiquity. When about 1836 he decided to remodel the river front of Andalusia, Nicholas Biddle demanded a portico based on the Hephaesteum (Theseum) at Athens, and although the full temple façade was never common in the Philadelphia area, it was certainly not unknown. Not even the most palatial of the New York mansions surpassed in size or elegance Phil-Ellena, the house of George W. Carpenter on Germantown Avenue. With its polygonal cupola and hexastyle Ionic portico, the Carpenter mansion was one of the sights of Germantown from the time of its erection in 1844 until its demolition about 1900. More modest than Phil-Ellena but no less attractive were the Doric charms of Powelton, the residence of John Hare Powel on the west side of Thirty-second Street, north of Race (Fig. 66). Considering the architectural importance of this fine house, it is surprising that it has received so little attention either from contemporary writers or from later historians. On the basis of its style, however, Powelton should probably be dated about 1830.

Biddle's architect for the additions to Andalusia was Thomas U. Walter, a young Philadelphian of German descent who had received his professional training in the office of William Strickland. Walter had come to Biddle's attention three years before when he won the competition for the design of Girard College over such older and more experienced men as Isaiah Rogers of Boston, Town & Davis of New York, and even Strickland himself. City Councils had been well enough pleased with Walter's design to award it the first premium and to designate its author the architect of the new building. Not so Nicholas Biddle, who had himself appointed Chairman of the Building Committee, and who felt that his experience with the Second Bank (Fig. 54), when coupled with his travels abroad, entitled him to expect that the new school be housed in nothing less than a "perfect, chaste specimen of Grecian architecture." By his own account it was Biddle who induced Walter to give up the more modest scheme with which he had won the competition in favor of a grandiose design (Fig. 67) based apparently upon a combination of the Temple of Olympian Zeus at Athens and Pierre Vignon's church of the Madeleine in Paris (c.1808).

But Biddle and his committee were not the only clients whom Walter had to satisfy. In bequeathing a portion of his large fortune to the city of Philadelphia for the education of poor, white male orphans, Stephen Girard had specified in detail the form that the principal building of his college was to take. There were to be four large rooms, 50 feet square, on each of the three floors. All rooms were to be vaulted and all the building—walls, stairways, and roof—was to be of marble. Useless ornament was to be eliminated. The problem of fitting Girard's requirements into Biddle's classic temple would have challenged an older and more experienced architect than Walter. As it was, the solution finally adopted made the best of a difficult situation (Fig. 68). By concentrating necessary support at the four corners, the vaulted ceilings permitted Walter to open the side walls with numerous windows. This worked well enough on the first two floors, but at the third level there was room for only tiny windows at floor height. These were clearly inadequate for light and air, and to supplement them an oculus had to be introduced in the center of each dome.

Walter's skill in concealing Girard's domes under the gable roof of Biddle's temple is noteworthy, but vaulted ceilings and spacious entrance halls are no compensation for poor acoustics, bad lighting, and an inflexible plan. Monumental in scale, impeccable in workmanship, and uncompromising in details, Founder's Hall is at once the most impressive monument to the Greek Revival in America—if not in the world—and at the same time the real critic of the historical approach to architecture. As long as Greek forms were only the means to an end, as Strickland had used them in the Philadelphia Exchange, they afforded unlimited possibilities for beautiful and expressive design. But the pursuit of too great archaeological accuracy could lead only to the end of the architectural road. As a monument to Girard, and perhaps also to Nicholas Biddle, Walter's Greek temple is magnificent; as the solution to the problem of providing for the needs of a boys' school, it is wholly inadequate.

Time has dealt more kindly with Walter's architecture than with that of most of his contemporaries. Among the more important of his buildings in the Greek Revival style, still standing in Philadelphia, are the first building of the Philadelphia Saving Fund Society at Third and Walnut streets (1839-40; pediment added 1881), the Preston Retreat at Twenty-fifth and Hamilton (1837; altered 1909) and the Philadelphia Contributionship on South Fourth Street (1836).

During the years when he was busiest as an architect, Walter was also active in a variety of professional and cultural institutions. He was a member of the Philosophical Society and a frequent lecturer at the Franklin Institute. The American Institution of Architects, which he helped to found in 1836, was not an immediate success, but it paved the way for the establishment in 1857 of the present American Institute of Architects of which he was the second president. Although he returned to his native city late in life, Walter's Philadelphia career really ended in 1851 when he succeeded Robert Mills as architect of the Capitol in Washington. The wings for the Senate and House of Representatives are from his designs, as is, of course, the great cast-iron dome based on St. Paul's in London, for which he is best known.

Even before Walter had left Philadelphia for Washington, the Greek Revival with which he had been so closely identified had lost much of its popularity. Especially was this true in the field of domestic architecture; for public buildings Greek and Roman models would occasionally be used throughout the nineteenth century. In 1844 William L. Johnston designed for the Mercantile Library the dignified, classical building (Fig. 69) that stood until well into the twentieth century on Fifth Street across from Independence Square. But by this time the first excitement of the rediscovery of Greek art has passed and strict archaeological accuracy is no longer demanded. Johnston's handling of the Corinthian order is as much Roman as Greek, and the rusticated first floor owes more to Palladio than to Stuart and Revett.

As late as the 1850's the classical style was still being used in Philadelphia for churches like that erected on the northwest corner of Seventh and Spring Garden streets (Fig. 70). The design of the First Reformed Dutch Church is especially interesting because it appears to be based on the Maison Carrée at Nîmes, the same Roman temple that had first interested Thomas Jefferson in the beauties of classical architecture seventy years before. The architect for the new church on Spring Garden Street was Stephen D. Button, a New Englander who had received his architectural training in New York. After having served as supervising architect of the capitol of Alabama at Montgomery, Button settled in Philadelphia in 1849 where he formed a partnership with his brother-in-law Joseph C. Hoxie. Both singly and together Hoxie and Button are among the most interesting and least known architects of a period that is only just beginning to receive from historians the attention it deserves.

Perhaps the last important structure in Philadelphia that may fairly be considered a product of the Greek Revival is the second building erected by the Library Company, this time at Broad and Christian streets. Built about 1875 from the designs of Addison Hutton, this is known as the Ridgway Library in accordance with the request of the donor,

Dr. James Rush, that the new building be named for his wife who was the daughter of Jacob Ridgway, a rich merchant of Philadelphia. As it had for Strickland's Second Bank half a century before, the Parthenon again seems to have served as the model for at least the central portion of this massive granite façade. Inconveniently located, difficult to heat, and in constant danger from fire, the Ridgway Library no longer serves the function for which it was built. The Library Company hopes to move to more suitable quarters in the near future, and Hutton's building, like so many others of its period, will probably be demolished.

THE GOTHIC REVIVAL

Philadelphians were attracted by the picturesque qualities of the Gothic almost as early as they learned to admire the chaste beauties of the Greek. Baltimore might claim the little chapel designed by Godefroy in 1806 for St. Mary's Seminary as the first Gothic church in America, but Philadelphia had in Latrobe's Sedgeley (Fig. 71) one of the earliest country mansions and in Dorsey's Chestnut Street residence (Fig. 72) one of the first town houses in the new style. St. Mary's chapel is still in use, but unfortunately Sedgeley and Dorsey's Gothic Mansion were demolished long ago.

The basis for the appeal of the Gothic style was not unlike that which had first accounted for the popularity of Greek and Roman antiquities. Coming after the classical bias of the Renaissance, the strangeness of medieval forms appealed powerfully to the Romantic mind. And because they knew little about the Middle Ages, men of the eighteenth century felt free to substitute fancy for fact. As Sir Joshua Reynolds (1723-1792) put it in his *Thirteenth Discourse*: ". . . whatever building brings to our remembrance ancient customs and manners, such as the Castles of the Barons of Ancient Chivalry, is sure to give . . . delight."

The word "Romantic" is related to *romant,* meaning a medieval tale, and throughout its history the Gothic Revival had a strong literary quality. Such authors as Milton, Spenser, and Chatterton had helped to open their readers' eyes to the beauties of medieval architecture that lay all about them. Those men of taste who had no ruined abbey or ancestral castle on their estates had, of course, to content themselves with imitations such as the ones supplied by Sanderson Miller, a kind of specialist in spurious ruins. And if, except for one or two doubtful examples, North America had little in the way of monuments of its medieval past, the writings imported from England and the local imitations of Charles Brockden Brown (1771-1810) whetted the American appetite for the gloomy architecture that was the stock in trade of the Gothic novel. This literary tradition was continued well into the nineteenth century by the immensely popular stories of Edgar Allan Poe (1809-1849) and Sir Walter Scott (1771-1832), who himself lived at Abbotsford, a Gothic castle of sorts.

As a definite architectural style, the Gothic Revival in England may be said to date from about 1750 when Horace Walpole (1717-1797) began the remodeling of Strawberry

Hill, his villa at Twickenham on the outskirts of London. Later Walpole, too, tried his hand at writing a Gothic novel, and today Strawberry Hill appears more a stage setting for its owner's moods and emotions than a serious attempt to create a building based on an earlier style. Although later critics were especially contemptuous of Strawberry Hill for its sham details made of plaster or painted on wall paper, it is nevertheless architecturally important for having made the Gothic style socially acceptable as well as for having stimulated a more careful investigation of medieval buildings. But it has been well said that something cannot be revived that never existed. Since there was no medieval precedent for mantelpieces and a number of the other features Walpole wanted to include in his remodeled villa, he created his own designs, using tombs as his principal source, but also borrowing from any other object that seemed to suit his purpose. This practice of regarding Gothic motifs as decorative elements to be applied to the surface with little regard for the structure beneath, and still less for the original purpose of the borrowed design, became one of the major characteristics of the Gothic Revival, especially in its earlier phases.

The origins of the Gothic Revival help to explain the form of Sedgeley, designed by Latrobe in 1799 to stand on the northern tract of the old Morris estate, bought by William Cramond at the sheriff's sale that same year. In this case the pointed openings and the drip moldings (labels) about them are all that identify the Gothic style. Otherwise Sedgeley appears to be a late Federal mansion with hipped roof and rounded central bay like that at Lemon Hill, nearby. Although not without medieval precedent, corner pavilions seem to have been elements especially favored by Latrobe. He used them earlier for the unexecuted design of the Tayloe house in Washington and later for the Waln mansion on Chestnut Street, mentioned briefly in the preceding section. Latrobe complained that Sedgeley had been mishandled by its builders, but even so, it was probably never one of his most successful designs. It deserves mention, nevertheless, because of its early date; with it Latrobe emerges as an innovator in the Gothic style as well as in that of the Greek Revival, more frequently associated with his name.

It is less easy to speak of "firsts" in connection with the revival of Gothic architecture than in the case of the re-emergence of Greek art after the archeological discoveries of the eighteenth century. This is because the medieval tradition in building had never been completely superseded. In England, for example, even such champions of classical architecture as Sir Christopher Wren, Nicholas Hawksmoor, and Robert Adam had occasionally tried their hands at designing in a style that they at least intended to be Gothic. But since it was clear that not even the most accomplished architects understood the Gothic very well, to assist those who desired to build in what was becoming the fashionable style, Batty and Thomas Langley brought out in London in 1742 their *Gothic Architecture Improved by Rules and Proportions*. The Langleys' objective was to discover, if possible, the principles that underlay Gothic architecture, and not, as is sometimes said, to make up rules of their own. In this they were not particularly successful, but their book went through several editions and, along with a number of others that included Gothic designs, was widely read in Europe and America.

Perhaps it was in such books as those put out by Batty Langley that John Dorsey found many of the ideas he incorporated in his Chestnut Street mansion (Fig. 72). As in the case of Sedgeley, the basic plan of Dorsey's house is predominantly classic in its balance and symmetry. Except for the two round attic portholes, the niches on the first floor, and the large central window that give the façade a somewhat ecclesiastical air, all the doors and windows are rectangular, rather than pointed. A measure of medieval verticality is introduced by the four "buttressing strips" with their pointed finials, but most of the other "Gothic" elements are only surface deep. And what unusual elements they were. Contemporary accounts mention oxeye consoles, Saracenic tablets, quatrefoil guilloches, shields, escutcheons, tablets, and "appropriate bas-relief sculptures"—all apparently made of artificial stone "by the celebrated Mr. Coade."

More immediate sources for many of the architectural elements combined on the façade of the Gothic Mansion may have been two buildings erected on Chestnut Street within a year of each other and just at the time when Dorsey must have been thinking about the design of his house. These were Latrobe's Philadelphia Bank (Fig. 73) and Strickland's Masonic Hall (Fig. 74), both important examples of the first phase of the Gothic Revival in America. Some connection between the Gothic Mansion and the Philadelphia Bank is perhaps also suggested by the fact that Robert Mills, then a young man at the beginning of his career, made the drawing for the engraving of Dorsey's house in *The Port Folio,* as well as supervised the construction of the Philadelphia Bank while its architect was absent in Washington on other commissions. In any case, Mills seems to have had his fill of the Gothic style for, with one or two minor exceptions, he never employed it later for any of his own buildings.

The design of the Philadelphia Bank represents one of the first American uses of the Gothic style for a commercial structure. By departing radically from prevailing practice, Latrobe doubtless wished to call attention to the business opportunities afforded by his client and at the same time to avoid any possible confusion with the Bank of Pennsylvania, located in its classical temple two blocks to the southeast. Such a distinction was the more necessary since the Bank of Pennsylvania had done everything in its power, first to prevent the establishment of the Philadelphia Bank, and then to hamper its success. Brick was used for the exterior of the new building, but the foundations and decorative details were of stone in the Philadelphia tradition. A flight of marble steps led to the entrance on Fourth Street, and on the Chestnut Street side, as well as in the rear, there was a pleasant garden surrounded by an iron fence. Writing three years after its completion, Dr. James Mease described the Philadelphia Bank as "the first correct specimen of the style, called, improperly, the Gothic, executed in the United States." Today Latrobe's building seems less a correct specimen of the art of any period than an interesting example of Batty Langley Gothic characterized by the application of medieval details to an otherwise classical building.

In some respects the interior was perhaps the most interesting part of the Philadelphia Bank. Except for the vault, all the first floor was taken up with an impressive banking room. For this Latrobe designed a Gothic ceiling, complete with fan vaulting executed in plaster by William Thackara, and including in the center a pendant framed in iron. Another flight of marble steps led to the second floor where was located the board room. By his own account, Latrobe had patterned this part of the bank after "a Gothic octagon Chapter House with one pillar in the center" from which sprang plaster ribs decorated with bosses of the same material. The basement contained the presses on which the banknotes were struck, and throughout the building the furniture was also from the designs of the architect.

Since there were no medieval counterparts to the banks being erected in the early part of the nineteenth century, Latrobe had to find the model for his board room in the chapter house of one of the English cathedrals. Judged by the historical standards then current, this was something of an anomaly, inasmuch as the medieval Church had considered the charging of interest an unethical practice. The Gothic style might be used with more propriety, however, for the design of a Masonic hall in view of the fact that medieval guilds had contributed importantly to the rise and development of Freemasonry. Perhaps considerations of this kind played a part in the decision to use the Gothic style for the new Masonic Hall on Chestnut Street between Seventh and Eighth, designed by William Strickland about 1808 (Fig. 74). Yet even in this case the use of the tall spire suggests that Strickland may have turned to ecclesiastical rather than secular sources for his models. Buttresses made of "parti-colored marble" and decorated with statues in niches offered a contrast to the brick walls, but in most other respects Strickland's design conformed to the pattern of other early Gothic buildings in Philadelphia. A large semipublic hall occupied most of the ground level, the second floor only being reserved for use by the members.

On the night of Mar. 9, 1819, the wooden tower and most of the interior of the Masonic Hall were destroyed by fire. Hill's aquatint shows the fire at its height being fought by members of the volunteer companies to whom the print is dedicated. Until comparatively recent times, fires of this kind were a major hazard in Philadelphia, as in all congested areas. The precautions that Franklin took to protect his houses have already been noted, and the Pennsylvania Hospital even went so far as to acquire the whole block south of Pine Street in an effort to insulate its premises. At Franklin's suggestion, the first volunteer fire company was organized in 1736, and by the Revolution there were at least eight or ten companies active in the city. Franklin also played an active role in the establishment in 1752 of the Philadelphia Contributionship for the Insurance of Houses from Loss by Fire (sometimes known from its symbol of interlocking hands as the "Hand-in-Hand"). After the Revolution, when the directors of the Philadelphia Contributionship reaffirmed their refusal to insure houses shaded by trees, the Mutual Assurance Company (known from the device on its firemark as the "Green Tree") was founded in 1784 to insure properties in this category. Since then, many nationally known insurance companies have become established in Philadelphia, but the Philadelphia Contributionship and the Mutual Assurance are still active and still continue their original practice, based on English precedent, of writing perpetual policies secured by a single premium. And even more important for the scholar, the files of surveys, maintained by these companies since their establishment, are primary sources for the study of Philadelphia architecture.

After the fire, the Hall on Chestnut Street was gradually repaired except for the tower, which was never rebuilt. But beginning about 1827, and continuing for a number of years thereafter, anti-Masonic sentiment limited the growth and prosperity of the lodges in the Philadelphia area. Under these conditions, the Grand Lodge decided in 1835 to sell its Chestnut Street building to the Franklin Institute and to purchase Washington Hall on Third Street in its place. It was not until mid-century that the Masons could again think of erecting another lodge, but when the Franklin Institute failed to keep up its mortgage payments, it was decided to repossess the old hall on Chestnut Street and to replace it with a new building.

The architects for the second Gothic Masonic Hall on Chestnut Street were Samuel Sloan and John Stewart, and a comparison of the façade (Fig. 75) of their building with that of the earlier one of Strickland illustrates the direction taken by the Gothic Revival during the second quarter of the nineteenth century. Instead of brick with the stone trim characteristic of Philadelphia buildings since early in the eighteenth century, brownstone was selected for the material of the new Hall. And even more important, instead of a few superficial details applied as decoration to a solid wall beneath, as in the case of Latrobe's or Strickland's earlier work, Sloan and Stewart have succeeded in making many of the Gothic elements an integral part of the structural system. In this case the verticality associated with medieval architecture is also made to dominate, although the symmetry and regularity of the façade attest to the continuing vitality of the classical tradition.

The plan of the new Hall conformed to the earlier practice of devoting a major portion of the ground floor of public buildings to shops or other commercial purposes that might be expected to provide a source of regular income. For the decoration of the Grand Lodge Room on the second floor, the Masons seem to have turned to the firm of Collins & Autenrieth. They were the artists, in any case, who supplied the design used by Max Rosenthal for the large colored lithograph here reproduced as Figure 76. Although paint and plaster doubtless accounted for much of the rich detail, if the Grand Lodge Room was in fact decorated as Collins & Autenrieth showed it in their drawing, it must have been one of the most elaborate Gothic interiors of the period.

The better understanding of Gothic architecture revealed by the new Masonic Hall in Philadelphia had its origins in developments in Europe, especially England. There the whimsical attitude characteristic of the style of Batty Langley and his contemporaries had been followed by a more careful and detailed investigation of medieval buildings. This scholarly approach to Gothic architecture was brought to the attention of architects by the large number of books on the subject that began to appear in the last quarter of the eighteenth century and continued well into the nineteenth. In 1798 Milner published his *History of Winchester,* and the same year Bentham and Willis brought out their *History of Gothic and Saxon Architecture in England.* But most important for the understanding of Gothic architecture in America were the books of John Britton. His *Architectural Antiquities of Great Britain* appeared in forty parts, the last in 1814, and a new volume was added to his *Cathedral Antiquities* almost yearly until 1835. As a result of the investigations of the antiquarian and architectural historian, the accomplishments of the Gothic Revival architect began to approach in scope and quality the descriptions found in the Gothic novels. Fonthill Abbey, designed by James Wyatt (1746-1813) about 1796 for

William Beckford (1760-1844), the richest commoner in England, had an octagon tower nearly three hundred feet high as well as a vast hall that would have done credit to Hollywood in the twentieth century. Even before the middle of the nineteenth century it was no longer sufficient to speak simply of Gothic architecture; not only was French Gothic distinguished from English and English from Italian, but it became customary to differentiate among the "Perpendicular," "Decorated," and "Norman" styles.

This discussion of the second Masonic Hall has done some violence to strict chronology, for there are several categories of earlier buildings that belong in any discussion of the Gothic Revival in Philadelphia. Prisons comprise one of the most important of these, as represented by the Eastern State Penitentiary, sometimes known as Cherry Hill from its location in an old orchard (Fig. 77). Since in the Middle Ages a castle had been designed to repel invaders, it no doubt seemed to the architects of the nineteenth century that the same battlemented walls that had kept the enemy outside might also serve to confine prisoners within. In fact, many of the planners of the early prisons were quite explicit concerning the way in which they wished the style of their building to reflect its purpose. "The exterior of a solitary prison should exhibit as much as possible great strength and convey to the mind a cheerless blank indicative of the misery which awaits the unhappy being who enters within its walls" was the way the Commissioners of the Eastern Penitentiary expressed their view on this point. From its beginning in 1821, the Eastern Penitentiary represented this prevailing Quaker philosophy on penal matters and did much to establish Haviland as the leading designer of a new type of prison soon to be erected in considerable numbers in Europe and America.

Like the Walnut Street Jail (Fig. 21) which it superseded, the Eastern Penitentiary was intended to continue the Pennsylvania system of solitary confinement by reducing to a minimum the contact between prisoners. In this way it was hoped to give ample opportunity for repentance and at the same time to protect good resolves already made. Idleness was not a part of this plan, however, and prisoners were required to work in their cells, to which small individual exercise yards were therefore attached. But the real innovation at the Eastern Penitentiary, and the one that brought it much attention, was the arrangement of the cell blocks in a radial plan. This permitted a minimum of supervisory personnel stationed in the central building to keep all the prisoners under constant and almost simultaneous surveillance. Since this plan seems to have been used earlier in Europe for hospitals for the insane, Haviland cannot be considered the originator, but he was the first to apply it successfully to the design of prisons. As they had come to the Walnut Street Jail before, persons interested in penal reform came from Europe, as well as America, to study the results achieved at the Eastern Penitentiary, and further evidence of the extent to which Haviland's plan was in advance of its time is seen in the fact that Cherry Hill is still in use for prisoners requiring maximum security. Largely as a result of the success of the Philadelphia prison, Haviland was asked to rebuild Strickland's Western Penitentiary in Pittsburgh, as well as to design new prisons at Harrisburg, Reading, and Lancaster. States other than Pennsylvania also sought his services, among them New York, New Jersey, Rhode Island, and Missouri.

In Philadelphia, the influence of the Eastern Penitentiary may be seen in the façade of the County Prison at Moyamensing, begun in 1831 from the designs of Thomas U. Walter (Fig. 78). The style of both prisons conforms to what was then known as the Castellated Mode, derived, as the name implies, from the military rather than the religious architecture of the Middle Ages, and to be recognized by the crenelated battlements and terminal towers. Frequently, as here, the use of the Castellated Mode also called for a central tower, based presumably on the medieval keep. Other features usually associated with a castle, such as the slit windows, heavy walls, and doors closed with portcullises, must also have seemed especially appropriate for a prison.

As a county prison, Moyamensing was too small to use Haviland's radial plan, but provision was made for the confinement of approximately four hundred prisoners in separate cells arranged in two blocks of three stories each. Guards located at the head of the corridors running the length of each wing provided the necessary supervision. The section of Moyamensing Prison reproduced as Figure 79 shows the typical cells; each measured 13 feet long, 9 feet wide, and 9 feet high, and all were roofed with brick arches and floored with heavy oak planks. The problem of sanitary facilities, always an important consideration in a prison where maximum security and isolation of the prisoners is desired, was solved by providing a hydrant and an individual water closet in each cell. One set of ducts brought in fresh air and another warm air from the furnaces in the basement. Like the Eastern Penitentiary on which is was based, Moyamensing was so far in advance of prevailing practice that it has continued in use up to the present, although its demolition is expected to take place during 1963-64.

When first built, Sedgeley stood apart from the type of house customarily found in America, but as the century progressed the Gothic became more and more the preferred style for country residences. Associative values accounted for part of this popularity. A. J. Downing (1815-1852), the writer and landscape gardener who served as a kind of arbiter of American taste in the period prior to the Civil War, expressed it this way:

> Not a little of the delight of beautiful buildings to a cultivated mind grows out of the *sentiment* of architecture, or the associations connected with certain styles. Thus the sight of an old English villa will call up in the mind of one familiar with the history of architecture, the times of the Tudors, or of "merry England," in the days of Elizabeth. The mingled quaintness, beauty and picturesqueness of the exterior, no less than the oaken wainscot, curiously carved furniture and fixtures of the interior of such a dwelling, when harmoniously complete, seem to transport one back to a past age, the domestic habits, the hearty hospitality, the joyous old sports, and the romance and chivalry of which, invest it, in the dim retrospect, with a kind of golden glow, in which the shadowy lines of poetry and reality seem strangely interwoven and blended.

Although he was willing to admit the beauty of other styles, Downing's own preference was clearly for the Gothic.

No doubt in selecting the Gothic as the style for his country house (Fig. 80) Turner Camac was not indifferent to the associative values mentioned by Downing, but there was probably also another basis for his choice. This was the growing belief that the character of a building should conform to its site. In the cause of artistic unity, Renaissance architects had carried the lines of their architecture into the design of the surrounding gardens, but it remained for the architects of the Romantic Period to reverse this process by making the style of a building dependent upon its natural setting. And of all the past styles at his disposal, the architect of the early nineteenth century usually considered the Rural Gothic the most appropriate to the country. Because of its steep roof, pointed gables, and decorative barge boards along the eaves, a cottage such as that of Turner Camac seemed to belong to the irregular terrain and less well-kept paths and lawns, more frequently found in the rural areas than in urban ones. To describe a setting of this kind, including its architectural accompaniment, the term "picturesque" was habitually used—a word meaning literally "like or suitable to a picture," for it was originally from the painters that many of the principles of Romantic aesthetic had been derived.

As in the preceding periods of American architecture, a variety of English publications supplied the models for Gothic cottages such as that of Turner Camac. But in America special emphasis was given to the verandah as a kind of out-of-door room, standing midway between the house and garden, where man and nature met. For the inclement seasons of the year, some of the functions of the verandah were taken over by a conservatory such as that at Mrs. Camac's, described by Downing as "the most tasteful and elegant" that he had ever seen.

There is no reason to suppose that by building a Gothic house the Camacs were seeking to consolidate their position in Philadelphia society, but considerations of this kind did help to account for the popularity of styles based on the architecture of the past. For the growing middle class, associated in America with the rise of Jacksonian democracy, its use by a past generation seemed to offer some assurance concerning the "correctness" of a given style. Especially were the newly rich advised to avoid any appearance of "newness" about their possessions, lest they advertise the recent nature of their wealth. Much as today Georgian furniture is sometimes used in the hope of suggesting a cultured background for the owner, a Gothic house might be favored in the nineteenth century because its traditional character seemed to imply for its occupant a family history of comparable antiquity.

However appropriate to the rural cottage and the battlemented prison, the Gothic style had originated in a Christian context, and many of the forms used by Revival architects had a strong ecclesiastical flavor. This point was touched upon in speaking of the tower of Strickland's Masonic Hall, and it might have been made with even greater cogency by referring to such features as the rose window incorporated in the façade of Latrobe's Philadelphia Bank (Fig. 73) and Sloan & Stewart's Masonic Hall (Fig. 75). The medieval cathedral occupied much the same position in respect to those seeking to work in the Gothic style as the pagan temple had to those attempting to adapt Greek forms to the needs of contemporary society. Once interested in the past, it did not take historians long to recognize that Gothic art was the product of medieval culture, or to identify as Christianity the one factor which, more than any other, separated the Middle Ages from the Ancient World. Given this new awareness of history, it was inevitable that nineteenth century architects would find in the Gothic style one of the most fruitful sources for the designs of churches.

Among the Philadelphia churches in the Gothic style, the new façade added about 1810 to St. Mary's Catholic Church on South Fourth Street probably comes closest to sharing the characteristics of the other buildings discussed previously in this section. Of quite a different character, but still belonging in the category of early Gothic buildings by reason of its choice and treatment of medieval forms, is the St. Stephen's Episcopal Church, begun in 1822 and still standing on Tenth Street between Market and Chestnut (Fig. 81). William Strickland was the designer of this interesting building, but it has been suggested that he found in St. Stephen's in Vienna the model for the twin towers of the west façade. On the other hand, the crenelations that surmount the towers and run along the roof lines are reminiscent of the Castellated Mode—further evidence, perhaps, of the mixed ancestry of most early Gothic designs. Although roughcast brick was used for the exterior walls of St. Stephen's, the towers were built of gray stone. Enlargement and remodeling considerably altered the interior in the late nineteenth and early twentieth centuries, but earlier accounts of the church speak of the richness of the decoration and of windows filled with colored glass imported from England.

One of the most important results of the study of Gothic architecture was a new interest in the liturgy and sacraments of the Church. In England, Augustus Welby Pugin (1812-1852) was the best known and most influential of the medieval scholars whose enthusiasm for the Middle Ages led them to identify the Gothic style with the Christian religion. By his *Contrasts: or, a Parallel between the Noble Edifices of the Middle Ages and the corresponding Buildings of the Present Day; showing the Present Decay of Taste*, published in 1836, Pugin sought to explain the evils of the Industrial Revolution in terms of a decline in the religious orientation of society. Not content with writing only, Pugin left the Church of England, became a Roman Catholic, built himself a private chapel at Ramsgate, and before he died insane at the age of forty had done the work of ten ordinary men, including the designs for all the Gothic details of the Houses of Parliament in London.

Most of his countrymen were not willing to join Pugin in embracing Roman Catholicism, but there were many who were anxious to see reintroduced into the ritual of the Church of England some of the color and emotion lost during the Reformation. To promote this aim, the Camden Society was founded in Cambridge in 1839 and in 1841 began the publication of the influential *Ecclesiologist*. Later, when it had become involved in religious controversy, the Camden Society found it expedient to change its name to the Ecclesiological Society, by which it is perhaps best known in America. As Kenneth Clark has pointed out, the Ecclesiological Society proposed to reverse Pugin's position; whereas he had believed that better architecture could result only from a revival of religion, the Tractarians proposed to revive religion by reviving Gothic architecture. More than any other agency, it was the Ecclesiological Society that kept the Gothic Revival alive.

Although it may have originated at Oxford and Cambridge, the agitation for doctrinal and liturgical reform was soon felt on the other side of the Atlantic. And in America, as in England, Gothic art and the Anglo-Catholic elements of the Episcopal Church became confused with each other, often to the detriment of both. In 1846, for example, Richard Upjohn (1802-1878), designer of New York's Trinity Church and one of the best-known American architects who specialized in ecclesiastical buildings, refused to design a

Unitarian church on the grounds that the beliefs of its Boston congregation were at variance with those of the Anglican Communion to which he subscribed. Two years later in Philadelphia, when the parish of St. Mark's was founded, the vestry applied to the Ecclesiological Society for a suitable design for their projected church. The Society responded by submitting drawings by R. C. Carpenter in the Decorated style of English Gothic, favored by that group.

The local architect engaged to supervise the erection of St. Mark's was John Notman. His principal modifications in the plans sent over from England are said to have been the removal of the tower from the west end to its present position at the south porch and some reduction in the scale of the piers of the nave arcade (Fig. 82). True to the tenets of the nineteenth century that good architecture was the product of a moral society, the vestry had signs posted adjuring those working on the construction of St. Mark's from profanity of all kinds and reminding them of the sacred character of the work in which they were engaged. Because it was founded with the express purpose of "restoring Catholic worship" in the Episcopal Church, St. Mark's is rightly regarded as one of the first American churches to show the influence of the religious revival identified in England with the Camden Society and Oxford Movement. The extent to which Notman was dependent upon the plans sent over from England is made clear when St. Mark's is compared with his other churches in Philadelphia. Although not without architectural merit of a different sort, neither St. Clement's at Twentieth and Cherry streets (1859) nor Holy Trinity at Nineteenth and Walnut streets (1857-59) has the archaeological correctness of St. Mark's.

Few parishes could hope to raise the funds for a church the size and character of St. Mark's. Rural communities, especially, had to be content with more modest wooden structures, and to meet the needs of those parishes that could not afford the services of an architect, Richard Upjohn in 1852 brought out *Upjohn's Rural Architecture*. In Philadelphia, this type of "Carpenter's Gothic" was probably best exemplified by the Floating Church of the Redeemer, customarily anchored at the foot of Dock Street, where it would be convenient for the seamen using the port (Fig. 83). Supported on the hulls of two boats of approximately 100 tons each, this delightful Gothic building had all the prerequisites of a church, including a tower at the west end and an interior painted to resemble brownstone. Although not unique, the Floating Church at Philadelphia was considered important enough that a model of it was selected for display in the American section of the Great Exhibition at London in 1851.

The Rural Gothic was also the style selected for the wooden "castle" of the fishing club known as the State in Schuylkill. Founded in 1732 as the Colony in Schuylkill, this unusual organization has been called "the oldest club in the English-speaking world with an uninterrupted existence." Although the present Gothic house in which the members of the State in Schuylkill gather to enjoy each other's company and to make and drink their famous punch dates only from 1812, it is counted one of the earliest wooden buildings still surviving in the Philadelphia area, as well as an attractive example of the early Gothic style. Before it was moved to a location in Eddington, Bucks County, on the right bank of the Delaware, the "castle" stood on a site near Gray's Ferry, to which it had previously been moved from the right bank of the Schuylkill near the present Girard Avenue Bridge.

No doubt the fact that verticality was a dominant characteristic of medieval architecture suggested the use of the Gothic style for the taller structures coming into vogue about the middle of the nineteenth century. For Dr. David Jayne, the youthful William L. Johnston in 1849 designed such an eight-story, granite building in the Venetian Gothic mode (Fig. 84). The growing congestion of the large cities made greater height desirable, but an even more persuasive argument was the prestige that could be expected to accrue to the owner of the tallest building in town. The owner, in this case, was taking no chances that his identity or the nature of his business might be overlooked. In the print that he published to advertise his product, the name of Jayne appears in at least three places, and a large mortar and pestle, symbol of those who work with drugs and chemicals, was perched on each of the front corners of the roof parapet.

When Johnston died before the Jayne building was completed, Thomas U. Walter was engaged to continue the work. It was presumably he who added the castellated wooden tower, not unlike that used for Moyamensing Prison (Fig. 78). The tower of the Jayne Building was never replaced after it burned on the night of Mar. 4, 1872, in one of the most spectacular fires that Philadelphia had seen, but the remainder of the building was repaired and stood until 1958, when it, too, was demolished as part of the program to preserve and emphasize the Georgian architecture of the old part of the city.

The Jayne Building was a masonry structure built in the traditional manner, having little in common with the skeleton construction of the modern skyscraper. But in its attempt to give visual expression to the tall commercial building, Johnston's design looks to the future, rather than to the past. Well into the twentieth century the Gothic would continue to be used for such important skyscrapers as Cass Gilbert's (1859-1934) Woolworth Building in New York (1910-13) and the Chicago Tribune Tower, designed in 1922 by Raymond Hood (1881-1934) and John Mead Howells (b. 1869).

Its vertical qualities may also have been a factor in the selection of the Gothic style for the new standpipe designed for the West Philadelphia Waterworks in 1853 (Fig. 85). *Gleason's Pictorial* referred to this structure as "a notable curiosity" and described it as a heavy shaft of plate iron, 5 feet in diameter and 130 feet high, resting on a 50-foot base of cut stone. Birkinbine & Trotter were the engineers for the new West Philadelphia Waterworks, but no mention is made of the source of the cast-iron stairway or the colossal iron figure of Washington standing at the top. It is probable, however, that these decorative details were to be supplied by Robert Wood & Co., mentioned earlier in connection with the casting of the replica of Rush's "Nymph and Bittern."

About the time that the figure of Washington for the waterworks of West Philadelphia was under consideration, the firm of Robert Wood & Co. was preparing a similar cast-iron likeness of Henry Clay to stand on top of a Doric column, also of iron, at Pottsville, Pennsylvania. Complicated figures of this kind would normally be cast in more than a hundred separate parts, although experiments were said to be underway to perfect the casting of large figures in a single piece. In the 1850's when the popularity of decorative cast iron was at its height, Philadelphia directories list a number of persons engaged in manufacturing cast-iron fencing, but of these Robert Wood (the firm name varies slightly from time to time) was the most important. Only a small proportion of the decorative iron was marked with the maker's name, and popular patterns could easily be pirated, but there is no doubt that the output of Robert Wood's iron works, on Ridge Road near Spring Garden Street, was enormous. It is becoming increasingly clear, in fact, that most of the ironwork for which New Orleans and Charleston are justly famous was made in the North, much of it in Philadelphia.

THE FANCY STYLES: EGYPTIAN, CHINESE, MOORISH

The Greek and Gothic may have been the past styles most favored in the Romantic Period, but a variety of others were also employed on occasion, usually for their association with quite specific ideas. One of the first of these other modes to receive wide acceptance was the Egyptian. Although none of the architects mentioned earlier chose the Egyptian style with any frequency, most of them found it useful for special purposes. Latrobe proposed a room decorated in the Egyptian mode to house the Congressional library (*c*.1808); Strickland used the style for the First Presbyterian Church in Nashville, Tennessee (1849), and even Dorsey's Gothic Mansion (Fig. 72) is said to have had an Egyptian boudoir. A thorough study of the Egyptian Revival has yet to appear, but when it does, it seems almost certain that Philadelphia will emerge as having had at one time or another more Egyptian buildings than any other American city.

Since it shared many of the massive and forbidding qualities of the Castellated Gothic, the Egyptian style was early used for the design of prisons. When, for example, Thomas U. Walter was commissioned in 1836 to add a debtor's wing to Moyamensing, he selected the so-called Temple of the Sun on the Island of Elephantine in Egypt as his model. And the name "Tombs" by which the prison of New York City is popularly known is also a survival from an epithet more appropriately applied to an earlier building designed by Haviland in the Egyptian manner.

Although a number of travel books about Egypt had appeared in the late eighteenth century and even earlier Egyptoid motifs had occasionally been used in the designs of such artists as Fischer von Erlach (1656-1723) and G. B. Piranesi, the archaeological approach to Egyptian antiquities may be said to date from the French campaigns of 1798-99. Napoleon had taken with him into Egypt a number of competent artists and scholars whose job it was to study and record the antiquities with which the invading armies came in contact. Almost as important a result of the Egyptian Campaign as the discovery of the Rosetta Stone were the handsome publications of the emperor's Director of Fine Arts, Vivant Denon, which did more than anything else to acquaint the Western world with Egyptian art. As a consequence, about 1803 Eugène de Beauharnais added an Egyptian entrance to his Paris mansion, and motifs like those in the books of Denon made their appearance in the furniture and interior decorations of the Empire style. Nor was it a coincidence that the first structure in America to employ Egyptian forms in the design was the Battle Monument in Baltimore, designed in 1815 by the French architect, Maximilian Godefroy.

Although in its earlier phases the Egyptian Revival may often be regarded as a symptom of French influence, before it had run its course the style had taken on a kind of national aura. Aside from the fact that as early as 1782 a pyramid was adopted for the reverse side of the Great Seal of the United States, there was a popular belief that the early inhabitants of North and Central America were descended from the Egyptians. And if the Hudson River were likened to the Rhine, the Mississippi was considered the American Nile. The seriousness with which this idea was taken in the nineteenth century is attested today by the existence of such cities as Memphis, Tennessee, and Cairo, Illinois.

The specifically religious connotation increasingly associated with the Gothic style restricted somewhat its use for secular or non-Christian purposes. Perhaps it was a consideration of this kind—or it may have been only a desire to achieve a design consonant with his client's name—that led the unknown architect to select the Egyptian style for the Odd Fellows' Hall, built in 1847 and still standing at Third and Brown streets. As the "Christian" style, the Gothic must also have seemed unsuitable for synagogues, and since the Jews had no distinctive architectural style of their own, the Egyptian was sometimes used. No doubt its characteristic forms seemed vaguely "Eastern" in their origins; the nineteenth century was seldom very precise about such matters. However that may be, in Philadelphia William Strickland used the Egyptian style for Mikveh Israel (1824-1860), on Cherry Street, as did Thomas U. Walter twenty-five years later, for the Synagogue Beth Israel (1849-1894) on Crown Street. Presumably it was the quality of permanence associated with the stone architecture and dry climate of the Nile Valley that also recommended the Egyptian style for offices of the Pennsylvania Fire Insurance Company on Walnut Street, opposite Independence Square. Built in two parts, the first probably by John Haviland about 1839, the second around 1900, this attractive little marble building may before long be the only surviving example of the Egyptian style in Philadelphia, now that Moyamensing is scheduled for demolition and the Odd Fellows' Hall has been put to commercial use.

None of these associative ideas, however, seems to account for the Egyptian doorway and the smokestack in the form of a lotus-bud column at the Spring Garden Waterworks (Fig. 86). Probably the explanation, in this case, is fundamentally a structural one. The characteristic slope, or batter, regularly given to the walls of Egyptian buildings, by increasing their strength, made them especially suitable for use as reservoirs. The best-known of such structures was the Croton Reservoir in New York City, which once stood on the site of the present Public Library, but there was another example in Albany and presumably in other American cities as well. Transference of the architectural style from the reservoir that held the water to the structure that contained the pumps was a natural one of the kind that architects in the nineteenth century habitually made.

Because funerary art composed a large part of Egyptian antiquities, it was to be expected that the Egyptian would be the preferred style for the architecture associated with American cemeteries. Thus when Dr. William Swaim died in 1847 he was buried at Laurel Hill in a tomb of "pure Egyptian design" surrounded by eight obelisks "inscribed with the name of the deceased in appropriate hieroglyphic characters." This is not to say, of course, that any design that includes a pyramid or obelisk belongs necessarily to the Egyptian Revival. Since the Renaissance and before, such forms had come to be regarded as sepulchral and commemorative symbols in their own right. Even the giant obelisk designed by Robert Mills as a monument to Washington, and usually cited as the outstanding example of the Egyptian Revival in America, may owe quite as much to the Italy of Bernini as to the Egypt of Denon.

There seems no question, on the other hand, that the new interest in Egyptian archaeology lies behind Henry Austin's design for the gateway of the Grove Street Cemetery in New Haven, Connecticut, or of that of Jacob Bigelow for the entrance to Mount Auburn in Cambridge, Massachusetts. In Philadelphia, the curious entrance to the Odd Fellows' Cemetery, which once stood on Islington Lane near Ridge Road, appears to have been designed about 1850 by J. C. Hoxie and S. D. Button, and some fifteen years earlier in the competition for the design of Laurel Hill Cemetery both Strickland and Walter had submitted the Egyptian designs that may still be seen in the collections of the Library Company. In the end, however, the classic design finally approved for Laurel Hill was that proposed by John Notman, who also was the architect for a charming Gothic chapel, now demolished, but to be seen in Koellner's lithograph (Fig. 87).

Laurel Hill was one of three American cemeteries known especially for their rural beauties. Contemporary writers mention the picturesque arrangement of the monuments of Mount Auburn in Cambridge, and the breadth of the design of Greenwood in Brooklyn, New York, but Laurel Hill was considered remarkable for the variety of its trees and shrubs, as well as for the fine views of the Schuylkill River that it afforded. As they watched the increasing numbers of persons who visited the cemeteries in their spare time, it seemed to some that the moral lessons that the cemetery offered were being disregarded. "The only drawback to the beautiful and highly kept cemeteries," one visitor is represented as remarking, "is the gala-day air of recreation they present; people seem to go there to enjoy themselves and not to indulge in any serious recollections or regrets." The danger that the cemeteries might become the amusement parks of the day is reflected in some of the rules that many of the boards of managers adopted. Not only were the gates to be closed at sundown and no children admitted without a parent or a guardian who would be responsible for their behavior, but more significant still, it was found necessary to prohibit the consuming of food and drink within the grounds or the admission of any "party carrying refreshments." One of the custodians estimated that between April and December of 1846 over 30,000 people visited Laurel Hill, many of them only to enjoy its rural beauties.

The popularity of rural cemeteries like Laurel Hill was cited by A. J. Downing and others in support of the argument for the establishment of public parks in America. Largely as a result of his editorials on this subject, Downing in 1851 was invited by President Fillmore to lay out the public grounds in Washington as a Romantic park instead of the formal mall that L'Enfant had originally intended. Downing did not live to see the Washington park completed, but in 1858 his young English partner, Calvert Vaux, now in association with Frederick Law Olmsted, won the competition for the design

87

of Central Park in New York City. In spite of the political schemes that from time to time seemed to threaten its development, the merits of Central Park were soon demonstrated, and similar projects were begun in other American cities, including Brooklyn, Boston, and Chicago.

Philadelphia was not far behind New York in the establishment of a public park, if indeed it was not really ahead of it. The delight Philadelphians had taken in the little common surrounding Latrobe's Pump House in Center Square (Fig. 41) probably influenced the Watering Committee in its decision to landscape the five acres adjacent to the Fairmount Waterworks (Fig. 52), established in 1812. To these first five acres on the east bank of the Schuylkill, 23 more were added before 1828, so that about 1838 J. C. Wild in the description accompanying his view of Fairmount could speak of graveled walks and fountains where "vast numbers of people promenade at all hours of the day."

As noted earlier, Lemon Hill was next purchased by the city in 1844, largely to prevent its being used for commercial purposes that might contaminate the water of the Schuylkill. But so attractive for picnics did Philadelphians find the grounds of the old Morris estate (Fig. 29), that in 1855 this property was also set aside as a common. Two years later 34 acres of Sedgeley (Fig. 71), adjoining Lemon Hill on the north, were added to the city's holdings and the acquisition of Lansdowne in 1866 brought another 140 acres to what was now becoming one of the largest public parks in the country. In the late 50's and 60's plans such as that reproduced as Figure 88 were prepared for the development of this extensive tract, and in 1867 an act of the General Assembly of the Commonwealth of Pennsylvania designated the land along the Schuylkill as a public park, to be known as Fairmount and to be held as a public trust for the enjoyment of the citizens of Philadelphia and for the protection of the city's water supply. In 1868-69 the park was extended to approximately its present size, and the need to provide suitable space for the Centennial Exhibition in 1876 resulted in further improvements under the direction of Herman Schwarzmann. With more than 3,900 acres within the city limits, Fairmount is today the largest municipal park in the world and one of the most beautiful.

The curving drive that appears in the water color of Turner Camac's Gothic cottage (Fig. 80), no less than the winding paths and roads of Palles' design for Fairmount Park (Fig. 88), are further evidence of the great change in taste that had taken place since Holme had used the grid plan for his design of Penn's great town. Known frequently as the "English Style" from the country of its origin, this more "natural" approach to landscape design had been formed in the eighteenth century from a variety of sources. Boredom with the geometric formality of Renaissance art, the love of Englishmen for walking in the out-of-doors, and the cool, moist climate of Great Britain, which fostered tall trees and fine lawns, all contributed to the new style. The fact that the landscape paintings of Claude le Lorrain (1600-1682), Gaspar Poussin (1613-1675) and Salvator Rosa (c.1615-1673) were especially favored as models for this new type of design helps to explain the use of such terms as "landscape garden" and "picturesque" in this connection. Nor should the philosophical and political appeal of the new style be overlooked. It was thought to be no coincidence that the same country that gave rise to the informal garden was also

88

known as the Mother of Parliaments. Freedom of design was associated with freedom of thought. The landscape garden, as Nikolaus Pevsner has made clear, was also the garden of liberalism.

The studied informality of the English garden also drew inspiration from the porcelains, lacquers, and painted papers imported from the East. In many ways, Oriental art was the antithesis of that of the West; in contrast to the balance and symmetry of geometric forms that were the basis of the classical styles, Chinese artists relied on asymmetrical compositions made up of irregular, curvilinear shapes. Again the appeal was to the unfamiliar, the distant in place, and the remote in experience. The British East India Company had been organized in 1600, and by the eighteen century the influence of trade with the East on the English way of life is attested by the appearance of a variety of new words such as chinaware, chintz, and of course tea, with its innumerable compounds: teaspoon, tea table, tea party, tea time, and the like. This relationship between the asymmetry of Oriental art and the irregularity of the new taste in landscape design did not go unnoticed on the Continent where, especially in France, the English garden was frequently referred to as being in the Anglo-Chinese manner.

In spite of the virtues attributed to Oriental peoples and their governments by many Westerners in the eighteenth century, the Chinese style continued to be regarded, for the most part, as something exotic, applicable more to man's pleasures and amusements than to the serious affairs of life. Perhaps this had something to do with the absence of reliable models upon which a Chinese architectural style suitable for Western use could be based. Yet even the superb furniture designed by Chippendale in the Chinese mode was usually intended for the private sitting room or boudoir rather than for the state apartments. Oriental styles were considered especially appropriate for the garden, however. Thus Sir William Chambers (1723-1796) used Palladian models for the London government building known as Somerset House, but for the Royal Gardens at Kew (1757-62) he designed a number of pavilions in a variety of exotic styles, including the large pagoda still visited yearly by thousands of sightseers.

The form of the pagoda at Kew was taken from Chambers' own book, *Designs of Chinese Buildings, Furniture, Dresses, Machines and Utensils* (London, 1757), and the same source probably supplied the model for the Pagoda and Labyrinth Garden erected in 1828 near Fairmount (Fig. 89). John Haviland was the designer of this unusual group of buildings, including the 110-foot pagoda constructed of colored brick, wood, and iron. A winding stair led to the top of the pagoda from which there was a fine view of the Schuylkill River, and as an added Oriental touch windbells were hung from the projecting beams of the roof. Except for the view, contemporary accounts fail to make clear just what other pleasures one could expect to find in a "labyrinth garden." Whatever they were, they do not seem to have attracted Philadelphians in sufficient numbers to make the project pay. Not even the proximity of the Pagoda and Labyrinth Garden to the popular Waterworks was sufficient to compensate for its remoteness from the city and the poor state of the roads. Almost from the start, the project was a failure, and the unfortunate promoter, P. A. Browne, who had also been associated with Haviland on the unsuccessful Arcade, heard himself referred to as "Pagoda Arcade" Browne.

A Chinese pagoda also served as the cupola on the house called China's Retreat, built before the end of the eighteenth century in Bucks County by Andreas Everardus van Braam Houckgeest, a Dutchman who had been engaged in the China trade before he became an American citizen. To be considered "Chinese," however, an American house need only have a curving roof and a few scallops on the barge board along the eaves. That, in any case, seems to be the justification for applying the term to the house that John Notman designed for Nathan Dunn at Mount Holly, New Jersey. Dunn's interest in having a Chinese house was to be explained by the years he had spent in the Orient. There he had assembled a large collection of Chinese objects, including wax figures in native costume, household articles, and curios of various kinds. In order to display his Chinese collection to the public, in 1838 Dunn rented the first floor of the building begun a year or two before at Ninth and Sansom streets by two of the sons of Charles Willson Peale when the success of their father's exhibits on the third floor of the Arcade made larger quarters desirable (Fig. 90).

Soon the building on Sansom Street was known simply as the "Chinese Museum," and visitors to Philadelphia frequently mentioned it as one of the principal attractions of the city. "Unique both in Europe and America" was the way one person expressed it, while another considered that a few hours in the Chinese Museum approached "closely to a visit to China." Obviously the less one knew about the Orient, the more exciting seemed the Chinese Museum. Finally, however, it ceased to be a novelty, and financial reverses led Dunn to transfer his collections to London where they were eventually dispersed. Without its most profitable tenant, the Philadelphia Museum Company failed along with the Bank of the United States, its mortgagor, in the panic of 1841, although final dissolution did not come until 1846. For almost ten years thereafter the Chinese Museum, as the building continued to be known, was used for a variety of entertainments and exhibitions, until on the night of July 5, 1854, it was totally destroyed by the fire that also consumed the National Theater adjoining it.

In addition to the Chinese, other Eastern styles also made sporadic appearances in America during the Romantic Period. Near Bridgeport, Connecticut, P. T. Barnum about 1848 built Iranistan, an Oriental villa inspired by Brighton, the lavish marine pavilion in England originally designed about 1805 for the Prince Regent by Humphry Repton (1752-1818) and including motifs probably suggested, in turn, by Thomas Daniell's *Antiquities of India* (London, 1800). Nor were such exotic forms confined to American private residences; at about the same time that Barnum was erecting his "Persian" palace, Henry Austin incorporated a variety of Indian and other Eastern motifs into the design for his otherwise Italianate railroad station at New Haven. Prior to 1860 Philadelphia produced nothing so exuberant as Iranistan or the New Haven Railroad Station, but in several of his popular books Samuel Sloan did picture a number of Oriental villas, recommended especially for locations along the Hudson or the Mississippi. A house based on the most elaborate of these designs was actually begun in 1861 at Natchez, Mississippi, by

90

Dr. Haller Nutt, who had made a fortune through the growing of cotton. Unfortunately the outbreak of the Civil War prevented its completion, but even in its unfinished condition, Longwood, as Nutt's Oriental fantasy was called, has remained a delightful relic of one of the more whimsical interludes in American taste, as well as an interesting example of the work of an important Philadelphia architect.

For understandable reasons, even those most closely connected with it were not always agreed as how best to describe the style of such a building as Longwood. Frequently it might go under the name of "Moorish," a much-abused word employed in the nineteenth century to mean almost any loose collection of vaguely Eastern motifs, ranging all the way from Byzantine to Mogul and including Persian, Arabic, and Saracenic. The difficulty of defining what, exactly, was Moorish had the advantage of making it almost impossible to say what was not. These exotic qualities of the style related it to the Chinese and inevitably recommended its use for garden architecture; Chambers chose it for several of the pavilions designed for Kew, and in America it became one of the favorite styles for bandstands and similar buildings erected in public parks. Much as the Gothic novel had helped to prepare the ground for the revival of medieval architecture, a growing interest in the Moslem culture of Spain was attributable in part to such books as Washington Irving's *The Conquest of Granada* (1829) and *Tales of the Alhambra* (1832), as well as to the travel accounts of A. F. Calvert.

Because of its Near Eastern origins, the Moorish, like the Egyptian, was occasionally used for synagogues such as New York's Temple Emanu-El (1868-1927) or the Plum Street Temple in Cincinnati, built during the Civil War. The dates of these two temples are a reminder, moreover, that the Moorish style came into prominence later, and remained popular longer, than either the Egyptian or the Chinese. This would apply also to the two most prominent Moorish buildings in the Philadelphia area, Horticultural Hall (Fig. 113) and Wanamaker's Grand Depot (Fig. 114), both of which date after 1860 and are therefore most appropriately discussed as part of the High Victorian style.

THE ITALIANATE STYLES

By the second quarter of the nineteenth century enough time had elapsed since Georgian builders had looked to Palladio and his contemporaries for their models that it was possible for architects to regard the art of Italy once again with a fresh eye. Although not as distant in place as the Orient, or as remote in time as classical Greece or the Middle Ages, Italy—especially Italy of the Renaissance—was sufficiently removed from the everyday experience of Americans to appeal to the Romantic interest in the unfamiliar. To the other revivals of the period may therefore be added the Italianate.

No one had more to do with stimulating interest in Italian architecture than John Notman, the young Scot who had settled in Philadelphia in 1831, and who was mentioned previously in connection with St. Mark's Church (Fig. 82) and the design of Laurel Hill Cemetery (Fig. 87). In 1845 Notman was also winner of the competition for the design of

91

a new building for the Athenaeum of Philadelphia, a private library operated, like its New England counterparts, primarily for the benefit of its shareholders (Fig. 91). By its avoidance of classical orders and dependence upon the detailing of windows and the heavy cornice for its effect, the Athenaeum ultimately goes back to the Renaissance architecture of central Italy. But the more immediate source of the design seems to be such English buildings as the Manchester Athenaeum (1836) and the London Reform Club (1837), both the early work of Sir Charles Barry (1795-1860).

For reasons of economy the directors of the Athenaeum felt obliged to dispense with a lecture room on the first floor in favor of offices that could be rented. Notman's dignified stairway was retained, however, as were the classical details of the great library room with its screen of Corinthian columns at the east end overlooking the garden. A pair of stone balls was later substituted for the candelabra at either side of the front entrance in the engraving, but otherwise the Athenaeum remains essentially as Notman had designed it. And since it was one of the first buildings to use brownstone, the Athenaeum must also have helped to inspire the later vogue for that material in Philadelphia.

Probably on the basis of his work at Laurel Hill, about 1837 Notman was engaged to design for the Rt. Rev. George Washington Doane, Protestant Episcopal Bishop of New Jersey, the house now recognized as one of the first Italian villas in America. Riverside, Bishop Doane's residence in Burlington, still stands as part of St. Mary's Hall, a Church school for girls, and other examples of Notman's work in this style are also preserved at Princeton, New Jersey. Nassau Hall has lost the upper story of the lateral towers Notman added after the fire of 1855, but Prospect (1849) now serves as the official residence of the president of the University. Although most of Notman's villas in the Philadelphia area appear to have been demolished, old photographs give some idea of the Italianate design of Fern Hill, erected in 1849-50 for Henry Pratt McKean, and Alverthorpe, built in 1850-51 by Joshua Francis Fisher.

In publishing designs for houses like that by Notman for Bishop Doane, Downing customarily referred to the style as the "Tuscan" or sometimes as the "Modern Italian," and similar houses were in fact being built in contemporary Italy, long the goal of the Grand Tour of Americans and Europeans alike. Not that American architects who used the villa style had necessarily been to Italy; English publications such as those of Robert Lugar (c.1773-1855), J. B. Papworth (1775-1847), Francis Goodwin (1784-1835), and John Claudius Loudon (1783-1843) offered a wide variety of designs in the Italian style that might be adapted for American use (Fig. 92). But, as in the case of the Rural Gothic, mentioned earlier, American houses, like that in Figure 92, differed most markedly from their English counterparts in the emphasis given to the verandah. Although used occasionally for public buildings such as Upjohn's City Hall at Utica, New York (1852-53), the Italian style was especially popular for suburban residences. Such prominent American architects as Henry Austin, Gervase Wheeler, and A. J. Davis all designed villas from time to time, and any doubts concerning their social acceptability must have been dispelled when the Prince Consort planned the very Italianate Osborne for Queen Victoria.

The reasons behind the selection of the Italian style for suburban residences were related to those that help to account for the choice of the Rural Gothic for country houses. Although they may not have attempted to adapt the building to the specific site in the manner familiar to modern designers, the Romantic architects did seek a style appropriate to the general environment. And since, by definition, the suburbs lay between the country and the city, the style appropriate to a suburban residence would share some of the regularity of the classical styles associated with the city, and some of the informality regarded as a primary characteristic of the Gothic, preferred for buildings in the country. To many, the Italian villa seemed best to meet these requirements; its plan and silhouette had something of the picturesque irregularity of the Gothic, while its characteristic brackets, round-headed openings, and balconies had obviously a classical origin. The villa, moreover, was capable of almost infinite modification. For those who had the means and the desire, a variety of bold towers, balconies, verandahs, and conservatories could be included, as in Figure 92, but where space or funds were a consideration, a few brackets along the eaves and perhaps a small cupola on the roof were all that were required to identify a simple cube as belonging to the Italian style. Villas of this kind made up a large part of the developments under construction in suburban West Philadelphia in the decades prior to the Civil War. Hamilton Terrace on Forty-first Street north of Woodland Avenue is a good example of one such street laid out about 1854 in the Italian style for Samuel A. Harrison, the industrialist and real estate promoter, by Samuel Sloan, from whose *Model Architect* Figures 92 and 93 are taken.

In plan and elevation the house in Figure 93 conforms to the Italian type, but in place of the usual brackets a medieval "corbel table" has been introduced, thereby transforming it into what its designer referred to as a "Norman villa." Such arbitrary combinations of elements from a variety of sources are especially common after the middle of the century when it becomes increasingly difficult to apply specific historical names to architectural styles. In 1851 Sloan & Stewart designed this impressive mansion for Andrew M. Eastwick who had it built on the grounds of Bartram's gardens below Gray's Ferry. Constructed of brick roughcast to imitate stone, Bartram Hall, as Eastwick called his estate, was one of the most important examples of the villa style to be erected in the United States. Visitors exclaimed over its marble mantels, the view from its 90-foot tower, and its shower baths with hot and cold running water. Of more interest today, however, is the irregular plan and unbalanced façade. Not since the Middle Ages had builders deliberately sought such asymmetry with all the freedom and convenience that it implies. Perhaps in the end this will prove to have been the greatest contribution of the picturesque aesthetic to the architecture of the twentieth century.

Although in practice the towers and cupolas of the nineteenth-century villas were put to a variety of uses—or in many cases used for nothing at all—in theory, at least, they provided an opportunity for such a view of the countryside as might be desirable in a suburban location. By eliminating the more rural features such as the towers, cupolas, and verandahs, the Italian style might also be adapted for use in the city, as in the case of the mansion built for Joseph Harrison, Jr., whose ample fortune had been made building railroads in Russia (Fig. 94). Completed in 1857 from the designs of Samuel Sloan, this great house stood on the east side of Rittenhouse Square between Chancellor and Locust streets. At the rear was a large garden shared with the adjacent row of houses on Locust Street. Until torn down with the Harrison mansion to make way for the Penn Athletic Club (now the U.S. Signal Corps), the Locust Street row of houses represented yet another instance of a type of community planning that had long interested Philadelphia architects. In Harrison Row could also be seen a simpler version of the standard repertory of Renaissance motifs, just as today the continuous marble moldings surrounding the round top doorways of hundreds of row houses throughout the city are remnants of a period when the Italian style was in fashion.

In describing the Harrison mansion Sloan was careful to point out to his readers the implication of the balanced design. "Its symmetrical and chaste character is in harmony with regular and cultivated scenery," he wrote, "rather than with an uneven and picturesque prospect," adding: "it should be located on a spot 'shaven by the scythe and leveled by the roller'; in other words, where the hand of art has been pruning, grading and refining, rather than amid the rugged and irremovable inequalities of nature." As published in Sloan's *City and Suburban Architecture* the plan of the Harrison mansion included a conservatory with an octagonal greenhouse, a 50-foot dining room, a domed picture gallery, and a billiard salon with a ten-pin alley, adjoining. Heat was supplied by a hot water system of a perfected type just coming into use. In 1912 Edward T. Stotesbury acquired the Harrison mansion, still considered a half-century after its erection one of the most sumptuous in the city.

The association of the Gothic style with the Ecclesiological Society and the high church elements in the Episcopal Church may have been a factor in the decision to use the forms of the Palladian Revival for the new Roman Catholic Cathedral on Logan Square (Fig. 95). Fathers Maller and Tornatore, two priests with architectural training, are believed to have developed the first plans, but much of the exterior design was evolved in the mid-50's under the direction of John Notman. The façade, particularly, is reminiscent of Palladio's Venetian churches, and the dome pictured in the lithograph is not unlike Bramante's unexecuted design for St. Peter's. As finally carried out, however, the west towers were omitted, and the dome was lowered by the elimination of the Corinthian colonnade when lack of funds forced the substitution of wood for the masonry construction originally planned.

The architect for the interior of the Cathedral of SS. Peter and Paul was Napoleon LeBrun. The son of a French diplomat who had come to the United States during Jefferson's administration, LeBrun had been born in Philadelphia and there received his architectural training in the office of Thomas U. Walter. Professional recognition for LeBrun came early in life; awarded the commission for the Catholic Cathedral when he was only twenty-five, eight years later, in partnership with G. Runge, he won the competition for the design of the Academy of Music to be erected on the southwest corner of Broad and Locust streets. The last was clearly an unusual opportunity, and by careful study of the characteristics of European opera houses, LeBrun and Runge were resolved to make the auditorium in Philadelphia the equal of any in the world. When told that the total cost

94

of the new building could not exceed $250,000, the architects are said to have replied that for that sum they could complete only the interior, leaving the exterior to be finished when more funds were available. But in architecture the temporary has a perverse way of becoming the permanent. The Academy has never received its stone exterior, and as an indication of the way it was intended to appear, we have only the architects' drawing (Fig. 96).

For the design of the interior of the Academy the architects seem to have had in mind the neo-Baroque style then coming into vogue in the France of Louis Napoleon. Crimson, cream, and gold were the dominant colors, and the light from hundreds of gas jets in the great crystal chandelier brought out the carvings on the tiers of boxes as well as above and beside the stage. But more important to the success of the Academy than its handsome decor were its remarkable acoustics. As in all matters of this kind, chance undoubtedly played a part in the result, but there are also indications that the Building Committee considered the problem carefully and that the architects went to unusual lengths to achieve this end. The surfaces of the walls were kept "soft" to absorb the sound and diminish the possibility of echoes, and to increase resonance several pits were introduced beneath the floor of the parquet and the stage, as shown in the section from Runge's monograph on the Academy (Fig. 97). Ventilation, too, received its share of attention; in order to expel through the cupola the heat from the gas jets, along with the bad air from the auditorium, a shaft, eight feet wide, was included in the center of the ceiling above the chandelier.

The completion of the Academy of Music seems also to have brought to an end LeBrun's association with Runge, and soon after the Civil War he forsook Philadelphia entirely in favor of New York City. There in partnership with his two sons, Michael (d.1913) and Pierre (d.1924), he continued to practice architecture under the name of N. LeBrun & Sons. Among the best known of the firm's buildings is the tower of the Metropolitan Life Insurance Co., patterned on the campanile of St. Mark's in Venice and at the time of its completion in 1910 the tallest office building to be found anywhere.

The most elaborate example of the Italianate Revivals in Philadelphia was not, as might have been expected, either the opera house or the Roman Catholic Cathedral. Rather it was the Presbyterian church (Fig. 98) built in 1855 on the southeast corner of Arch and Eighteenth streets from the designs of Joseph C. Hoxie. Of a style called simply "Roman" in one contemporary account, the bell towers and central cupola, rising to a height of 170 feet, gave the design of this remarkable building a distinctly Baroque cast. Even after the removal of these features, the West Arch Street Presbyterian Church stands up well against the very much larger Cathedral of SS. Peter and Paul, two short blocks away, a consideration to which its builders were probably not indifferent. The fondness of the period for combining the characteristics of one style with those of another is again seen here in the Gothic qualities of the "tracery" of the windows, derived from models of the early Renaissance rather than those of the later periods to which the bell towers and cupola seem more closely related. The Corinthian order of the exterior is continued in the auditorium where originally opaque panes of glass in the ceiling and dome shed a soft light on what is still one of the most spacious interiors in the city. Today Hoxie has been nearly forgotten, but in the 1850's and 1860's he was one of the most successful architects in the

95

state. Singly and in partnership with S. D. Button, his brother-in-law, mentioned earlier as the designer of the First Reformed Dutch Church (Fig. 70), he designed some of the most important houses in Philadelphia. He seems also to have made a specialty of churches, for examples of his work in this category are found throughout Pennsylvania and as far west as Ohio.

The view of the Department for Males of the Pennsylvania Hospital for the Insane has been included here (Fig. 99) not as much for the modified Italianate style of its architectural design as for the attitude toward man and society that it represents. Quaker Philadelphia had early set a high standard of humanitarianism by its establishment of alms houses, hospitals, and better prisons. Such social consciousness was the exception at the time the Walnut Street Jail and the Pennsylvania Hospital were built, but by 1850 this point of view had gained wide acceptance throughout the Western world and especially in America. Free schools and the education of women were two such areas in which the nineteenth century made important progress. Another was the care and treatment of the insane, heretofore regarded as little more than animals.

In questions of behavior, environment seemed to the nineteenth century the deciding factor. This point was made in connection with the attempt of the Ecclesiological Society to revive religious faith by reviving Gothic architecture, but it might be applied also to the treatment of the mentally ill. Even before the medical basis for insanity was understood, an attempt was made to relieve mental illness by improving the patient's surroundings. Credit for leading the agitation for a more humane attitude toward the insane goes to Dorothea Dix (1802-1887), who began her work of reform in Massachusetts; but the most widely accepted method of treatment was worked out by the Philadelphia alienist, Dr. Thomas Kirkbride. Under this system maximum isolation of the patients was sought through the use of a building made up of extended wings arranged in an echelon plan. Any suggestion of a prison was to be avoided, and from the surrounding park, usually landscaped in the English manner as in Figure 99, special therapeutic advantages were expected to be derived.

The pioneer example of Kirkbride's system was the Department for Mental and Nervous Diseases of the Pennsylvania Hospital, erected at Forty-fourth and Market streets between 1836 and 1841 from the plans of Isaac Holden. As a young man Samuel Sloan had been employed as a foreman at the Pennsylvania Hospital and in this way formed a friendship with Dr. Kirkbride. Thus, when a new department for male patients was needed in 1856, the commission went to Sloan who, largely on the strength of Dr. Kirkbride's recommendation, was already recognized as a kind of specialist in hospitals for the insane. More than thirty such institutions are said to have been erected from his plans, a number of them in states as far away as Kentucky, Alabama, Minnesota, and Connecticut. In 1851 Sloan's design for a public school was also selected by the Board of Comptrollers; this meant that between 1852 and 1857 his firm held a virtual monopoly of school design in Philadelphia, and after 1855 in much of the state of Pennsylvania.

The upper cornices of the Academy of Music were made of iron, and by the middle of the century the relative cheapness of this material and the ease with which it could be cast into a variety of complicated shapes contributed to its growing popularity. Although earlier buildings erected in England and midwestern United States had made use of cast-iron plates fastened together in various ways, the development of iron-fronted structures on the Atlantic seaboard is usually associated with the name of James Bogardus (1800-1874) in New York. Bogardus' earliest building of this type was completed in 1848, and two years later in Philadelphia the Penn Mutual Life Insurance Co. followed suit with a cast-iron building for its new offices on the northeast corner of Third and Dock streets. In drawing his plans for the Penn Mutual Building, G. P. Cummings had supposed that he was designing a masonry structure, but when it later developed that it would be more economical to cast the Italianate details in iron than to carve them in stone, the same forms were translated into the new material without substantial change. Further status was conferred upon cast iron by its use in T. U. Walter's additions to the Capitol in Washington, including, most importantly, the great dome erected during the years of the Civil War.

Speed and economy also recommended cast iron for the fronts of the commercial buildings erected on lower Market Street during the 1850's and 1860's. Only the possibility of casting the elaborate decorative details in some such material as iron made economically practical such a building as that designed by S. D. Button about 1857 for Dale, Ross & Withers (Fig. 100). In his use of iron supports Bogardus may have taken an important step toward the achievement of the type of skeleton construction that makes possible the modern skyscraper, but most of the architects who used cast iron in the third quarter of the nineteenth century did so as a cheaper substitute for masonry. Presumably the construction that lies behind Button's façade did not differ materially from that of any building made of brick or stone. There seems to have been a brief resurgence in the popularity of the iron fronts in the 1880's before changing taste and new building codes at last rendered them obsolete. The Penn Mutual Building was demolished in 1956, and most of the other iron fronts in Philadelphia are gradually disappearing. Among the best examples that still remain is the Lit Brothers department store at Eighth and Market streets, erected from the designs of Collins & Autenrieth.

Cast iron must also have played a part in the interior decoration of many of the more fashionable stores such as that of Charles Oakford (Fig. 101). Once the mold had been made, it was relatively inexpensive to turn out Roman cornices by the yard and classical ornaments in almost unlimited quantity. Iron was also the preferred material for elaborate gas lighting fixtures such as the ones on the counters in Oakford's store. Those ornamental details that did not lend themselves readily to casting might be cut from wood by the means of the jigsaw, which by the middle of the century was rapidly displacing the skilled carver from his traditional role in architectural design. So well did his model hat store prosper that in 1856 Oakford admitted his two sons to the firm and in 1860 moved his whole establishment to the fashionable Continental Hotel, opened that same year on the site formerly occupied in part by the Chinese Museum (Fig. 102) and now by the Benjamin Franklin Hotel.

In Philadelphia, as in other cities, the first hotels were simply converted houses like the Bingham mansion, noted earlier (Figs. 27 and 53). Although many of its distinctive

97

features had appeared in earlier buildings such as James McComb's City Hotel in New York (1794), James Hoban's never-completed Union Public (Blodgett's) in Washington (c.1795), and the Exchange Coffee House Hotel in Boston (1809), the first example of the modern luxury hotel is usually considered to have been the Tremont House in Boston, designed by Isaiah Rogers and opened in 1829. The Tremont established Rogers as the leading American authority on hotels during the period prior to the Civil War; in Charleston, South Carolina, the Charleston Hotel, in Cincinnati the Burnet House, and in Nashville the Maxwell House were all built from his designs. In contrast to those of Europe, American hotels by charging comparatively modest rates for their rooms catered to the middle classes, earning thereby the title of "Palaces of the People." As it was later by the motion picture and television, public taste in the nineteenth century was considerably influenced by the style chosen for the latest hotel, and there, too, many an American had his first experience with a bathtub and the flush toilet.

Throughout the nineteenth century Philadelphia was often referred to as the "City of Homes," and possibly the distinction of its private residences may help to explain the absence of public hotels of the importance of the Astor in New York or the St. Charles in New Orleans. The Merchants' Hotel on Fourth Street between Market and Arch, designed by William Strickland about 1837 and now a warehouse, was as near as Philadelphia came to possessing a first-class hotel in the period prior to 1850. In 1852 the Girard House, designed by John McArthur, Jr., and Edward Collins was opened on the northeast corner of Chestnut and Ninth streets, across from the buildings then occupied by the University of Pennsylvania, on the present site of Gimbels department store. The Girard House was owned by the Edward brothers, who also built from McArthur's designs the following year the La Pierre Hotel (later called the Lafayette) on Broad Street where the Land Title Building stands today.

In general the architectural styles employed for American hotels paralleled those used for other types of buildings. Isaiah Rogers' Tremont House did much to popularize the Greek Revival for hotel design, but gradually Doric columns gave way to the angle quoins (squared stones) and balconies of the Italian Renaissance. The design of both the Girard House and the La Pierre made restrained use of Italian forms, and this was also the style selected for the Continental (Fig. 102), designed in 1857 by John McArthur, Jr., who in this period emerges as Philadelphia's principal architect of hotels. By selecting brownstone for the Chestnut Street façade, as well as in the use of the other motifs of the Renaissance *palazzo*, McArthur was continuing for the Continental a style first introduced in Philadelphia a decade before in Notman's Athenaeum (Fig. 91). A difference not discernible to the eye, however, was the use of cast iron for the cornice of the hotel.

Accounts of the Continental Hotel boast that the brownstone stair that rose from the main lobby (Fig. 103) was the only "self-sustaining" (i.e., free from the wall) example in the country. And of even more interest was the elevator, referred to at the time as a "vertical railway." Historians would probably not agree with the owners of the Continental that theirs was the second elevator in the country (the first one being in the Fifth Avenue Hotel in New York), but there is no doubt that it was a very early example or that hotels played an important part in the development of all aspects of the mechanical plant, including not only elevators but central heating, plumbing, and ventilating as well. Since even the finest hotels were usually obsolete within twenty or thirty years, architects in order to attract the public had to be on the alert for the latest mechanical devices and the most fire-resistant construction. Not a few of the pushbuttons associated with American culture by Europeans were first developed for use in luxury hotels.

In addition to the lobby, the ground floor of the Continental was taken up with public rooms and shops such as that of Charles Oakford, mentioned earlier. On the second floor a promenade, 165 feet long, led to an exterior balcony, and on either side were arranged the larger public parlors and dining rooms. As in the case of other major hotels of the period, many of the special rooms and suites must have been lavish in their appointments. Commenting upon the furnishings of a rival hotel in New York, *Putnam's Magazine* spoke of the bridal chambers as so "scandalously spendid" as to make timid brides "shrink aghast at its marvels of white satin and silver brocade." Estimates of the size of the Continental differ somewhat, but it seems to have provided accommodations for at least 1,000 guests.

One contemporary account referred to the Continental as a "monster" towering over everything else in the city. But even larger than many of the hotels and opera houses of the period were the "Frigate Houses" built by Philip Justice at the United States Naval Yard on the Delaware below Wharton Street. The largest of these, erected in 1822, was 270 feet long, 103 feet high, and 84 feet wide, making it one of the most conspicuous objects in the area.

Ship-building in Philadelphia dates almost from the founding of the city, for as early as 1683 William West had established his shipyard at the foot of Vine Street, and this was soon followed by others. By the time of the Revolution, abundance of good materials and the enterprise of such men as Bartholomew Penrose and his descendants had made Philadelphia one of the major ship-building cities in the world. The lithograph reproduced as Figure 104 shows the Sectional Floating Dry Dock in the shipyard of J. Simpson & Neill at the foot of Christian Street. By this device the entire hull of a vessel could be exposed for repairs in the light and air, instead of in the cramped quarters of the conventional dry dock. Sparks's shot tower lies to the right, and beyond it are the shipyards of Joshua Humphreys who designed and built the frigate "United States," America's first battleship. In 1875 the Pennsylvania Railroad acquired this area in Southwark along the river between Prince and Wharton streets when the Navy Yard moved to its present location on League Island.

Many of the most important buildings erected in Philadelphia during the first half of the nineteenth century are seen in their relationship to each other and to the city as a whole in the lithograph based on a painting by J. Bachman (Fig. 105). In the center foreground is the Permanent Bridge, now widened to accommodate the railroad tracks, and the larger structure just beyond it on Market Street is the first city gas works. Since it was built in 1836 at the height of the Greek Revival, the gas works had smokestacks in the form of gigantic Doric columns, and the largest storage tank used as guides twelve sets of

99

classical columns, arranged in groups of three, four tiers high. Cast iron was used for the guides, and to judge from R. A. Smith's description their location conformed to accepted classical practice: the Tuscan order was employed for the first row, Doric for the second, Ionic for the third, and Corinthian for the fourth. In the lower left corner of Bachman's view is the Wire Bridge and the Waterworks, with the Fairmount Reservoir beyond. The classic temple at the extreme left is, of course, Walter's Girard College, and slightly to the southwest of it lies Haviland's Eastern Penitentiary, to be distinguished by its radial plan. Nearer the center, the domes of the West Arch Street Presbyterian Church and the Cathedral of SS. Peter and Paul are conspicuous features—the latter showing the high drum with its classical colonnade as planned but never built. To the right of center is Strickland's St. Stephen's Church, and in the upper right-hand corner may be seen the Frigate Houses.

100

VICTORIAN ECLECTICISM
(c.1860–c.1890)

A COMPARISON OF THE SYNAGOGUE ERECTED IN 1869 FOR THE CONGREGATION RODEPH Shalom (Fig. 106) with such earlier buildings as the Second Bank (Fig. 54), St. Mark's (Fig. 82), or the Pagoda (Fig. 89) suggests the change in taste which separates most of the architecture of the first half of the century from much of that of the second. Fraser, Furness & Hewitt are still eclectic architects in that they rely on past styles for the sources of their architectural forms, but the remote in time and place has ceased to have the same fascination that it held for an earlier generation. The builders of the period of Rodeph Shalom no longer seek to conjure up visions of Greek philosophers engaged in solemn contemplation beside the blue Aegean, of monks at their devotions in the dim light of medieval cloisters, or of Chinese mandarins in temple gardens. By becoming more familiar, history has lost some of its power to excite the imagination; the designers of Rodeph Shalom seek neither mood nor archaeological correctness. To be sure, the association of Arabic architectural motifs with a religion of Near Eastern origin is consistent with the earlier practice of using Egyptian and Moorish styles for synagogues, but here Gothic forms are combined with the horseshoe arch and onion-shaped dome in a fashion that has little historical relevance.

The propriety of identifying an American architectural style by the name of an English queen, especially a queen who ruled for sixty-three years, is perhaps open to question. But most of us are willing to overlook the fact that Victoria came to the throne in 1837 because it has become convenient to associate her name with taste after the Great Exhibition of 1851, rather than with that before it. In terms of English art this is the style of Alfred Waterhouse (1830-1905) and G. E. Street (1824-1881), and particularly of Sir George Gilbert Scott (1811-1878) and the Albert Memorial (1863-72). And that is the sense in which the word is used here.

Nor does it seem inappropriate to call the style of Rodeph Shalom by a name which implies that English sources had something to do with its distinctive design. For behind the insistent polychromy of the arch voussoirs of alternating colors lies the Venetian Gothic popularized by John Ruskin (1819-1900). Unlike Stuart and Revett, Palladio, and Vitruvius, Ruskin was not a professional architect. Today we should probably call him an essayist and art critic, but his *Seven Lamps of Architecture,* first published in 1849, had as profound an influence upon Western taste as any book ever written. In the *Lamps* Ruskin sought to disentangle the Gothic style from Catholic ritual, even though by his insistence upon the ethical basis of art he owed more to Pugin and the earlier Gothic Revivalists than he was willing to acknowledge. For northern countries Ruskin favored the medieval styles of England, but it was his praise of Italian Gothic in the *Stones of Venice* that inspired the polychromy which perhaps as much as anything else identifies the High Victorian style.

101

In its use of alternating red and ocher, as well as in the flat ornament based on stylized plant forms, Rodeph Shalom owes much to Ruskin.

Further evidence of the Victorian love of color in architecture is seen in the selection of green serpentine stone for the buildings erected by the University of Pennsylvania on its new campus in West Philadelphia. Called "Collegiate Gothic" even then, the ornate structure illustrated in Figure 107 was one of four buildings erected in the 1870's from the designs of Thomas W. Richards, who held an appointment as Instructor in Drawing on the faculty of the University. Except for the east and west towers removed in this century, College Hall, as it is known today, retains much of its original appearance. Green walls are set off by base courses of brownstone, cornice and gables of lighter "Ohio stone," and polished red granite columns supporting an entrance porch constructed of what the architect referred to as "Franklin stone." Geometric tracery in the large window above the porch identifies the location of the original chapel, and old guide books speak of a variety of laboratories and lecture rooms, as well as special apartments for the faculty, trustees, provost, and student societies. Even by modern standards College Hall has much to recommend it, and when it was built it must have represented one of the most advanced academic plants in the country. It seems also to have had the approval of the trustees, for in 1874 they promoted Richards to be the University's first Professor of Drawing and Architecture.

But of the events of the second half of the nineteenth century none had more profound effects on American art and taste than the preparations made in Philadelphia to celebrate the completion of one hundred years of American independence. For one thing, the approach of the Centennial served to focus attention once again on the State House, which had led a somewhat uncertain existence since it had ceased to be a state or federal capitol. Purchased by the city in 1818 when it seemed as though the state legislature might be going to demolish all the buildings on Independence Square and sell the land for building lots, it had been put to a variety of uses during the next half century. Lafayette's visit of 1824 served briefly to stimulate interest in the sites associated with the Revolution; William Strickland was commissioned in 1828 to erect a new spire on the State House patterned on that removed in 1781, and two years later John Haviland began the restoration of the Assembly Room on the east end of the first floor. It must have been about this time that the simple doorway on Chestnut Street was replaced by the more elaborate one framed with Corinthian columns that appears in Poleni's drawing (Fig. 108). In front of the doorway stands J. A. Bailey's statue of Washington, erected in 1869 with funds provided by the children in the public schools of Philadelphia.

The appearance of the Assembly Room following Haviland's restoration is shown by Max Rosenthal's water color of 1856 (Fig. 109). William Rush's statue of Washington stands at the east end of the room, and on the walls are the portraits of more than one hundred Colonial and Republican figures purchased by the city at the sale of Charles Willson Peale's Gallery in 1854. The fact that there might be a dog pound in the cellar or a refreshment stand in the front hall did not prevent the East Room from being used for exhibitions and official receptions during the 40's and 50's. In 1848 the body of John

102

Quincy Adams lay in state there, and this custom was again followed at the time of the death of Henry Clay and the assassination of Lincoln.

In preparation for the observance of the centennial of American independence, City Councils set up a committee to restore the Assembly Room to what was considered to be its pre-Revolutionary appearance. Peale's small paintings were replaced by larger portraits of the founding fathers. The president's dais was rebuilt, and four columns thought to have originally supported the ceiling were reintroduced. Various miscellaneous objects that had found their way into the room (including the block of marble intended as the city's contribution to the Washington Monument) were removed, and furniture believed to have been in the East Room in 1776 was assembled from public and private sources.

As the first century of American independence approached its close, a number of individuals and organizations suggested ways whereby the centennial year 1876 might most appropriately be celebrated. Of these proposals, that of the representatives of the Franklin Institute of Philadelphia for an international exhibition in their city received the most favorable attention. Accordingly, on February 24, 1870, the City of Philadelphia, the Franklin Institute, and the Commonwealth of Pennsylvania together memorialized the Congress to "stimulate a pilgrimage to the Mecca of American Nationality, the Home of American Independence," by authorizing an International Exhibition of Arts, Manufactures, and Products of the Soil and Mine. In March of the following year the United States Centennial Commission was created by an act of Congress, and subsequent legislation provided for a Board of Finance composed of twenty-five directors with authority to issue capital stock to the limit of $10 million. By the summer of 1873 arrangements had progressed sufficiently far that President Grant was able to issue a proclamation that the exhibition would be held in 1876 and inviting foreign nations to participate. On the following day, July 4, 1873, the Commissioners of Fairmount Park made available 236 acres of land bordering on the Schuylkill and extending from Lansdowne Avenue to Belmont.

The idea for an international exhibition was not of course either new or original. Historians would trace its origin at least as far back as the fairs of the Middle Ages, but the proponents of the Philadelphia Centennial undoubtedly had in mind more recent examples. In the second half of the nineteenth century important international exhibitions had been held at London (1851 and 1862), New York (1853), Paris (1855 and 1867), and Vienna (1873). Together these offered valuable precedent and experience upon which the commissioners might draw as they made their plans for an exhibition in Philadelphia.

Following the pattern set by the Crystal Palace designed by Joseph Paxton for the London Exhibition of 1851, the Committee on Plans and Architecture first thought in terms of a single building to cover 44 acres, a portion of which was to be so designed that it might remain as a permanent structure to be known as Memorial Hall. It was also intended that a second temporary building would be constructed near by and that this would serve during the exhibition as an art gallery. These, in brief, were the terms of the first unlimited competition announced by the committee in 1873. The authors of the ten best projects were each to receive $1,000 and to be given the privilege of submitting designs in a second and final competition.

103

By July 15, 1873, when the first competition closed, forty-three designs had been received; the majority were from Philadelphia and New York, but some came from as far away as San Francisco and New Orleans. Unknown amateurs were represented as well as established architects. Plans varied considerably among circles, squares, and rectangles and, in recognition of the patriotic basis of the exposition, the star received rather more prominence than was perhaps architecturally desirable. Many of the designs showed the influence of earlier European exhibitions, and most of them included a large central dome or some form of a tower that would serve to give the building an appearance of dignity and importance and at the same time afford the visitor who ascended it a view of park and city.

Of the ten architects who were selected to submit designs in the final competition, four were awarded additional premiums. Fourth place went to the brothers Henry A. and James P. Sims of Philadelphia, who received an award of $1,000 for a design that included a permanent memorial building resembling somewhat a Gothic cathedral. Henry Sims, the elder of the two brothers, had come to Philadelphia from Canada about 1860, and there in the fifteen years before his early death at the age of forty-three had designed several churches and a number of country houses, as well as helped to form the Philadelphia Chapter of the American Institute of Architects. Together with his younger brother, James, Henry Sims served as architect for the Girard Avenue Bridge, erected between 1872 and 1874, to replace an earlier wooden structure (Fig. 110). Although not as famous as the Colossus or the Permanent Bridge, the Girard Avenue span was considered at the time of its erection the widest bridge in the world; by way of it many of the thousands of sightseers who attended the Centennial Exhibition reached the west bank of the Schuylkill.

Two other Philadelphia architects, John McArthur, Jr., and Joseph M. Wilson, placed third in the final competition with a brick and iron structure surmounted by a 500-foot tower which, had it been built, would have been at that time the highest in the world. McArthur was mentioned earlier as the designer of the Continental Hotel, and both he and Wilson figure prominently in the history of Philadelphia architecture of the latter half of the nineteenth century. Second place was awarded by the Committee to the neo-Baroque design submitted by Samuel Sloan, the Philadelphia architect mentioned in the preceding section for his contributions to the Italianate revivals. But for the design that included the largest dome and the most elaborate decoration the Committee reserved first place and the prize of $4,000. This was submitted by the same firm of Collins & Autenrieth that earlier had been associated with the Grand Lodge Room for Sloan's Masonic hall (Fig. 76). Grandeur is likely to be expensive, however, and when the commissioners found that the winning design would cost nearly $8 million to build, they decided to abandon the original plan to erect one large structure in favor of a variety of smaller buildings devoted to specific purposes. There was precedent for this decision, since a number of separate pavilions had been tried with considerable success at the Paris Exposition of 1867. In the end the Centennial Exhibition was housed in almost two hundred buildings of many shapes and styles. Most of these have disappeared but their original appearance and location are suggested by such panoramic views as that published in *Harper's Weekly* (Fig. 111).

Considerations of cost probably also played a major part in the Commission's decision to dispense with the services of the architects who had placed in the competitions and to rely instead on those already in the employ of the Commission or practicing in nearby cities. The large Gothic structure of wood and glass at left center of the balloon view is Agricultural Hall, designed by James H. Windrim. A native Philadelphian, Windrim attended Girard College and after a brief apprenticeship with John W. Torrey had entered the office of John Notman. Perhaps the influence of Notman's Holy Trinity should be seen in the design with which in 1867 Windrim won the competition for the new Masonic temple at Broad and Filbert streets (Fig. 112). In view of the fact that he was only twenty-seven at the time and that the winning design seems a somewhat mechanical performance, it is possible that Windrim's activities as a Mason carried more weight with the Building Committee than his professional qualifications. In any case, the Masonic Temple was an important commission, and its successful completion in 1873 undoubtedly had much to do with bringing its architect to the favorable attention of the Commissioners for the forthcoming Centennial Exhibition. Although Windrim's building in Fairmount Park covered seven and one-half acres and provided 236,572 feet of exhibition space, it was the smallest of the five major structures. Someone estimated, in fact, that half the population of Philadelphia could have been accommodated at one time in the Main Exhibition Building (Industrial Hall), which formed a large rectangle 1,876 feet long, visible in the center of the aerial view from *Harper's* (Fig. 111). Both this building and the similar but smaller Machinery Hall, located a short distance to the west, were designed by Henry Pettit and Joseph M. Wilson. Unlike many of the other structures of the Centennial, both these buildings were largely devoid of decorative details and their essentially utilitarian character may have been suggested to Pettit by his study of earlier European exhtions as well as by the engineer's training that he and Wilson shared.

Like Agricultural Hall, Industrial Hall and Machinery Hall were temporary structures and both were demolished shortly after the close of the Exhibition. Horticultural Hall and Memorial Hall, on the other hand, were intended from the first as permanent buildings that would remain as ornaments to the Park and monuments to the Exhibition, and it is therefore surprising that their design was turned over to a young and largely unknown engineer in the employ of the Fairmount Park Commission. This was Herman J. Schwarzmann, the son of a fresco painter of Munich, who had come to the United States about 1864 when he was a young man in his early twenties. In addition to the large permanent structures, Schwarzmann was also responsible for the Women's Pavilion, Judges' Hall, and the Carriage Building. After the close of the Exhibition, Schwarzmann moved to New York and there in partnership with Alfred Buchman continued to practice architecture until shortly before his death in 1891.

By far the most substantial and elaborate structure on the Exhibition grounds, and the only one of importance that remains standing today, was the building known then, and now, as Memorial Hall. Standing north of the Main Exhibition Building in the eastern portion of the Centennial enclosure, it is situated on a commanding rise of ground above the nearby Schuylkill River. The cost of the building was paid by the state of Pennsylvania, since it was expected that it would remain as the home of the Pennsylvania Museum of Art or possibly as a legislative hall, should it later be determined to move the capital of the Commonwealth from Harrisburg to Philadelphia, as some had proposed. And Memorial Hall did, in fact, serve as the museum of Philadelphia from the close of the Exhibition of 1876 until the erection of the present building on Benjamin Franklin Parkway. Fortunately, its abandonment as a museum did not mean the destruction of Memorial Hall. Following years of neglect, it is now undergoing extensive repairs to adapt it to use as a modern recreation center for the Philadelphia area.

Horticultural Hall (Fig. 113) was less fortunate. After being damaged by high winds in the fall of 1954, it was pulled down in spite of the fact that it was one of the most interesting examples of the Moorish style to be found anywhere and by any standard a major monument of American architecture of the nineteenth century. In its use of glass and iron Schwarzmann's design was reminiscent of Paxton's building for the London Exhibition of twenty-five years before and thereby typified the interest of the period in new materials and methods of construction. At the same time the Moorish style chosen for its decorative details continued the romantic love of the exotic that had colored American taste throughout the preceding half century, especially for the architecture of gardens, expositions, and resorts. In this and other respects Horticultural Hall looked to the past, rather than to the future; it was perhaps the last great building of its kind that would be devoted to the subject of horticulture, for the second century of America's independence would see her transformed from a nation concerned predominantly with agriculture to one engaged largely in industry. Even in 1876 Machinery Hall with its great Corliss engine was challenging Horticultural Hall and the various agricultural exhibits for the interest of the visitors to the Centennial.

In his *Centennial Portfolio* Thompson Westcott expresses his regret that in a few months all the buildings that had sprung up "as if by magic" would in the same fashion disappear, leaving only Horticultural Hall and Memorial Hall "to tell the story of the greatness of the Exhibition to succeeding generations." Possibly more remains of the Centennial than Westcott expected; the Catholic Total Abstinence Fountain is still in place, as are the houses erected by Ohio and Great Britain nearby. The Wisconsin Building was moved to Bala-Cynwyd where it still serves as a private residence, and other structures were moved or re-erected at nearby resorts such as Atlantic City and Cape May. After first serving a number of other purposes and undergoing extensive alterations, the Japanese Pavilion today functions as the station of the Pennsylvania Railroad at Strafford on the Main Line. Such a list of the relics of the Centennial could probably be extended, but Westcott was undoubtedly right that for most people Memorial Hall would remain, as those who built and named it intended from the first that it should, the principal symbol of the exhibition that celebrated the first century of American independence and thereby exerted an almost incalculable influence upon American art and taste.

Perhaps the design of Horticultural Hall had something to do with the selection of Moorish forms for Wanamaker's new department store, opened for business the same year as the Centennial (Fig. 114). The name "Grand Depot" customarily applied to this rambling structure prior to about 1885 was a survival from the use of the sheds at Thirteenth and Market streets as the freight station of the Pennsylvania Railroad. Most of his contemporaries must have thought John Wanamaker mad to consider moving his Men's and Boys' Clothing Store from modest quarters on the southeast corner of Sixth and Market streets to an abandoned railway depot with two acres of floor space. But even more revolutionary for the time was the concept of offering many kinds of goods under one roof, all clearly marked, with the same price for every customer. Yet, as everybody knows, the idea worked. Within a few months after the new store was opened women's apparel was added to the men's and boys' and before the end of the first year, a mail-order department was established to serve the areas outside the city. Now a "retail dry goods store," instead of one devoted entirely to clothing, in 1877 Wanamaker's arranged its 129 counters in concentric circles and provided 1,400 stools on which its customers might sit while making their selections. By 1885 the number of employees had grown to five thousand, and a list of the separate departments would fill a good-sized page.

Schwarzmann may have used Moorish forms for Horticultural Hall because of the relationship of its function to that of the garden, long associated with the more exotic architectural styles, but for the design of Memorial Hall he appears to have relied more on current European models, especially those of the immensely influential Ecole des Beaux Arts in Paris. In this he was following in the path of earlier American architects who since the middle of the century had shown an increasing willingness to accept the leadership of the French in matters pertaining to the arts. Even T. W. Richards had thought it desirable to introduce mansard roofs on the Collegiate Gothic buildings for the University of Pennsylvania (Fig. 107). In this case the result of such hybridization was a style then sometimes referred to, logically enough, as the Franco-Norman—just the kind of unhistorical combination of architectural forms in which the Victorian Period took delight.

Samuel Sloan claimed the house built for a Dr. Evans near West Chester in 1860 as the first mansard roof in the Philadelphia area, and although there were certainly earlier examples in New York and elsewhere, it appears that what a contemporary writer referred to as the "Mansard Madness" did not reach Philadelphia in a virulent form until the mid-1860's. One of the earliest and most attractive examples of the style is the Union League club at Broad and Sansom streets, built in 1865 by John Crump from the designs of John Fraser. With its graceful curving stairway leading to the front door, the "League" has always contrived to look more like the public's concept of a great private mansion than a large men's club and thereby to convey the impression of dignified hospitality remarked upon in the local press on the occasion of its opening. About the time that the Union League was being completed work was beginning on the mansion on Chestnut Street at Nineteenth, designed by John McArthur, Jr., and therefore among the first Philadelphia houses to employ the mansard roof (Fig. 115). McArthur's client was the same Dr. David Jayne mentioned earlier as having purchased the Arcade (Fig. 63) and for having built the most important of Philadelphia's early tall buildings (Fig. 84). Unfortunately, Jayne did not live long enough to enjoy his fine house, but his family resided there until the opening years of the twentieth century. In 1922 the Jayne mansion was razed to make way for the Aldine Theater.

107

The popularity of French architecture in the United States was largely the result of the building campaign of Napoleon III, which had made Paris under the Second Empire one of the most brilliant of the European capitals. For the style of his new buildings Napoleon looked back to the French Renaissance when capable architects such as François Mansart (1598-1666) had succeeded in giving the classical motifs derived from Italian sources a distinctly national appearance by the addition of such forms as the steep roofs associated with his name. Impressed by the buildings of Paris, whether seen in books or at first-hand, rich Americans such as Dr. David Jayne insisted on mansard roofs for their mansions, while American architects were also employing the French Renaissance style for a variety of other purposes. James Renwick (1818-1895) chose it for Vassar College at Poughkeepsie and the Corcoran Art Gallery (c.1873) in Washington. As early as 1862 Boston commissioned G. J. F. Bryant (1816-1899) and Arthur D. Gilman (1821-1882) to design its new City Hall in this fashionable style, and the next two decades saw the erection throughout the United States of innumerable railroad stations, banks, stock exchanges, and insurance companies, all under the spell of France.

But the principal exponent of the French style for municipal buildings was unquestionably Alfred B. Mullett, who was the architect of the State, War, and Navy Building in Washington (1871-87). Although born at Taunton, England, Mullett had come to the United States in 1845 when his parents settled in Ohio. For a time prior to the Civil War he was associated in architectural practice with Isaiah Rogers, but his preference for French Renaissance forms was probably the result of his previous training at European schools. In 1865 President Johnson appointed Mullett to the Office of the Supervising Architect of the United States Treasury Department, and during the next decade he seldom departed from his favorite style for the scores of government buildings erected under his direction throughout the country. Post offices in Boston, St. Louis, New York, and Chicago, customhouses in Portland, Maine, and Madison, Wisconsin, and a mint in San Francisco are only a few of the best-known examples.

Nor was Philadelphia overlooked in the dispensing of federal funds. On the site formerly occupied by the President's House (Fig. 31) and more recently by Strickland's buildings for the University of Pennsylvania (Fig. 60) John McArthur, Jr., supervised the construction of a new post office based on Mullett's design (Fig. 116). Built between 1873 and 1884 at a cost of over $7 million, the Philadelphia Post Office was a good example of the use of the French Renaissance manner for municipal buildings. As it had for many other structures of the period, the Louvre seems to have been the inspiration of the central pavilion on Ninth Street for which the American sculptor Daniel Chester French (1850-1931) provided the decorative figures. In the 1870's so elaborate a style doubtless seemed particularly expressive of the wealth and importance of the federal government, although today Mullett's designs are not usually regarded as constituting one of the more distinguished periods of American architecture.

The Philadelphia Post Office was demolished about 1935 to make way for the present U.S. Court House, and most of the other buildings of the period patterned on the forms of the French Renaissance are also rapidly disappearing. Fortunately, the greatest example of the style in America—or anywhere at all, for that matter—still stands. This is, of course, the Philadelphia City Hall (Fig. 117).

The story of the City Hall is too long to be recounted here, assuming it could be unraveled. As early as 1860 the commission for the design of the new City Hall was given to John McArthur, Jr., in preference to Samuel Sloan or George S. Bethell, who had also submitted drawings. At first the Commissioners of Public Buildings seem to have had in mind several smaller structures, rather than a single large one, and as late as 1869 there appear to have been those who considered a location on Independence Square preferable to that at the junction of Broad and Market streets. A number of McArthur's earlier drawings for the City Hall are classical in character; some make use of the Corinthian order and at least one includes a Roman dome reminiscent of that on the Capitol in Washington. But the Civil War brought to an end the first phase of planning for a new municipal building in Philadelphia, and it was 1870 before the project was taken up again. By that time the enthusiasm for the French Renaissance was at its height, and as finally constructed between 1871 and 1881 the City Hall was a conspicuous example of that style.

With McArthur on the City Hall was also associated Thomas U. Walter, now an old man at the end of his career. Some have seen Walter's hand in the elegance of detailing, others in the monumentality of the tower, but we shall probably never be able to identify precisely his contribution to the whole. When built, the City Hall was the largest office building in the world. Its size is a symptom of its American origin, but it is also a basic characteristic that distinguishes much of the architecture of the High Victorian Period from that of the earlier part of the century. On the basis of such buildings as the Philadelphia City Hall the last half of the nineteenth century has sometimes been called "The Age of Elegance." Such grandeur is not easily come by, and if the effective handling of space be regarded as the essential of great architecture, then the interior court, when taken together with such rooms as the council chamber and mayor's apartments, entitle City Hall to favorable consideration with any of the best architecture of the past or present. The faults of the French Renaissance style were chiefly those of any formula too uncritically accepted and too often repeated.

In the decades following the Civil War few architects could resist the twin influence of Ruskinian Gothic and the French Renaissance. Not even Frank Furness, certainly one of the strongest spirits of the age, was entirely immune, as his design for the Pennsylvania Academy of the Fine Arts gives evidence (Fig. 118). Mansard roofs of French origin are here combined with the Gothic forms and love of color made popular by Ruskin. And to this unlikely union Furness has brought his own love of violent contrasts. The rough brown stone of the lower portions of the façade is juxtaposed to the patterned brick and smooth lighter stone above. The columns are polished pink granite, and before it deteriorated from exposure to the weather, a Greek statue stood on the pedestal above the doorway, silhouetted against the geometric tracery of the Gothic window.

Furness and his two partners, John Fraser and George W. Hewitt, have been mentioned previously as the designers of Rodeph Shalom (Fig. 106). This must have been one of the earliest important commissions of the firm, since only two years before, young Furness

109

had returned from New York where he had gone shortly after the Civil War to study in the office of Richard Morris Hunt (1827-1895). As one of the first American architects to study in Paris at the Ecole des Beaux Arts, Hunt, on his return to this country, in 1857 had established in his own office a studio for the training of young architects, based on the French atelier system.

But it is not as much the Renaissance tradition fostered by the Ecole that Furness' style resembles as the architectural projects of Eugene Emmanuel Viollet-le-Duc (1814-1879), the great French theorist and restorer of Gothic buildings. How closely the spirit of many of Furness' buildings echoes that of the illustrations in the *Dictionnaire de l'architecture française* (1854-68), and especially the *Entretiens sur l'architecture* (1863-72), has often been remarked. But to call attention to one of the sources of Furness' architectural ideas is not to suggest that his work is a copy of any past period or of any earlier architect; the more Viollet-le-Duc's designs are studied in this connection, the bolder and more inventive Furness appears. As a practicing architect Viollet-le-Duc was concerned largely with the restoration of Gothic buildings, and his most unusual ideas got no further than the pages of his books; but Furness had the opportunity and the daring to express his in brick and stone.

"Daring" is probably the right word to apply to the building designed by Furness in 1879 for the Provident Life and Trust Company. Even without name or number it is easily spotted among its conventional neighbors in Baxter's view of the north side of Chestnut Street between Fourth and Fifth Street (Fig. 119). The writer in *The Evening Telegraph* probably spoke for the majority of his contemporaries when he described the anxiety with which he had watched the process of construction: ". . . there has been a constant strain on the public mind as to what might be coming," he wrote. "This strain has finally been relieved by the last stones having been set in their places. Can it really be," he then goes on to inquire, "that this is a coming American Nineteenth Century style which we are slow of heart to recognize?" The writer of the comments in the *Telegraph* must have found the interior of the Provident scarcely less disturbing than the exterior. Green and white Minton tiles covered most of the walls of the great banking room, which extended the full height of the building and was lit at the top by skylights supported on polychromed iron trusses. The pyramidal roof in Baxter's view may not have been a part of the original design but the stumpy columns certainly were, and these united with the cantilevered tower and harsh clash of form and textures to make the Provident one of Philadelphia's most controversial buildings. When the bank was finally demolished in 1960, the controversy broke out anew; for everyone who believed that the city was losing one of its architectural treasures there were at least two others who felt that an eyesore was at last being removed. Without taking sides in an argument that has already been effectively decided, it might be suggested that the future has a vested interest in any building that after seventy-five years is still spoken of in superlatives, even if some of them are unfavorable. All Furness' major banks have now been demolished, leaving only the Centennial Branch of the First National (now the First Pennsylvania Company) at Market and Thirty-second streets as evidence of this important aspect of his professional activity.

But even those Philadelphians who cared least for the Provident could hardly disown entirely either it or its author. Furness was one of them, first and last, as perhaps no other architect has ever been. His father was Dr. William H. Furness, an ardent abolitionist and minister of the First Unitarian Church at Tenth and Locust streets (Fig. 57). Except for his military service during the War (when he was awarded the Congressional Medal of Honor for valor) and his brief period of study in the office of Hunt in New York, Furness seems seldom to have left the city of his birth, and only rarely did he have a commission outside the Philadelphia area. Not, of course, that he was alone in his perverse disregard for the generally accepted standards of aesthetic beauty. In England the designs of William Butterfield (1814-1900) have points of similarity and there were even American contemporaries who shared some of his ideas of architectural form. But Furness did regularly and boldly what others did occasionally and usually timidly.

It is not surprising that when he came to Philadelphia in search of professional instruction, Louis Sullivan (1856-1924) found Furness the only architect with whom he cared to study. Both men regretted it when the panic of 1873 brought an end to their association only a few months after it had begun, but Sullivan was always grateful that his introduction to the architectural profession had been in an office where standards were high and creative talent clearly in evidence. In a number of ways Sullivan and Furness had much in common, not only in their attitude toward architecture, but also in their love of free, flowing ornament made up of natural forms not unlike those of the style to be known in Europe as *Art Nouveau.* Furness was the most original architect that Philadelphia produced, prior to the twentieth century, and Sullivan, as everyone knows, was the only man whom Frank Lloyd Wright was willing to call Master.

Like others in all professions, Furness seems to have grown more conservative as he grew older. Although to the last his style retains its individual characteristics, the designs of the 80's and 90's no longer stand out as sharply from the main stream of late Victorian architecture as did the Academy of Fine Arts and the Provident Life and Trust Co. Bank. In this category of later structures is the building erected for the Library Company at Locust and Juniper streets about 1880 (Fig. 120), perhaps best described as a kind of *tour de force.* The clue is found in the gracefully curving steps and the statue of Dr. Franklin in the pediment, for the whole façade is, in fact, a Victorianization of Thornton's earlier building on Fifth Street (Fig. 26). It is easy to imagine that Furness enjoyed this opportunity to play with Georgian forms in much the same fashion as earlier he had distorted Gothic motifs for his own expressive purposes.

Among Furness' last commissions was the Library of the University of Pennsylvania, opened in 1890. The butt of many a campus joke and now considerably altered, it must have been a model of advanced planning when first built. Earlier writers stress its economy, convenience, and utility, and to imagine the original appearance of the main reading room with its great open fireplace is to hope that the architects of the new library, now in the process of construction, will somehow contrive, in terms of the present day, to provide the student with so a humane an atmosphere for study.

About 1881 Furness entered into partnership with Allen Evans, who ten years before had left the office of Samuel Sloan in favor of that of Furness & Hewitt. Two years after the completion of the University Library, Furness, Evans & Co. (there were a number of silent partners) received their largest commission and one that occupied their attention from 1892 to 1894. This took the form of an addition to the Broad Street Station, the first portion of which had been erected from the designs of Wilson Brothers & Co. and opened to the public in 1882. As constructed, the addition was considerably smaller than that shown in the preliminary study, reproduced as Figure 121, but it was still several times the size of the original station seen at the right of the architects' rendering. In its final form the new addition contrasted with the original even more markedly than in the earlier studies, but in all his proposals Furness seems to have intended to continue the use of similar Gothic forms carried out in the same materials: rough granite and brick in a variety of plain, molded, and enameled forms. Terra cotta, then a relatively new material in America, had been used by the Wilson Brothers, but its application was considerably extended by Furness. Among the examples of decorative sculpture Karl Bitter (1867-1914) provided for the Broad Street Station are said to have been some of the largest pieces of terra cotta ever fired. Furness also continued the general plan of the earlier building. In each case the waiting rooms lie behind the large windows of the second story, just as the smaller openings of the upper stories indicate the presence of the offices of the Pennsylvania Railroad. The location of the waiting rooms above the street level is readily understood when it is remembered that, because the Broad Street Station was in the center of the city, the railroad tracks, after crossing the Schuylkill, were raised high on a massive masonry foundation, dubbed the "Chinese Wall" by Philadelphians. Thus one passed directly from the waiting rooms to the train house carried above Fifteenth Street on heavy iron girders and extending to the rear a full city block. The 300-foot span of the new train shed made it the largest in the world—so large, in fact, that in order not to interrupt train service the old shed was not demolished until the new one had been built over it.

The 3,000 tons of metal that went into the new train shed for the Broad Street Station are a reminder of the increasing interest of late Victorian architects in the structural aspects of iron. By mid-century, buildings such as Paxton's Crystal Palace had demonstrated the advantages of a structural system based on metal supports, but in spite of evidence of this kind iron continued to be thought of primarily as a medium from which complicated shapes could be cast more economically than they could be cut in stone. Had the Broad Street Station been built a few years earlier, many of the decorative details carried out in terra cotta might very well have been cast in iron. When iron was used structurally, it was most frequently as an occasional beam or as isolated supports in an otherwise masonry building. Understandably, the structural possibilities of iron and steel first attracted the attention of engineers concerned with the erection of bridges or of architects engaged in solving a variety of contemporary problems, such as those posed by railroads, department stores, and libraries for which there was no clear historical precedent. But even here, metal structural members were usually regarded as something to be disguised inside a masonry shell, or, if exposed, to be kept separate from the more traditional (and therefore more

112

"architectural") parts of a building, as in the case of the train shed of the Broad Street Station.

Somewhere between the traditional architectural solutions of the past and the unexplored world opened by new materials and methods of construction, brought in by the Industrial Revolution, lay the structural and aesthetic problems of the tall building. The answer offered by Addison Hutton in the new Girard Life Insurance, Annuity and Trust Co. erected on the northeast corner of Broad and Chestnut streets in 1888, was typical of many (Fig. 122). Hutton will be recalled as having designed ten years before the severely classical Ridgway Library on South Broad Street, and there was probably little in his earlier association with Samuel Sloan that would suggest satisfactory answers to the problems raised by the multistoried commercial building. Commenting on the new structure on Chestnut Street, one periodical mentions in passing the fact that Hutton had submitted five previous schemes before finding one acceptable to the client, and if the earlier designs resembled that finally executed, such indecision is easily understood. The concern of the medieval builders with height had early recommended the Gothic style for tall structures, as in the case of the Jayne Building (Fig. 84), and this tradition is continued by Hutton. Instead of Gothic, however, the models used here are the Romanesque forms made popular in America by the work of Henry Hobson Richardson (1838-1886). Moreover, in this case Hutton seems to have been at no pains to disguise the specific sources of his design: the great piers with their connecting arches are paralleled by similar features on the Marshall Field Warehouse in Chicago (1885-87) and the tower on the corner is of the Salamantine variety also used by Richardson a few years earlier for Trinity Church in Boston (1872-77). In all probability a good deal of metal was employed in the Girard Building, but the effect, nevertheless, is of a masonry structure erected in the conventional manner.

Hutton belonged to a growing minority of architects who for one reason or another chose to practice alone, for a significant aspect of the architectural history of the last quarter of the nineteenth century was the growing importance of American architectural firms. Even so marked an individualist as Frank Furness found it convenient to have partners in his architectural practice. As early as 1873 Chicago had its Burnham & Root and 1880 saw the establishment of Adler & Sullivan in that city. On the east coast from New England to Florida scores of clubs, railway stations, hospitals, hotels, libraries and palatial private residences gave evidence of the popular success of McKim, Mead & White (founded 1879) or of Carrère & Hastings (1885); it would take still another firm, Shepley, Rutan & Coolidge to carry on the tradition and practice of H. H. Richardson. Wherever industry or fashion prospered, the substantial architectural projects of the day favored the designer who could command an extensive organization of specialists.

In this period Philadelphia can claim no architectural firm of the stature of those of Chicago or New York, but at least one deserves mention; this is the organization that Joseph Wilson founded with his younger brother John under the name of Wilson Brothers & Co. Established in 1876, the Philadelphia firm thus followed Burnham & Root by three years, but preceded Adler & Sullivan by four, McKim, Mead & White by three, and Carrère & Hastings by nine. In the sixty years that lay between the founding of Wilson

Brothers & Co. and the closing of the last of its successor firms in 1936, there were few types of buildings that the partners and their associates did not undertake. The Observatory at West Point Military Academy is their work and so were the stations of New York's Third Avenue "El." In size the firm's commissions ranged from the burial vault for the Fraser family in Greenwood Cemetery, Brooklyn, to the sprawling State Hospital for the Insane at Norristown, Pennsylvania. Most of the commissions were in Pennsylvania, but there were also a number in New York, New Jersey, and the New England states; some were as far west as Colorado and Oregon, and as far south as the Carolinas. Nor was the firm's practice limited to the United States; a few structures, such as the market house at Demerara, were built as far from Philadelphia as Cuba, South America, or Australia. Small cottages, large hotels, churches, schools, hospitals, libraries, commercial buildings, and bridges by the score—apparently no building was too large or too small, too near or too far, for the firm to undertake.

The founding of Wilson Brothers & Co. in 1876 reflects the association of Joseph Wilson with the buildings of the Centennial Exhibition in that year, and doubtless the fact that both he and his brother John were essentially engineers who had received their training with the Pennsylvania Railroad also explains the selection of the new firm to design the first part of the important Broad Street Station, noted earlier (Fig. 121). Even more unusual for its period than the Broad Street Station, however, was the building erected by the firm for Drexel & Co. on the site formerly occupied by Thornton's Library Hall (Fig. 26). Claimed at the time of its construction in 1885 to be one of the most sumptuous structures in the country, the Drexel bank was remarkable particularly for the spaciousness of its main room, which the client specified must rise to the full height of the building without interior supports of any kind. But scarcely was the new bank completed when it was decided to add six more stories, and when the neighboring Independence Bank, true to its name, refused to sell at any price, Drexel simply built around it. The presence of the Independence Bank, as well as the incorporation of the earlier structure, helps to explain several of the otherwise incongruous features in the final design of the Drexel Building (Fig. 123). Instead of the Romanesque or Gothic styles often favored for tall buildings at this time, the new bank on Chestnut Street was decked out in classical forms, perhaps thought of as more suggestive of the conservative qualities desirable in a financial institution, as well as an oblique reference to Drexel's predecessors among the merchant princes of the Renaissance.

When the enlargements were finally completed about 1889, the Drexel Building towered 135 feet above the sidewalk to form one of the most conspicuous features of the Philadelphia skyline. But the most interesting aspect of the design was the ingenious way in which the architects had solved the problem of supporting the six additional stories that now rose above the banking room and for which there was therefore no suitable footing. The solution adopted was as bold as it was simple; massive iron pilasters were bolted to the inside walls of the bank to serve as bases for the series of large iron frames formed roughly in the shape of the letter A, shown in the architects' working drawing (Fig. 124). Rising through four stories to a height of approximately fifty feet, these giant A-trusses supplied a permanent but concealed scaffolding on which some of the girders framing the building were made to rest and from which others were suspended. Indicative of the scale of the drawing is the fact that the iron pin that fastens the diagonal beams to the supporting pilasters in the lower corners is eight inches in diameter. Although common enough in later structures, the A-frame was unusual at the time it was employed in the Drexel Building and its use may have been suggested to the Wilson Brothers by their experience with iron bridges for the Pennsylvania Railroad.

On the Chestnut Street side of the Drexel Building, the floor beams appear to have been imbedded in the masonry of the side walls, as indicated in the drawing, but in the rear sections the girders rested on iron columns located inside the pilasters of the exterior masonry shell. In this portion of the building, at least, the walls supported mainly themselves and had little or nothing to do with the stability of the floors within. This fact is made clear by extant working drawings as well as by newspaper accounts which mention that at one time during the erection of the building the metal frame of four stories could be seen above the walls. In the use of an iron frame essentially independent of its surrounding masonry the Wilson Brothers were going considerably beyond the older type of mill construction without, however, achieving the full "skeleton" form which implies that the metal frame provides the support not only of the floors, but of the exterior walls as well. Although Chicago deserves credit for the development of the type of skeleton construction on which the modern tall building depends, examples like this make it clear that Philadelphia architects were also following closely the new technological developments.

The Drexel Building was among the last large structures to use wrought and cast iron throughout. About 1883 the Bessemer process, introduced into Pittsburgh, flooded the American market with cheap rolled steel. William Le Baron Jenney (1832-1907) used steel for a portion of the Home Insurance Building (1883), and the question arises as to why the Wilson Brothers did not use it also. Cost may have been a factor (in 1890 Jenney used iron for the sixteen-story Manhattan Building in Chicago on the grounds that steel was too expensive). More probably, the Wilsons were thoroughly familiar with the properties of iron and were reluctant to use a new material in a building involving structural problems of the complexity of those mentioned here.

Characteristic of late Victorian architecture about 1890 was the design of Willis G. Hale for the remodeling of the Bingham House at the corner of Eleventh and Market streets (Fig. 125). The consequences of the division between structure and ornament, inherent in the Romantic view of architecture from the first, are here all too apparent. Always alert to the vagaries of prevailing taste, the hotel proprietors no doubt demanded a design that would combine some of the more obvious features of the popular Richardsonian Romanesque with the steep roof and clustered chimneys of the French châteaux, still considered fashionable. And as if this were not enough, here and there over the surface are disposed a variety of swags and cartouches of the kind especially favored in the more academic circles that looked for leadership to the Ecole des Beaux Arts. In spite of the elegance of its suites and the undeniably picturesque appeal of its exterior, the design of the Bingham

115

House contained the symptoms of a kind of architectural indigestion that invited professional therapy. The style of many of the buildings of the next quarter-century may fairly be viewed, in fact, as representing a reaction to the earlier eclectic excesses of men like Willis Hale.

CREATIVE ECLECTICISM
(c.1890-c.1920)

THE BASIC QUALITIES THAT DISTINGUISH THE ARCHITECTURE OF THE LATE NINETEENTH AND early twentieth centuries are more easily identified than defined. Eclecticism continues to be the dominant theme, as it had been for nearly a century, but now, more often than not, the styles of the past are handled with a new awareness of the aesthetic principles that appear to underlie them. To this aspect of eclecticism may fairly be applied the term "creative," provided its use to describe the architects of the Late Victorian Period is not understood as implying the absence of that important quality in their predecessors. Viewed in this context, the word will be found to have two meanings: on the one hand, the grasp of an architectural idiom of a past style was often so complete as to enable the architect to design freely and "creatively" within it—to make it, as it were, his own; on other occasions, a knowledge of traditional styles seems to have had the effect of freeing the architect to "create" new forms, based on the past, but so tastefully adapted and so imaginatively combined that they tend to lose their historical identity. History does not repeat itself, and stylistic parallels between the art forms of different periods are apt to be misleading. But if the point is not pressed too far, this later phase of eclecticism may be thought of as bearing somewhat the same relationship to the style of the High Victorian Period as did the Federal manner to the preceding Middle Georgian. Both the late nineteenth century and the late eighteenth have in common the fact that each represents the last phase of a mature style, and both reveal something of the same finesse and sophistication in the handling of architectural elements.

In Philadelphia this changing attitude toward traditional architectural forms is well illustrated by the design of Frank Miles Day for the rebuilding of Horticultural Hall after a fire had destroyed a previous building in 1893 (Fig. 126). Until its demolition in 1917 to make way for the Shubert Theater, Horticultural Hall stood next to the Academy of Music on South Broad Street, and the selection of Day as the architect for the new building may well have been based upon the favorable reception of his design for the nearby Art Club, erected a few years earlier at 220 Broad Street (since 1943 occupied by the Keystone Automobile Club). The Art Club appears to have been Day's first important commission after his return from several years of study and travel in Europe—then considered an essential foundation for a successful architectural career—and although it may be, as some have suggested, that the student's sketchbook is here too clearly in evidence, there is also apparent the same disciplined use of historical ornament that marks all Day's best work. And therein lies perhaps the greatest difference between the eclecticism of the late nineteenth century and that of the earlier Victorian and Romantic periods. Ornament for Day and his contemporaries is seldom solely literary or pictorial; it is used instead for essentially

117

architectural ends, to define volumes and voids and to establish their relationship to each other.

In the simplicity of its cubic form, the clear separation of the two stories, and the deep shadows cast by the overhanging roof, Horticultural Hall is reminiscent of a Florentine palace of the Renaissance. Similar sources must also account for the other details, as well as the classical composition of the whole, but Day has so well assimilated his models that he has been able to recast them in forms that evade precise identification. Especially is this true of the flat band of ornament frescoed in reds, yellows, and sultry browns that takes the place of the classical cornice and seems closer to the contemporary work of Louis Sullivan than to anything to be found in Renaissance Italy.

In 1892 Day formed an association with his elder brother, and later, after H. Kent Day's retirement in 1912, with Charles Z. Klauder (1872-1938). Dutch and Flemish sources may have inspired the design for a house on West End Avenue and 94th Street in New York City, French châteaux for the roof of the twelve-story building of the American Baptist Publication Society at 1422 Chestnut Street, and Italian palaces the clinical amphitheater of the Medico-Chirurgical Hospital at Seventeenth and Cherry streets, but whatever the source of his design, and whether developed independently or in collaboration with others, Day seldom lost the sense of architectural form that set his earlier work apart from that of most of his predecessors and many of his contemporaries.

At about the same time that Frank Miles Day was beginning his professional career, two other young Philadelphians, formerly draftsmen in the office of Theophilus Parsons Chandler (1845-1928), founded the firm of Cope & Stewardson. Chandler is remembered today principally as having established the Department of Architecture at the University of Pennsylvania in 1890 and as the designer of such Philadelphia buildings as the Swedenborgian Church at Chestnut and Twenty-second streets, the Penn Mutual Life Insurance Co. (now demolished) at 1921-1925 Chestnut Street and the John Wanamaker residence at Twentieth and Walnut streets. But of more influence on the designs of the new firm than Chandler's somewhat heavy style was the direct contact of its members with European architecture; John Stewardson had been a student at the Ecole des Beaux Arts, and Walter Cope had spent a year abroad in study and travel. And these first impressions were strengthened and extended by later visits; sketches made by one or the other of the partners in Italy, Flanders, England, Normandy, and Spain are clearly the basis for many of the motifs that appear throughout the designs of the firm. In 1887 the first two partners were joined by a third in the person of John Stewardson's younger brother, Emlyn Lamar, who had graduated from the University of Pennsylvania the preceding year.

During the first year of the new firm's existence it was called upon to design Radnor Hall, the earliest of a series of buildings for Bryn Mawr College. There in Denbigh Hall (1891), Pembroke Hall (1894), Rockefeller Hall (1904), and the Library (1906) may be traced the evolution of the Collegiate Gothic style for which the partners are best known. In turning to the late English Gothic for the design of American colleges and universities, Cope & Stewardson had in mind Oxford and Cambridge from which the tradition of higher education in the United States was thought of as having been derived. Especially

118

to those familiar with the great English universities, the appeal of ivy-covered cloisters, battlemented towers, and oriel windows was understandably great, and Cope & Stewardson were asked to provide a similar academic setting for such other American universities as Princeton (Blair and Little halls and the old gymnasium) and Washington University in St. Louis, Missouri (School of Architecture, University Hall, Busch Hall). Haverford was one of the few eastern colleges to swim against the current, and for Roberts and Lloyd halls, Cope & Stewardson used a modified Georgian style presumably considered more in keeping with a Quaker background.

No doubt impressed by the buildings at Bryn Mawr, the Trustees of the University of Pennsylvania chose Cope & Stewardson to design the dormitories at Thirty-seventh and Spruce, begun in 1895, but only completed in recent years (Fig. 127). This seems to have been the firm's first major work within the city limits, and in many ways it represents Cope & Stewardson at their best. If a case for Creative Eclecticism can be made, it must rest on the evidence of buildings such as these.

The need to provide hundreds of rooms of similar size could easily produce an architectural design of overwhelming dullness. But whatever the faults of the dormitories at the University of Pennsylvania, monotony would not seem to be one of them. Instead of the more severe Tudor Gothic used at Bryn Mawr and Princeton, for their work at Pennsylvania Cope & Stewardson turned to the Jacobean style, mentioned briefly in the first section as representing in English architecture the moment of transition between the Middle Ages and the Renaissance. And precisely because the dormitories are Gothic at one moment and classic at another, they contrive for the most part to be neither.

By varying the shapes and levels of the courts, Cope & Stewardson created at Pennsylvania a series of architectural adventures of which even the most callow undergraduate cannot be wholly unaware. At one moment confined and intimate, the next spacious and formal, the five courts provide a setting for almost any mood. While half-glimpsed vistas beckon just ahead, the care and imagination lavished on the smallest details make any haste to pass them by seem churlish. But a work of art is more than the sum of its parts, and to dissect the various motifs and styles that go to make up this rich composition is to miss the point. The Palladian openings, pilasters, balustrades, oriels, dormers, and clustered chimneys are never ends in themselves but always disciplined and integrated parts of an exceptionally rich style wherewith the architects sought to provide a fitting background for the many dimensions of the intellectual life associated with a university.

The use of the Jacobean style also permitted Cope & Stewardson to give up the colder gray stone of the Tudor Gothic in favor of mellow bricks set off with white stone trim. The circumstances that surrounded this change were later recalled by James F. Jamieson (1867-1941), a Philadelphia architect associated with the firm: "I remember well his [John Stewardson's] cabling from England for us to stop all work on the plans for the dormitories at the University of Pennsylvania because our designs called for stone; and he, having just seen the buildings of St. John's, Cambridge, was converted to the idea of using brick. When he presented to the office his beautiful water colors illustrating his point, we were all immediately convinced of the sureness of his taste—and the beauty of Pennsylvania's dormitories is the best comment on how right he was. Again, when we had half completed the south wall of the dormitories on Pine Street, he was dissatisfied with the appearance; the color of the mortar was wrong! And he persuaded his own firm to shoulder the expense of tearing down the wall and rebuilding it with mortar of the right color." Jamieson's recollections reveal not only the importance of direct European contacts in the formation of the style of Cope & Stewardson, but also the fidelity to their work of many of the architects of their generation.

With the advantage afforded by the perspective of half a century, it now seems clear that these European contacts, frequently renewed and refreshed, explain, as much as anything else, the essential differences that separate much of the architecture of the end of the nineteenth century from that which immediately preceded it. It was therefore especially appropriate that when a tragic skating accident ended Stewardson's career in his thirty-ninth year his friends should have founded a traveling scholarship in his memory. In spite of two world wars and the dwindling value of the dollar, the Stewardson Scholarship still assists promising young architects to have at least a few months abroad. No doubt since Stewardson's day their goals have changed somewhat, but the need to expand horizons still remains.

The house designed in 1890 for Messrs. Neil and Mauran (Fig. 128) and still standing at Twenty-second and Cypress streets illustrates the highly individual style of the fourth Philadelphia architect whose name is usually associated with the new spirit of Creative Eclecticism. This was Wilson Eyre, who had been born thirty-two years before in Florence, Italy, but of American parents. When his parents opposed his wish to be a painter, Eyre decided to become an architect instead, although his professional training seems to have been limited to a year or two at the Massachusetts Institute of Technology, followed by five years in the Philadelphia offices of James P. Sims, to whose practice he succeeded in 1882.

The sensitive drawing reproduced in Figure 128 is typical of Wilson Eyre, and it is unfortunate that, as built, the house on Twenty-second Street did not follow it more closely. But even the changes made in the slope of the roof and the shape and spacing of the windows were not sufficient to destroy the artist's feeling for proportion and the expressive qualities inherent in the materials. "Nothing is so offensive as a building overloaded with ornament," Eyre told his classes at the University of Pennsylvania, and the crisp lines of designs like this show how faithfully he followed his own advice. Although the origin of Eyre's style seemed to lie in the medieval past, his architectural forms are so imaginatively handled, particularly in his earlier work, that they may be said to lose much of their historical character. Here is something of the same individuality that distinguishes the style of Frank Furness, but played, it need hardly be added, in a quite different key. Where Furness' designs are masculine, even brutal, Eyre's are often infused with a whimsical quality that seems to make them more a part of the world of imagination and childhood fantasy than of Philadelphia in the 1890's.

In his country houses, especially, Eyre's simple use of simple materials achieves an effect not unlike the designs of McKim, Mead & White frequently referred to as the "shingle style" or occasionally, and for less cogent reasons, as "Queen Anne." Behind both McKim, Mead & White and Wilson Eyre lies, of course, the Arts and Crafts Movement in England, beginning with William Morris (1834-1896) and continuing in the work of such later men as C. F. A. Voysey (1857-1941), Charles R. Mackintosh (1868-1928) and, particularly, Norman Shaw (1831-1912). For Morris, it will be recalled, Philip Webb (1831-1915) had designed the Red House at Bexley Heath, Kent, based upon the theory, unusual in 1860, that a country house would be most successful in the measure as its design was a product of its plan and its materials, without conscious reference to any historical style. Eyre probably did as much as anyone to establish the tradition of distinguished country houses for which the Philadelphia area was known in the late nineteenth and early twentieth centuries, a tradition continued by later architects such as Mellor, Meigs & Howe, Robert R. McGoodwin, and Edmund B. Gilchrist. Together with Walter Cope and others, Eyre was also active in' the T-Square Club, which sought to encourage creative talent, especially among the younger members of the profession, and whose *Yearbooks* are such important records of the architectural thinking of the period.

In 1893 the decision of the trustees of what was then known as the Free Museum of Science and Art to commission an ambitious structure to house their archaeological collections brought together in collaboration the four architects whose individual styles have been discussed above. A glance at the gigantic scheme that this group effort produced (Fig. 129) will make clear that what is today the Museum of the University of Pennsylvania at Thirty-third and Spruce streets is but a fragment of the building originally planned. Of the entire complex only the west court (at the right of the illustration) was completed by 1899. In 1912 the right rotunda behind the west court was built, and in 1926 a portion of the middle section was added, but without the great central dome.

Some insight into the evolution of the design of the University Museum is afforded by surviving drawings that show variants of the final plans worked out in several different styles, including the Classic. But, as often with the most important buildings of this period, it is easier to describe the traditional sources of the individual motifs than to find a historical or geographical name applicable to the style as a whole. To be sure, the rotundas of the Museum seem based on the lanterns of the Romanesque churches of northern Italy, and of Lombard inspiration also are the wall arcades and porches. But what, then, of the early Renaissance loggia of the central section and the Japanese gateways that lead into the two lateral courts? Ralph Adams Cram (1863-1942), who, if anyone, could be expected to have an eye for such matters, was delighted with the Museum at the same time that he was puzzled by it: "The thing baffles and amazes," he wrote. "What is the basis, Lombard, Tuscan? Or are the hints of these influences accessories only, accidents? . . . One feels that American architecture should show at least its chain of ethnic continuity. Of this there is nothing in the Archaeological Museum. Does this prove that the theory is wrong . . . ?" Modern critics would undoubtedly reply that such theories were indeed wrong and that the Museum was a distinguished building precisely because its designers had succeeded in blending and remaking ideas taken from many periods and many places into a new artistic unity, explicable, in the last analysis, only in terms of itself.

121

Even more difficult to identify than the style of the Museum is the distinctive contribution of each of the several architects. In retrospect, it seems especially remarkable that four men who held such definite views concerning architecture should have succeeded so well in subordinating their individual styles in the interest of a single unified design. Perhaps Cram came as near the truth as anyone when, in another context, he assigned to each of the architects of the Museum one of the qualities he considered essential to great architecture: to Day "good taste," to Eyre "personality," and to Cope & Stewardson "poetry." The drawing reproduced here is unquestionably the work of Wilson Eyre, and probably his was the general scheme adopted for the Museum. The "personality" of Eyre seems to appear also in the handling of many of the materials, especially the dark brick with the unusually wide joints and the interesting patterns achieved with small pieces of inlaid marble. Cram's "poetry" is hardly an architectural term, but it does better than most to describe the landscaped courts with their reflecting pools and the simple but forceful massing of the surrounding buildings, so similar in spirit to that of Cope & Stewardson's dormitories at Pennsylvania. And as for Day's exquisite "taste," surely the fine proportions enhanced by the restrained but telling use of ornament owe much to him.

Although the Middle Ages continued to be a major source of inspiration for the architects of the late nineteenth century, Georgian forms steadily increased in popularity. The more archaeological aspects of the Georgian Revival are well represented in Philadelphia by the Law School of the University of Pennsylvania, designed by Cope & Stewardson in 1898 and based upon the style of Sir Christopher Wren, specifically his work at Hampton Court. Usually the historical reference is a more general one, however, leaving unanswered the question of whether the architect had taken English or Colonial sources as his models. The latter became increasingly important as, in the wake of the celebration of the centennial of their independence, Americans became more and more interested in their own country and its arts.

To many, Georgian forms must have seemed peculiarly appropriate for a city with so distinguished a colonial past as Philadelphia. No doubt considerations of this kind lie behind the choice of the style for the Philadelphia Racquet Club on South Sixteenth Street, completed in 1907 from the designs of Horace Trumbauer (Fig. 130). Except for an enlargement in scale, this may appear at first glance to represent a fairly direct borrowing from Georgian models like Cliveden (Fig. 17) and Independence Hall (Fig. 22). But the employment of such unusual features as the attic story (required, of course, by the need to provide for court tennis and other sports) and a Greek rather than the customary Roman cornice make it clear that something of the same freedom in the handling of traditional forms, mentioned earlier in discussing the work of other major architects of the period, is also operative here.

In many ways the Racquet Club has stood time's test better than most of the buildings of its period, and this is the more remarkable since its architect had received a minimum of what could be considered a professional education. When he opened his own office in 1892, Trumbauer, unlike most of his professional contemporaries, had never been to Europe, and behind him lay only eight years in the office of George W. and William D.

Hewitt, which he had entered in 1884 as an errand boy. The epigrammatic epitaph proposed for Sir John Vanbrugh (1664-1726) might serve equally well for Trumbauer:

Lie heavy on him, Earth, for he
Laid many a heavy load on thee!

But the characteristically heavy hand with which Trumbauer approached the problems of architectural design did not prevent his receiving the patronage of Philadelphia's richest families. This was the era before the imposition of the graduated income tax, when architects were apt to be required to produce designs expressive of the worldly success of their clients. In this spirit of conspicuous consumption Trumbauer provided for P. A. B. Widener and W. L. Elkins their enormous residences, as impressive in their own way as are the palaces that Richard Morris Hunt and McKim, Mead & White were designing for others such as the Vanderbilts at Newport. Nor should we forget Grey Towers, the Jenkintown residence of William Welch Harrison, designed by Trumbauer early in his professional career. Now fortunately preserved as part of Beaver College, this superb pile is as near to being a Gothic castle as anything Philadelphia ever built.

Universities, clubs, and archaeological museums were projects particularly well suited to the talents of such leading Philadelphia architects as Frank Miles Day and Wilson Eyre. Less appropriate to their subtle and highly personal styles was the commercial building, and possibly for that reason John Wanamaker in 1902 turned to Chicago and Daniel H. Burnham for the design of the new store (Fig. 131) wherewith he proposed to replace the Grand Depot (Fig. 114).

In the decade between 1885 and 1895 Chicago architects had assumed national leadership by reason of their handling of the structural and aesthetic problems inherent in the tall building. It will be recalled that it was H. H. Richardson's Marshall Field Wholesale Store in Chicago that Addison Hutton chose as one of the models for his Girard Life and Trust Building (Fig. 122), and such a source appears to lie behind the use of piers and arches for the center section of the John Wanamaker store. But for the Romanesque details favored by Richardson and his followers, Burnham has substituted those of the Renaissance, notable especially in the pilasters of the ground floor and the cornice that surrounds the flat roof after the manner of an Italian *palazzo*. Behind the limestone sheath of the Wanamaker store lies, of course, a steel frame which Burnham ignored to the extent that his design is based on the traditional three-part division, inherited, via the Renaissance, from classical antiquity and consisting of base , body, and capping member—the composition, in short, of the classical orders. Not even Richardson and Sullivan had been able to free themselves completely from this traditional approach to architectural design, and its use by earlier architects in Philadelphia is illustrated by the work of Hutton and the Wilson Brothers (Fig. 123). But to suggest that in some respects the design of the exterior of the Wanamaker store looks backward rather than forward is not to deny its competence, both structural and functional. Viewed in somewhat different perspective, it appears as an imaginative reconciliation of the principles of Renaissance design with the demands of modern steel construction, apparent in the regularity of the fenestration and the proportion

123

of voids to solids. When built, Wanamaker's was one of the major department stores of the world and the great covered court is still among the finest spaces in the city, which the passage of half a century has failed to rob of its power to delight.

In partnership with John Wellborn Root (1850-1891), Burnham had earlier in his career made important contributions toward the evolution of a modern style for the tall building, and his later use of Renaissance forms in designs like that of the John Wanamaker Store is to be explained by the delight with which he and a majority of his countrymen viewed the classical beauties of the Columbian Exposition, held in Chicago in 1893. As first conceived by Burnham and Root, the Chicago Fair was to have been a panoply of many styles in a riot of colors and materials. But Root died before the plans had progressed beyond their first stages, and Burnham was completely won over by his colleagues from the East who favored a unified design based on the Renaissance tradition of the Ecole des Beaux Arts where many of them had studied and to which all of them looked for professional leadership. Except for Henry Ives Cobb's Fisheries Building in the Romanesque tradition of Richardson and Louis Sullivan's Transportation Building, which probably owed more to Oriental sources than most of his admirers now care to admit, the prevailing theme was overwhelmingly Classic. On all sides were to be seen triumphal arches, Roman orders, and classical entablatures peopled with a multitude of half-clothed figures, all composed of a gleaming white mixture of plaster and cement. For the Administration Building Richard Morris Hunt designed a domed structure, dignified but dull, and McKim, Mead & White's Agricultural Building followed much the same pattern.

Disgusted by the uncritical amazement and delight with which the vast crowds viewed the wonders of what was soon called "The White City," Louis Sullivan prophesied that its influence in American taste could be nothing less than an "appalling calamity." From the Fair, Classicism did indeed spread its white mantle over most of the country, and the dominance of the French Ecole in the professional training of American architects was assured for another generation. But this was hardly an unqualified evil; adherence to the practices and principles of the Ecole probably raised more indifferent architects to a high level of mediocrity than it dragged down the rare genius from the heights to which undisciplined inspiration might otherwise have led him. And if most of the classical buildings erected during the late nineteenth and early twentieth century contributed little to the enrichment of American life, Philadelphians owe to the influence of the Fair and to McKim, Mead & White the altogether satisfying building of the Girard Trust Company at the corner of Broad and Chestnut streets (Fig. 132). Forget that the choice of the Classical style was dictated by the long-standing principle, emphasized by the Ecole, that conservative financial institutions should be housed in structures whose appearance would convey to the public a sense of the stability that comes from established traditions and experience. Architecture, like the other arts, is not reducible to a set of rules; even those who fairly question the kind of thinking that permits the use of a Roman temple as the basis for the design of a twentieth-century bank, when they view the Girard Trust nestling like some *objet de vertu* in its setting of drab office buildings, would not be without it. Together with McArthur's

124

City Hall and Fraser's Union League, it does much to prevent Broad Street from appearing as banal as most of the other commercial thoroughfares throughout the country.

The influence of the World's Columbian Exposition was not confined solely to architecture, however. A principal reason for the undeniably impressive appearance of the White City had been its formal organization around the major and minor axes established by lagoons, the work of Frederick Law Olmsted. So it was that in the wake of the Fair, while architects busied themselves with neoclassical façades, planners and landscape designers set about the creating of esplanades, malls, and vistas of all kinds—occasionally impressive but more frequently tiresome to eye and foot alike. Inspired by Olmsted's lagoons, Burnham proposed a new plan for Chicago, and similar motivation lay behind the determination of the McMillan Commission to recast the public grounds of Washington, D.C., in the seventeenth-century mold originally favored by L'Enfant in place of the Romantic park designed by Downing. The membership of the McMillan Commission was made up largely of men who had planned the Columbian Exposition, and it is doubtful if the present mall that stretches somewhat drearily from the Washington Monument to the Capitol would be there today had it not been for the favorable reception of the Chicago Fair.

Few of the attempts to introduce Baroque planning into an American city were more spectacular—or in some ways more successful—than the Benjamin Franklin Parkway in Philadelphia. From the moment it was first seriously considered to the day it was opened to traffic in 1918 this great boulevard was close to twenty-five years in the making and during that time nearly every major architect and local group concerned with the arts had some part in its planning or execution. As early as 1892, City Councils included a plan for a parkway in an ordinance passed in April of that year. But since this did not receive the mayor's approval, the idea was not pressed until early in 1900 when some eighteen institutions joined together to form the Art Federation. Later this group merged with still another under the name of the Parkway Association. In this way a variety of plans were developed by Wilson Eyre, Paul Cret, and others, and although details differed, most of the schemes had in common the Baroque concept of a great diagonal vista that would serve to break the monotony of Philadelphia's gridiron plan. In 1909 Mayor Reyburn directed that provision be made for such a parkway in the official plan of the city drawn up in that year.

A temporary halt in the plans for the parkway ended in 1917 when the idea was taken up again, this time by the Fairmount Park Art Association. In view of the importance assigned the great boulevards of Paris by those interested in reviving Renaissance planning in America, it was perhaps logical that the final plans for a parkway in Philadelphia should be the work of a French designer. This was Jacques Auguste Henri Gréber, a writer and urban planner, said to have come to Philadelphia to design the gardens of Edward T. Stotesbury. As president of the Fairmount Park Art Association from 1909 to 1916, Stotesbury must have been thoroughly familiar with the history of the parkway project and could therefore have been expected to advance the qualifications of Gréber as a man well able to consolidate the previous plans in a fashion most likely to secure their adoption.

As finally developed, Gréber's plan (Fig. 133) afforded an uninterrupted vista from

125

the heights of Fairmount, where a new museum was to be erected, to McArthur's City Hall with its lofty tower. In many of its essentials, the Greek temple form of the Philadelphia Art Museum may also have been Gréber's, replacing the Roman design developed in 1895 by James Brite (d. 1942) and Henry Bacon (1866-1924), although the actual construction was carried out under the direction of a group of architects: Horace Trumbauer (probably the choice of the Wideners), C. C. Zantzinger, and Charles L. Borie, Jr. (presumably the selection of Eli Kirk Price, a member of the Park Commission and later director of the museum). The exterior of the new building was finished by 1927, but the first gallery did not open until the following year, and some portions of the vast interior still await completion.

At the foot of Fairmount on the main axis of the Parkway, the final plan called for an oval area enlivened by fountains such as had been included in several of the earlier schemes and no doubt owed its inspiration to piazzas like that designed by Bernini for St. Peter's in Rome. In the triangular areas immediately to the east Gréber proposed new buildings for the Pennsylvania Academy of the Fine Arts and the Pennsylvania Museum and School of Industrial Art. Neither was ever erected, nor was the enormous Episcopal cathedral planned for the north side of the Parkway about midway between Fairmount and Logan Square. Gréber must have realized, as many American planners apparently had not, that a vista is not in itself sufficient to retain spectator interest for long unless reinforced at strategic points by important structures. The dome and tower of the cathedral would also have supplied a vertical accent midway between the City Hall and the Art Museum. Such a point of interest was the more necessary since it was proposed to substitute rows of trees for the continuous façade of buildings that had lined the Parkway in several of the earlier plans.

Under Gréber's scheme the position of Logan Square was kept as Holme had planned it (Fig. 2), but the middle was turned into a great circle for pedestrian and vehicular traffic. In the center was the fountain composed of allegorical figures representing the Delaware, Schuylkill, and Wissahickon rivers, carried out about 1924 from the designs of Alexander Sterling Calder, son of the sculptor associated with McArthur on the City Hall and father of the artist well known today for his mobile abstractions. Calder was assisted in the development of the design for the fountain by Wilson Eyre and his partner, since 1912, John Gilbert McIlvaine (1880-1939). LeBrun and Notman's Cathedral of SS. Peter and Paul was left undisturbed on the east side of the Square, but for the north side Gréber turned to the Place de la Concorde in Paris, originally laid out by Jacques-Anges Gabriel (1698-1782) between 1753 and 1763. Thus the Ministries of War and Navy in Paris formed the basis for Gréber's vision of Trumbauer's Free Library (1927), as well as that of Morton Keast's Municipal Court (1938-41), adjacent. Keast had been associated earlier with John T. Windrim (1866-1934), son of the designer of the Masonic Temple at Broad and Filbert streets (Fig. 112), and himself the architect of the new building for the Franklin Institute, erected on the west side of Logan Square in 1934.

Unrelated in scale to the rest of the city and a nightmare to the unwary motorist, the Parkway can easily be criticized. Individual elements are occasionally coarse, and few of the buildings can be called distinguished in their own right. But when the various parts are

126

seen in relationship to each other, the whole takes on a grandeur that is not unimpressive. To stand at City Hall and see the classical façade of the Museum, enframed in trees and rising above the splashing water of Calder's fountain, is to experience a little of the excitement conveyed by the great Baroque plans of Europe: of the Champs Elysées, of Versailles, and of Bernini's Rome. Few American cities can claim as much.

127

MODERN PHILADELPHIA
(c. 1920-1960)

THE YEAR SELECTED HERE TO MARK THE BEGINNING OF THE MODERN PERIOD HAS LITTLE DIRECT relevance to Philadelphia. But it does serve to express the fact that, however deep in the past lie the roots of modern architecture, its first fully coherent manifestations appeared in the decade following World War I. In this sense the earlier work of even the most important innovators—such men as Peter Behrens (1868-1940) in Germany, Otto Wagner (1841-1918) and Adolf Loos (1870-1933) in Austria, Henri Van de Velde (1863-1957) in Belgium and Germany, H. P. Berlage (1856-1934) in Holland, Auguste Perret (1874-1954) in France, and Frank Lloyd Wright (1868-1959) in America—by continuing to echo, however faintly, the historical styles of the past, or by failing to exploit fully the new materials and structural methods made available by the technology of the twentieth century, must be regarded as preparing the way for a modern style, rather than as belonging to it.

In Philadelphia, the earlier tradition of Creative Eclecticism was continued into the 20's and 30's by a number of competent architects, of whom Paul Philippe Cret was the best-known and certainly the most influential. Educated at the Ecoles des Beaux Arts of both his native Lyons and Paris, Cret had come to the United States in 1903 at the age of twenty-seven to accept the post of Assistant Professor of Design at the University of Pennsylvania. During the next forty years, his teaching and example had a decisive influence on the direction taken by the architecture of his adopted country. Even in such early buildings as the Pan-American Union on Constitution Avenue in Washington, D.C. (designed between 1908 and 1910 in collaboration with Albert Kelsey), or the somewhat later Rodin Museum on the Benjamin Franklin Parkway in Philadelphia (designed in 1929 in association with Jacques Gréber) can be seen Cret's tasteful handling of the classical tradition favored by the Ecole and noted previously in connection with the work of McKim, Mead & White. But it is especially in such a design as that for the Federal Reserve Bank of Philadelphia, erected on the northeast corner of Tenth and Chestnut streets between 1932 and 1936, that Cret's peculiar talents are most clearly revealed (Fig. 134).

By placing the eagle above and Bottiau's allegorical reliefs at each side, Cret identifies the entrance to the bank without altering the regular rhythm of the piers. Although the few ornamental details, like the general organization of the design, are Greek in origin, they have been restated so freely to satisfy the specific architectural problem at hand that only the classic spirit remains as a kind of timeless residuum. Here, as in all that he did, Cret sought to express what he himself referred to as the "principles of composition not new, to be sure, but somewhat neglected during the past hundred years, such as the value of restraint, the value of designing volumes instead of merely decorating surfaces and the value of empty surfaces as elements of composition." In its free adaptation of the architec-

129

tural forms of the past to the requirements of the twentieth century, the Federal Reserve Bank is not unlike better-known examples of the period such as B. G. Goodhue's Nebraska State Capitol (1926) and Bacon's Lincoln Memorial in Washington, D.C. (1917). It was the qualities characteristic of such buildings that the American Institute of Architects stressed in the citation that accompanied its Gold Medal Award presented to Cret in 1938: "He has brought to the land of his adoption the sound sense, the clear logic, the discriminating taste that belong to the classic tradition of an older civilization. Thus armed, he has met and mastered without standing still those problems that are inherent in new materials in a new world. . . ."

For all its classicism, the design of such a building as the Federal Reserve Bank probably owes more to modern technology and structural method than might appear at first glance. Nor were Cret and his colleagues unaware of or uninterested in the new developments then more often associated with the engineer than with the architect. For the Edward G. Budd Manufacturing Company they designed passenger railroad cars and even a locomotive in 1937 for the Reading Lines. Of more recent interest here, however, was the part played by the firm in the erection of a number of the major bridges of the period. All three of the bridges that span the Delaware River at Philadelphia—the Delaware River Bridge (1926), the Tacony-Palmyra Bridge (1929), and the Walt Whitman Bridge (1958) —are the work of the engineering firm of Modjeski & Masters and of the architectural firm of Paul P. Cret or, in the case of the last bridge, of its successor, which bears the names of Cret's four partners, Harbeson, Hough, Livingston & Larson. In each case the architects sought to relate what they considered to be the characteristics of good design to structural problems which could only be solved in terms of the new technological advances.

In the architect's rendering (Fig. 135) the Delaware River Bridge (now renamed the Benjamin Franklin Bridge) seems to soar over the river with a confidence and grace which has been likened to some majestic water bird in flight. At either end huge masses of concrete faced with stone convey the feeling of solidity appropriate to their function as anchors for the great cables from which the bridge is suspended. The hand of Cret is especially evident in the classical qualities of these anchorages where decoration is held to a minimum: a few simple but effective cornices, a balustrade, and a single balcony on each of the towers. In contrast to such massive strength of form is the delicate pattern of the cables and the comparative lightness of the steel members of the bridge whose main span of 1,750 feet made it the longest suspension bridge in the world when it was built. Viewed in the perspective of Philadelphia history, the Delaware River Bridge appears as another addition to the distinguished roster of Philadelphia structures that had earlier included the first covered bridge in America (Fig. 34), the longest single span (Fig. 50), and the first wire suspension bridge open to general traffic (Fig. 51).

Of the architects practicing in Philadelphia in the twenties, not even Cret used the forms of the past more tastefully or with greater professional success than did the firm of Mellor, Meigs & Howe. It must therefore have come as something of a shock to Philadelphia in 1928 when George Howe withdrew from his profitable association with the firm and set himself up in a small office with the intention of practicing what he then referred to as the "modern system of design." On the surface there might seem little in Howe's background to presage such a step. Scion of a well-to-do family with important Philadelphia connections, a graduate of Groton, Harvard and the Ecole des Beaux Arts, Howe was described by his colleagues as looking upon architecture with "seriousness but with detachment, more as a hobby than as a career."

In spite of the change in his professional views, Howe was able to take with him from his old firm (where the partners had practiced more as individuals than as a group) an important corporate client in the President and Board of Managers of the Philadelphia Saving Fund Society for whom he had previously designed several branch offices. One such branch was the small Elizabethan structure erected in 1926 to test the economic advantages of the location at Twelfth and Market streets for use as the more centrally placed site of the new offices projected by the bank. In 1929 the Board decided to put into effect its plans for a large multistory building capable of producing income from the rental of office space as well as providing for the banking activities of the Society.

As Howe was quick to point out, in the evolution of the design for the new building (Fig. 136) he took as his models the work of such European architects as Walter Gropius (b. 1883) and Ludwig Mies van der Rohe (b. 1886) in Germany, J. J. P. Oud (b. 1890) in Holland, and Le Corbusier (b. 1888) in France. And as further preparation for the task he had set himself, Howe also entered into partnership with William Lescaze, a man he described to the President of the Philadelphia Saving Fund Society as someone "who had long been studying and practicing the new system." Trained in Europe under Karl Moser (1860-1936), Lescaze had come to the United States from his native Switzerland as the protégé of the Swiss consul in New York. Among his first commissions in this country was the interior of the New York apartment of the symphony conductor, Leopold Stokowski, through whom he may have met William Wasserman, then engaged in planning his house with George Howe as the architect.

When Howe and Lescaze presented their design for the new building, the Board of the Philadelphia Saving Fund Society refused to accept it. Those who did not find it downright ugly considered that at best it looked like a loft building. Could not a few more verticals at least be introduced on the exterior? But on such matters of principle the architects stood their ground. Patiently Howe explained that since "in the steel frame of the skyscraper the actual supports of the external casing are not the vertical columns but the continuous horizontal brackets which run around the building at each floor, the logical way to build is to set horizontal courses on these brackets and not to form verticals by breaking the apparent lines at right angles to the natural supports." Without Howe's tact in replying to such criticisms and without his reputation for impeccable taste and his Philadelphia connections, it is doubtful that so radical a departure from prevailing practice could have been made acceptable to the directors. In a sense Howe made modern architecture respectable in Philadelphia.

The drawing reproduced here does not show atop the building the great neon sign, twenty-seven feet high, which has made the letters PSFS known to every Philadelphian. When the President of the Society asked him to "design a branch bank around an electrical

131

sign," Howe had already become interested in the work of modern European architects in his efforts to reconcile architectural form with modern technology. In the final design of the bank this reconciliation was brought about to his satisfaction, and therein lies the importance of the PSFS Building—no one now calls it by any other name. It was the first large commercial structure in America to exploit fully the new materials and the new methods of construction that they made possible as the basis—and the only basis—of modern architectural design. Instead of obscuring the metal frame, as had their predecessors, with a masonry sheath and decorative details derived from the styles of the past, Howe wrote the Board of Managers that he and Lescaze proposed to design the new bank around the principle that "fundamental necessity . . . was an opportunity rather than an obstacle." To the principles of the lintel and the arch used by men since the opening of recorded history, steel in the twentieth century added for the first time the cantilever on a large scale, thereby eliminating any need for corner supports, previously such important elements in architectural design. And as the term "skeleton" applied to modern construction correctly implies, the supporting members of a structure like the PSFS Building are isolated from the external covering which is, in fact, only a "skin" stretched over the spaces they create. Reduced to a practical necessity for safety and protection from the weather, the wall no longer serves a structural function.

Once over their initial opposition, even the most skeptical members of the Board must have been impressed with the effects achieved by Howe and Lescaze through their forceful and elegant disposition of strong forms and rich materials. Following long-standing tradition in Philadelphia, the first floor of the bank is rented as shops and therefore finished with a continuous glass façade trimmed with black marble of mirror surface. An even larger expanse of glass, surrounded by a broad area of highly polished gray granite, marks the banking room projecting over the shop fronts below. At the extreme right is the entrance, narrow but dramatic in its height. These smooth and curving surfaces set the banking area apart from the twenty-eight angular tiers of the office tower above, whose floors extend like "ribs" from the dark gray brick "spine" (the architects' words). In this upright slab, set off by contrasting forms and textures, are the stairs and elevators that serve the rental spaces of the building. And throughout the design stainless steel and glass, arranged with careful attention to proportion, function as a kind of unifying theme.

As the new building for the Saving Fund Society was nearing completion, it was one of two American skyscrapers (the McGraw-Hill Building in New York of 1931 by Hood & Fouilhoux was the other) included in the publication that accompanied the architectural exhibition at the Museum of Modern Art in 1932. In referring to a building such as that by Howe and Lescaze as belonging to the "International Style," the authors sought to suggest the dispersion of the style and the contribution of many architects from various countries, rather than to imply the total absence of individual traits or national distinctions. Reduced to its simplest terms, however, the International Style might be identified by three primary characteristics: emphasis on volumes of space (in contrast to mass and solidity), regularity imposed by modern materials and structural methods (but not symmetry or balance in the classical sense), and expression of the essential qualities inherent in the materials (never applied ornament of any kind). The fact that the country's oldest saving institution should commission a building which by its adherence to these principles was the most radical American structure of its day will seem strange only to those who have forgotten their Philadelphia history. Behind the PSFS Building lie such illustrious predecessors as Blodgett's Bank, the Bank of Pennsylvania, the Second Bank of the United States, the Philadelphia Bank and the Provident, all outstanding in one way or another and most of them no less radical departures from prevailing practice when they were built.

Shortly before his death in 1955, George Howe contributed still another important architectural landmark to the Philadelphia scene. This was the publishing plant of *The Evening and Sunday Bulletin,* erected on a six-acre site at Thirtieth and Market streets and designed by Howe in collaboration with Robert Montgomery Brown. Of gray glazed brick relieved only by the owner's name spelled out in large black letters and the concrete columns sheathed in stainless steel exposed on the first floor of the office section, the Bulletin Building is chiefly remarkable for the skillful adaptation of architectural form to the complex requirements of the modern newspaper. Covered sidings accommodate up to fourteen railroad cars from which the paper passes to two press lines, each over three hundred feet long and together capable of producing nearly three thousand copies of *The Bulletin* during every minute of operation. Visited by thousands of persons each year, the Bulletin Building has attracted wide attention wherever there is interest in the application to newspaper publishing of the economy and speed inherent in contemporary production-line techniques.

The Great Depression which, by lowering prices, made it easier for Howe and Lescaze to use rich materials for the PSFS Building, also brought a temporary end to the construction of important commercial structures. Attention turned, instead, from the single building to the planned community sponsored by local and federal governments. One of the first such projects, and one still widely regarded as among the most successful, is the block of apartments named for Carl Mackley, a local martyr killed during a strike in 1930, and situated at Juniata Park in the northeastern part of the city. Built in 1933 for the hosiery workers of Philadelphia, this project was designed by Oskar Stonorov, in association with Alfred Kastner, and erected under the direction of W. Pope Barney (Fig. 137).

By putting underground the access to the garages and other service areas (lower right corner of the drawing), the site was kept free for the development of the spaces between the four rows of apartments. Here are to be found small informal parks, play areas, and even a pool with a sandy beach. Reflecting Stonorov's European training, the Carl Mackley Houses conform to the principles of the International Style in their lack of applied ornament of any kind. The effectiveness of the design depends, instead, upon the patterns created by windows and recessed balconies in the otherwise smooth surfaces of the walls, as well as upon the contrast of the blue trim with the buff terra cotta facing. Intended from the first as a self-contained unit of three hundred families, the project included an auditorium for entertainment and a store for the simpler shopping needs of the area. Although the immediate sources of the planned community represented by the Carl Mackley Houses are European rather than American, the project nonetheless takes its place as an important

133

modern example of group housing, a matter that had engaged the attention of Philadelphia builders almost since the founding of the city and had produced such earlier forms as the Sansom and Colonnade rows (Figs. 33 and 64).

By the end of the Second World War both the architectural profession and the public at large had generally come to accept the modern system of design for which George Howe had fought fifteen years before. The dominance of the Ecole des Beaux Arts was ending in the architectural schools of the country, and the capitulation of the last bastions of academic eclecticism was being hastened by the presence in America of such pioneers of the modern movement as Mies van der Rohe and Walter Gropius. If anything, the enthusiasm for modern design was perhaps too general and too complete; designs once vital were aped and unwittingly parodied until they became clichés copied by multitudes of architects with all the unthinking acceptance with which their predecessors had adopted the Venetian Gothic or the French Renaissance. For this at least part of the blame may rest upon the mass production techniques of American industry, easily supported by the new aesthetic principle of regularity. Builders and architects were supplied with a virtually unending catalog of prefabricated standard parts that tended to inhibit creativity, always a part of significant design.

During the last decade Philadelphia has doubtless contributed its share of bad buildings. But it has also produced some remarkably good ones, although probably not everyone will agree concerning the right of many structures to be placed in either category. In selecting four examples for illustration and brief comment here, no implication is intended that these are necessarily the best or that only these are worthy of notice.

Modest in scale, but thoroughly satisfying in nearly every detail, is the new Mercantile Library erected at 1021 Chestnut Street in 1953 from the designs of Martin, Stewart & Noble (Fig. 138). In the midst of one of the busiest commercial thoroughfares in the city this elegant little structure has the task of selling reading as its neighbors sell shoes or carpets. And the advantage seems to be all with it. Rarely has so much well-ordered space been defined by so little material. Across the façade is stretched a transparent barrier of glass held in place by narrow mullions of sparkling stainless steel, machined and joined with a jeweler's precision. Aside from the aesthetic properties of the materials, the only ornament is the name spelled out in handsomely proportioned and well-spaced letters over the entrance. The whole design is an invitation to enter; and as an added inducement there is visible from the sidewalk a tiny urban garden in the rear: a tree, a bush, a vine, and a fountain.

Another recent building to have a generally enthusiastic reception is the Lankenau Hospital and Health Center at Overbrook, designed by Vincent Kling (Fig. 139). Founded in 1860 by German-born immigrants who had come to this country following the Napoleonic wars, the present institution takes its name from John D. Lankenau, president from 1869 to 1901. After nearly a century of service to the community, Lankenau Hospital had outgrown its original site opposite Walter's Founder's Hall at Girard and Corinthian avenues, so that, when the property of the Overbrook Golf Club became available shortly

134

after 1950, it was decided to move to the present location off Lancaster Avenue, just west of City Line.

To the extent that the design of Lankenau depends for its effect upon the horizontal pattern created in the plain walls by bands of windows reflecting the structural system, it conforms to the general practices of the International Style. Variety is achieved by varying the heights and positions of the several units as well as by exploiting the different levels of the site. The introduction of occasional oblique elements and the use of continuous horizontal sunshades for the Nursing Wing also adds interest and variety to the silhouette. Built of Roman brick of a warm salmon color, Lankenau owes not a little of its success to its high location and commanding view over the rolling terrain of the old golf course. Its designers were well aware of the potential advantages of the site, and to hear of their concern for its psychological effect upon the patients and their families is to be reminded of the interest of the nineteenth century in this same subject. Those who set the Pennsylvania Hospital for the Insane (Fig. 99) in its romantic park would have understood this aspect of Kling's design. With such buildings as Lankenau, Philadelphia continues its tradition of leadership in the designing of structures for the medical profession, begun two centuries before with the Pennsylvania Hospital (Fig. 35).

Once the principle of skeleton construction in the tall building is accepted as a basis for architectural design, there is nothing inherent in the system to require that the covering of the spaces created by the metal frame be of any particular material, or even that it extend over the entire form, for that matter. Marble is one of the materials used to good effect for this purpose, as in the case of the Pennsylvania State Office Building at Broad and Spring Garden streets, erected in 1958 through the collaboration of three firms: Carroll, Grisdale & Van Alen; Harbeson, Hough, Livingston & Larson; and Nolen & Swinburne (Fig. 140). Here the flat surfaces of the slab shape are enriched on two sides by alternating windows flush with the wall with others having projecting frames, thus creating a lively checkerboard pattern.

In contrast to this emphasis on mass in the upper floors is the open character of the ground floor from which the curtain wall has been omitted so that the vertical supports encased in stainless steel stand unveiled and the building seems to rest on tall stilts. By this device (used earlier in concrete by Le Corbusier for the Unité d'Habitation in Marseilles, among others, and more recently in bronze-sheathed steel by Mies for the House of Seagram in New York) garden areas are made to extend beneath as well as around the building, and the pedestrian, instead of feeling hemmed in, moves as though through a series of outdoor rooms of varying character. Appropriately, therefore, not the least effective part of the State Office Building is the landscape design (Fig. 141) of Ian L. McHarg, a young Harvard-educated Scotsman who is now Chairman of the Department of Landscape Architecture at the University of Pennsylvania. Pools and planting are organized in a series of gradually descending levels whereby a considerable difference in grade is skillfully absorbed without risking the unsettling optical effect to be anticipated if a building set on stilts were further elevated on a high platform or terrace. An elegantly simple, square dish-shaped fountain, lighted at night, dominates and unifies the design.

135

Few problems are more difficult of solution for the modern architect than those involving additions to earlier eclectic buildings. For this reason the design achieved by the firm of Geddes, Brecher, Qualls & Cunningham for the extension of the Moore School at the University of Pennsylvania is all the more remarkable (Fig. 142). Except for the use of the same materials, or materials of similar appearance, the new building makes no attempt to conform to the Jacobean style of the Towne School on the left or to the thoroughly commonplace character of the Moore School, a former factory, on the right. A conflict of scale and style is avoided by setting the addition back a few feet, as if to disclaim the intention on the part of the newcomer of engaging in any kind of direct competition with its older neighbors.

Entered only from the Moore School, the new addition is precisely what it appears to be: four floors of work area, each approximately sixty feet square. To keep this space free of interior obstruction, the vertical supports are placed around the periphery of the building, and the elevator, stairs, and other services and facilities are located in the two towers at either end, whose blank brick-faced walls serve also to insulate the modern design of the addition from the traditional forms of the flanking structures. Horizontal spandrels of precast concrete support the floor slabs at the same time that they help to give to the exterior design the strongly sculptural quality that sets it apart from so many of its glossy contemporaries. The U-shape given these members not only contributes needed strength and rigidity, but also expresses the position of the floors and ceilings with a clarity unusual even in a period when such revelation of a structure is often taken for granted.

A vertical section of the new addition to the Moore School (Fig. 143) best illustrates the structural system, as well as the ease with which the temporary cement block partitions can be adjusted to future needs. To form the deep grid of the floor slabs, concrete was poured around disposable cardboard boxes, a device to eliminate costly wooden forms. Through the interstices of the monolithic slab run the utilities, which are therefore always within easy reach from the open grid below: an important consideration for those making future changes in the division of the work space on any floor. Lights placed in alternate coffers create a strong checkerboard pattern at night, but one perhaps more to be enjoyed from the exterior of the building than from within, where the pipes and wires are also visible. On front and back the wide openings in the concrete frame are filled with brown-tinted glass protected and warmed on the interior by finned convectors running between the vertical members. Well-spaced mullions in the large glass areas add to the abstract design and provide smaller units capable of being individually controlled. Although critics were not wanting to point out minor faults in the extension to the Moore School, its general excellence has been recognized by a variety of awards including the National First Honor Award of the American Institute of Architects.

In addition to the necessity of providing suitable modern structures for the expanding needs of the city, Philadelphians, in the decade following World War II, were also faced with the problem of preserving important structures still surviving from earlier periods. Many of these were in danger of demolition, and nearly all were located in the old section of the city then little more than a slum. This situation inspired the efforts of a

136

number of individuals and groups who, in turn, succeeded in interesting the State of Pennsylvania and the federal government in the rehabilitation and development of the area around Independence Hall. Now, nearly twenty years after the first concentrated efforts in this direction, the Mall stretching north from Chestnut between Fifth and Sixth streets is being developed with state funds. In this way large numbers of unattractive and nondescript buildings have been cleared away, the neighborhood considerably improved, the fire hazard to the State House reduced, and ease of access to the shrine of American independence facilitated for its many visitors. When it is completed and the planting has become established, the Independence Mall will form an impressive vista stretching to the approaches of the Benjamin Franklin Bridge. It has, of course, nothing whatever to do with the original plan of Philadelphia and in its vast scale is in danger of dwarfing the State House, which is its sole reason for being.

Since 1948 the federal government has also been engaged in the development of the Independence National Historical Park to the east of Independence Hall. In this area the problem was very different from that on the north, since here are to be found many structures of the greatest historic and architectural importance. Of some of these it is now necessary to say that they *were* to be found, for the decision of the Park Service has been to demolish everything built after the Greek Revival. In fact, the excitement with which large numbers of persons in Philadelphia and elsewhere have set about restoring and re-creating what they believe to be a Colonial environment makes it abundantly clear that the Romantic delight in the past, usually associated with the nineteenth century, is by no means dead in the twentieth. The policy of the Park Service has meant the restoration and preservation of such important buildings as Blodgett's Bank, the Second Bank of the United States, and the Philadelphia Exchange, but it has resulted in the demolition of the Jayne Building, the Penn Mutual Life Insurance Building, and the Guarantee Trust Co., to cite only the most important examples mentioned earlier. Here again the scattered eighteenth-century structures that remain will presumably be surrounded by parklike areas, doubtless very attractive, but bearing little or no relationship to the original setting, which did much to account for the scale and general character of such buildings as the Second Bank and the Carpenters' Company. Even though experience suggests that in many cases future generations are not likely to consider pleasant parks adequate compensation for the structures demolished to make way for them, in fairness it must be admitted that the retention of commercial buildings of the nineteenth century in an environment of this kind raises problems, practical and aesthetic, for which no one seems to have found a really satisfactory solution.

An attitude toward older structures somewhat different from that of the National Park Service is exemplified by the plans for the redevelopment of Society Hill, the area lying southeast of the Park and mentioned earlier as having once belonged to the Free Society of Traders. Private groups such as the Old Philadelphia Development Corporation and the Philadelphia Society for the Preservation of Landmarks have long urged the saving of what has been called the finest collection of Colonial and early Federal structures in the country. But in its program to arrest the progressive deterioration of this section the Redevelopment Authority has not faced the same difficulties as the Park Service. Because this was never the center of major commercial activity in the nineteenth century, few if any significant structures of that era are endangered by the Authority's proposal to remove buildings incompatible with a residential neighborhood and to provide for the restoration of early houses through rent or sale to persons interested in preserving and maintaining them.

As a basis for its decisions, the Redevelopment Authority has had the advice of the Philadelphia Historical Commission, appointed by the mayor in the spring of 1956, and charged with the continuing responsibility of searching out and recording those buildings possessing the greatest historical importance. The creation of a wholesale produce center in South Philadelphia has already made it possible to remove the markets from the Dock Street area and to restore the headhouse (Fig. 32) to something approaching its former appearance. In some of the vacant places left by the demolition of undesirable buildings, greenways and footpaths are planned that will open vistas of historic landmarks in the Independence National Park deep within the residential section. In others are projected multistory apartment houses like those designed by I. M. Pei & Associates (Fig. 144). Since the introduction of such tall structures poses a threat to the scale and character of their small Georgian neighbors, they have understandably met opposition from many quarters, especially from those who have been impressed by the results achieved at Williamsburg. The City Planning Commission and other proponents of this plan would doubtless reply that only in this way can the density of population be brought to a point that will justify garden areas and at the same time support the facilities required to make this an attractive residential community. Presently under consideration for the river front are such projects as a marina, a heliport, an aquarium, an ice-skating rink, and a variety of exhibits and restaurants. However later critics may judge the rehabilitation of the Society Hill area, the plans now being developed must be considered an imaginative response to the difficult question of how the past can best be made to serve the present.

In this respect the views of the Planning Commission and the Redevelopment Authority seem more in keeping with Philadelphia tradition than some of the other schemes for the embalming of the Georgian structures of the city. When even its greatest buildings outgrew their immediate usefulness or stood in the way of new developments, Philadelphia has usually been ready to tear them down and to erect something different in their place. However much we must regret the continuing destruction of important structures that has gone on almost from the founding of the city, there is something heartening in this steadfast refusal of earlier Philadelphians to content themselves with preserving the architectural monuments of their illustrious past. The Protestant groups who first settled Penn's great town brought with them no more important an artistic tradition than had the colonists of most other American cities, but they brought something that in the long run proved more important: freedom and independence of thought. Because they were not afraid of new ideas, whether in the field of politics, social reform, or the arts, Philadelphians were among the first to try new architectural forms and theories. They produced the most advanced hospitals, the most progressive prisons, several of the most ambitious churches, and some of the earliest and most beautiful municipal parks. Their bridges were longer, wider, and deeper than others of their day. Whenever a new style made its appearance in America it was apt to be found in Philadelphia first; here were a number of the earliest and finest Federal buildings, the first examples of the Greek and Gothic styles, the first and most numerous Egyptian structures, and one of the largest and handsomest buildings in the Moorish manner. Among its neighbors, only Philadelphia can boast a pagoda the size and character of Haviland's. It was Philadelphia that inspired, fostered, and supported such original spirits as Frank Furness and Wilson Eyre, and in the 1930's only it, of all American cities, could claim an outstanding example of a tall building in the International Style.

In the best Philadelphia tradition of experimentation and innovation is the Alfred Newton Richards Medical Research Building, designed by Louis I. Kahn (Fig. 145). Better known, perhaps, as a teacher than as a designer, Kahn has here put to the test a number of the theories associated with his name. Arranged in a series of seven pavilions, three of which are scheduled for completion later, the Medical Research Building is based upon Kahn's principle of "served" and "servants" spaces. The glass-enclosed elements contain "studios," capable of being divided as future conditions may require, and serviced by the utilities located in a central pavilion and in the towers whose unusual height is explained by the need to carry off fumes from the laboratories. On the interior of Kahn's building there is no pretense of affording art for the sake of art; wires, pipes, and ducts are left exposed where they can be put to use most quickly and economically, and the character of the space will finally be determined by the uncompromising realities of medical research, rather than by any classical rules of proportion. The strong visual impact of the exterior, no less than the arrangement of the interior, is the result of a logical expression of a plan carefully worked out in terms of scientific requirements. The blue glass used in some of the transoms to reduce glare combines with the rose-purple brick of the massive towers, the lighter values of clear glass, and the exposed precast concrete structural members to form a powerful abstract pattern of great originality. In a recent highly laudatory article, Kahn's design was described as "accomplished, adult, humane." Accomplished and adult it certainly is, but for many its logical organization and unusual forms, so much a part of the experimental method and so little related to previous experience, may well appear cold, oppressive, and perhaps somewhat forbidding. Only to later generations who have accustomed themselves to living in a world dominated by science are they likely to appear humane.

Even before it was finished, the University's research center was being hailed in many quarters as the greatest building of the last decade, if not of the century. The historian is understandably cautious about such contemporary judgments, especially of a structure not yet occupied. But there can be no doubt of the importance of Kahn's design or of the widespread influence it is certain to exert. Together with other recent buildings mentioned here, the Alfred Newton Richards Medical Research Building reasserts for Philadelphia its long-standing claim to architectural leadership and holds promise of a future for the old city no less vital than its distinguished past.

139

NOTES TO THE ILLUSTRATIONS

INTRODUCTION

IN ADDITION TO THEIR OFTEN VERY CONSIDERABLE ARTISTIC MERIT, ARCHITECTURAL PRINTS and drawings frequently supply valuable evidence of buildings later altered or destroyed. This is especially true of the work of such Philadelphia artists as the elder Birch, Breton, Kennedy, and Evans, who had as one of their conscious objectives the accurate recording of the rapidly changing urban scene for the benefit of future generations. "This Work will stand as a memorial of [the] progress for the first century," William Birch wrote in the introduction to his views of Philadelphia, published in 1800. In this he spoke more truly than he knew, for of the twenty-seven architectural subjects selected for illustration not more than four can be said to retain today any substantial part of their original appearance.

But if architectural prints and drawings are indispensable for the study of the past, as a group they also comprise a special body of material which needs to be used with some caution. Together with the "once was," the artist may occasionally offer us glimpses of the "intended" or perhaps only the merely "hoped for," and it is not always easy, even for the historian, to distinguish the one from the other. It is well to remember, in this connection, that most architectural prints were originally created for some practical purpose that went beyond the artistic value for which they are collected today. More often than not, the publication of a handsome view of a building was expected to advance the reputation of the designer, raise money for the construction fund, thank the donor for gifts already made, or advertise some commercial enterprise. Many prints doubtless served several purposes, but whatever the specific objectives, it was usually to the artist's advantage to represent his subject in the most favorable light possible. A few deft strokes of the pencil and decorative details might be added, offensive surroundings eliminated, and unfinished projects completed. Thus the appearance of a building in a print or drawing should usually be taken as evidence of the intention of the designer rather than as an accurate representation of the completed structure. As in the twentieth century the public's concept of architectural style probably owes almost as much to the skill of the professional photographer as to the designers of modern buildings, so also, in an earlier age, American architecture, like that of Europe, was known very largely through the eyes of the printmaker. It is not unlikely that in the nineteenth century the design of numerous buildings was predicated quite as much upon their need to appear to advantage in engraved or lithographic form as upon more specifically architectural objectives.

As the tempo and complexity of American life increased in the nineteenth century, the sources of American architectural prints become nearly as numerous and varied as the activities and subjects represented. Sheet music, certificates of membership, shares of stock, diplomas, advertisements for business, and the so-called "trade-cards," which came in a wide range of sizes and shapes, are but a few of the many sources that provide useful as well as attractive views of Philadelphia architecture. Even the newsboys of the *Public Ledger* handed out as their "Annual Greeting" for 1861 a view of the interior of Independence Hall "engraved expressly" for the purpose. Nor should it be forgotten that before the development of photography and modern photolithographic processes, many capable artists must have devoted a large portion of their time to providing illustrations for books and periodicals. It may usually be assumed, in fact, that most small prints were originally intended for inclusion in a publication of some kind, even though it may not always be possible to identify the source. Atkinson's *Casket* (later *Graham's Magazine*), *The Port Folio, Ballou's* (later *Gleason's*) *Pictorial Drawing-Room Companion, Harper's Weekly, The American Architect,* and a variety of similar periodicals all contain useful material for the study of the iconography of Philadelphia.

Original drawings in a considerable number have also been included among the illustrations. A few of these were obviously intended as the basis for prints; some were made to preserve a record of an important building threatened with destruction; still others were drawn by the architect, or at his direction, for presentation to a client or possibly for inclusion in an exhibition. In a variety of such ways drawings supplement the architectural prints and are particularly helpful in illustrating buildings of the twentieth century when the camera all but eliminated the usefulness of the print as a factor in architectural history.

In making the final choice of illustrations, the main objective has been to find views that reveal clearly the architectural character of the most important buildings. This has meant that a number of prints and drawings, delightful in themselves, have had to be omitted because they did not seem to do justice to the architectural subject. On the same basis a few others have been included although they may have been published frequently elsewhere or are of somewhat doubtful artistic quality. Wherever possible, however, views have been selected with which the reader is less apt to be familiar and which there is some reason to consider as works of art in their own right. This is especially true of the drawings, most of which are not well known, and a number of which are here published for the first time. An effort has also been made to include among the illustrations representative examples from the work of most of the important artists who have selected their subjects from the Philadelphia scene.

Early prints of Philadelphia are largely confined to plans and maps like those drawn by Thomas Holme in 1682 (Fig. 2), Nicholas Scull and George Heap (*c.*1750 and later; Fig. 1), A. P. Folie (1793), and John Hills (1796), and to the Scull and Heap "East Prospect" of the city, published in 1754 (end papers). Prior to the end of the eighteenth century individual buildings were rarely depicted except for the elevations of the State House that appeared on the Scull and Heap maps (Fig. 1) and a few scarce and rather crude views such as that of the Old Court House, issued *c.*1764 (reproduced in Stokes and Haskell,

Pl.B-19). A helpful list of the early maps and views of Philadelphia in the collection of the Library of Congress has been compiled by P. Lee Phillips and published in 1926 by the Geographical Society of Philadelphia.

The first important series of architectural prints to appear in Philadelphia, and perhaps anywhere in the New World, was the book of engravings published by William Birch & Son entitled *The City of Philadelphia, in the State of Pennsylvania North America; as it appeared in the Year 1800.* On his arrival in Philadelphia from England in 1794 the elder Birch had been much impressed, as he says in the introduction to his book, by the sight of a city that "less than a century" before had been "in a state of wild nature" and that in that short time, as if by some magic power, had been raised "to the eminence of an opulent city." This seems to have been the basis for his desire to picture the beauties of his adopted city for others, especially Europeans. In the execution of his engravings of Philadelphia the elder Birch was assisted by his son, Thomas, whom he had apparently trained, and who is sometimes credited with preparation of the preliminary water colors like that for the plate of "Morris' Folly" (Fig. 30). The finest known copy of the first edition of Birch's views is usually considered to be that now owned by the Free Library of Philadelphia. The first edition of the Birch views contained twenty-eight plates, including a plan of the city; this was followed by a second edition, published in 1804, and made up of twenty views, of which seven were entirely new and thirteen represented reworked plates of the first edition. In the second edition Birch identifies himself as an "enamel painter," and the son is no longer listed as having a part in the publication. This was followed in 1808 by *Country Seats of the United States* in which a majority of the twenty plates are devoted to estates in the vicinity of Philadelphia. The third and last edition of the views of Philadelphia to appear during Birch's lifetime was published in 1827-28. This was a miscellaneous collection of engravings that had appeared separately as well as in the first and second editions of the views. In later years prints were occasionally pulled from the surviving plates that Birch had not intentionally defaced before his death in 1834. Martin P. Snyder discusses Birch's career and gives a useful check list for all the editions, including restrikes, in *The Pennsylvania Magazine* for July, 1949.

Apparently Birch's principal reason for bringing out a third edition of his views was the competition he expected from the engravings of Philadelphia subjects which, beginning about 1827, were published by Col. Cephas G. Childs, a native Pennsylvanian from Bucks County not far from Philadelphia. Issued originally in parts, but collected under the title *Views in Philadelphia and its Environs, from original Drawings taken in 1827-30,* the engravings for which Childs is best known are considerably smaller than those of Birch, vary somewhat in size, and represent the work of a number of artists. From the twenty-five plates published in this series, views of Old Swedes' Church (Fig. 9), the First Congregational Unitarian Church (Fig. 57), the U. S. Mint (Fig. 58), Sedgeley (Fig. 71) and St. Stephen's Church (Fig. 81) have been selected for reproduction here.

Although the views of Philadelphia usually associated with Childs' name are metal engravings, he was also among the first American printmakers to experiment with the new planographic technique of lithography, which was becoming popular in the second quarter of the nineteenth century. The ease, speed, and economy of this new process greatly increased the number and variety of prints of Philadelphia subjects that appeared between about 1830 and the Civil War. The broad subject of lithography in the United States is covered by Harry T. Peters in *America on Stone* (Garden City, 1931), and on a more specialized level we are fortunate in having Nicholas B. Wainwright's *Philadelphia in the Romantic Age of Lithography* as a guide.

At first the lithograph was regarded primarily as a convenient means of reproducing paintings, but gradually it came to assume a more independent status as artists learned to design directly on the stone. The gilders, William B. Lucas and David Kennedy, who operated a looking-glass store on south Third Street, were among the first in Philadelphia to establish the new process as a commercial enterprise. The partnership was terminated in 1833 by the death of Lucas, but in the four years of its existence the firm of Kennedy & Lucas turned out a considerable variety of prints, including the illustrations for the first edition of Watson's *Annals of Philadelphia* (1830) and a number of architectural subjects of which the view of St. Peter's, here reproduced as Figure 12, is a good example.

The artist who drew many of the views lithographed by Kennedy & Lucas, including that of St. Peter's Church and the illustrations of Watson's *Annals*, was an Englishman named William L. Breton. It is strange that so little attention has been paid to Breton, because he is responsible for the drawings that form the basis of our impressions of the appearance of many early buildings such as Joshua Carpenter's house (Fig. 3), the Slate Roof House (Fig. 4), the Letitia Street House (Fig. 6), and the Old Court House (Fig. 8).

Kennedy and Lucas seem to have had to depend primarily upon the income from their store, and financial success also eluded Col. Cephas G. Childs and his two successive partners, Henry Inman and George Lehman, in their efforts to establish a lithographic press on a commercial basis. To satisfy a debt, Childs in 1834 turned over his interest in the firm of Childs & Lehman to Peter S. Duval, a young French lithographer whom he had induced to return with him from Paris three years before. For the new firm of Lehman & Duval financial prospects gradually improved so that when, four years later, Lehman decided to withdraw, the younger partner was able to continue alone. By the time of his retirement in 1869 Duval had become the leading lithographer in Philadelphia and one of the most successful in the country.

Lithography was also the preferred technique of the Swiss artist who, coming after Birch and Childs, was responsible for the third major series of architectural prints of Philadelphia subjects. These were the work of John Caspar Wild who may have come to Philadelphia as early as 1831. There in 1837 he entered into partnership with J. B. Chevalier for the purpose of producing lithographic views of the city, to be sponsored in turn by the *Saturday Courier*. The views of the University of Pennsylvania and the Naval Home (Figs. 56 and 60) were not the first subjects Wild attempted, but they were included among the twenty plates which, together with a page of descriptive text for each, comprised the *Views of Philadelphia, and its Vicinity* issued in 1838. Wild made at least six more lithographs of Philadelphia subjects, including the four-part Panorama from the roof of the State House, before he left Philadelphia permanently in 1838 for the Midwest.

146

Although Chevalier continued in business as a lithographer after Wild's departure, he does not seem to have taken much in interest in the *Views,* the rights to which passed into the hands of J. T. Bowen who in 1848 reissued them in color over his own name. In *The Pennsylvania Magazine* for January, 1953, Martin Snyder discusses Wild's activities in Philadelphia and gives a check list of his views of the city.

The John T. Bowen who acquired the rights to Wild's *View of Philadelphia* was an English lithographer who in 1838 had transferred his business from New York to Philadelphia. There in his "lithographic establishment" at 94 Walnut Street (old number) he soon built up a large trade and in the process earned the reputation of being "the best lithographer and colorer" in the country. Known especially for its color work, the firm's prints are best exemplified by the plates in the octavo edition of John James Audubon's *Birds of America* (1839-44). After her husband's death in 1856 Bowen's wife carried on the business, later forming a partnership with John Cassin, the Philadelphia ornithologist, under the name of Bowen & Company.

The success that Bowen had achieved with his hand-colored plates led Duval and others to experiment with lithographs printed in color. The first efforts in this direction were fairly crude, but before the middle of the century the process had been perfected to a point where it had gained wide acceptance. From this period in the firm's history dates the delightful view of the Northern Liberties and Spring Garden Waterworks in the Egyptian manner, issued in 1852 (Fig. 86). In 1848 Duval also began the use of steam power to operate his presses, an achievement duly noted on most of the prints produced thereafter in his establishment.

The prominence of lithographers such as Bowen and Duval may help to explain why Currier & Ives, the most prolific of all American printmakers, did not think it worthwhile to include many Philadelphia subjects in their offerings. The view of the Girard Avenue Bridge (Fig. 110) is one of the few attractive views of Penn's great town by the New York firm (Frederic A. Conningham, *Currier and Ives Prints; An Illustrated Check List,* New York, 1949).

Wainwright has estimated that by 1856 there were as many as sixteen lithographic firms in Philadelphia of which Duval and his three principal rivals, Sinclair, Wagner & McGuigan, and Rosenthal, were the most important. Together they must have employed close to a hundred artists, most of whom are known to us today as little more than an occasional credit line on an old print. Many of those who worked in the lithographic shops appear to have been foreign-born artists who were unable to find a market in Philadelphia for their paintings and so turned to making prints as a means of earning a living.

We are also indebted to Nicholas Wainwright (*The Pennsylvania Magazine,* July, 1960) for information concerning one of the most talented and successful of these foreign artists who worked in Philadelphia in the mid-nineteenth century. This was Augustus Koellner (Kollner or Köllner), an emigrant from Germany, who settled in Philadelphia in 1840 and there during the remaining sixty-six years of his life produced a great variety of paintings, lithographs, and engravings that cover a wide range of subjects. Only a small part of Koellner's work could be considered architectural; many of his most attractive prints were done for the American Sunday School Union, and throughout his life he seems especially to have favored subjects that included horses. The view of Laurel Hill Cemetery (Fig. 87) is one of seven Philadelphia subjects that were part of the collection of fifty-four *Views of American Cities* drawn by Koellner and published between 1848 and 1851.

Related to the "trade-cards" (most of which were not cards at all) were the street panoramas popular in Philadelphia shortly after the middle of the century. Among the first of these was the "Panorama of Chestnut Street" put out by Julio Rae about 1851 and featuring the business establishments on both sides of the street between Second and Tenth. By displaying prominently the signs of the firms that had contributed to the project, Rae and his associates hoped to interest Philadelphia businessmen in these lithographic views as a means of advertising. The idea was again revived in 1857 on a somewhat larger scale by DeWitt C. Baxter and continued, according to Joseph Jackson, until about 1882. At first "Baxter's Panorama" was engraved on wood, but later the publishers turned to lithography. Figure 119 is a view typical of many of the blocks on Chestnut and Market streets that Baxter drew. Below were listed the names of the participating firms with blank spaces to indicate those that could not, or would not, pay for this privilege.

Although lithography became increasingly popular with the illustrators and print makers of the nineteenth century, the older varieties of engraving, in use since the fifteenth century, were never entirely abandoned. Many periodicals continued to use engravings, frequently on wood (and therefore, since they are essentially a relief process, not really "engravings," in spite of the name applied to them), and there were always those who preferred the crisp line made by the engraver's burin to the pictorial effects of the lithographer's crayon. One of the leading Philadelphia engravers was John Sartain, who had immigrated to America from England in 1830. There he settled in Philadelphia where until his death in 1897 he continued to be closely associated with numerous publications as both engraver and publisher. The view of the Philadelphia Exchange, Figure 59, is a good example of Sartain's use of mezzotint for an architectural subject. David McNeely Stauffer lists many Philadelphia prints in his *American Engravers upon Copper and Steel* (New York, 1907), to which Mantle Fielding added a supplement in 1917.

In the eighteenth and nineteenth centuries, most foreign visitors to America included Philadelphia on their itineraries, and those who had some training as artists often left sketches of what they saw there. As a British officer during the Revolution, Archibald Robertson's visit to Philadelphia in 1777 was not, of course, a matter of choice, but the several wash drawings of the city included in the portfolio of his work in the New York Public Library reveal their author as an exceptionally talented draftsman. Also from the collections of the New York Public Library is the water color of the Philadelphia harbor that J. L. Boqueta De Woiseri painted about 1810 (Fig. 36) from approximately the same point on the Jersey shore as that used by George Heap for his "East Prospect" sixty years before. Views of Philadelphia were also included in the more than fifty water colors of American scenes that the Russian diplomat Pavel Petrovitch Svinin made between 1811 and 1813 while he was secretary to the Russian consul-general in Philadelphia. Svinin's sketches have been published by Avraham Yarmolinsky, and, from the originals now in the

148

Metropolitan Museum of Art, the Pennsylvania Academy of the Fine Arts and the Pump House in Center Square are here reproduced as Figures 37 and 41.

The camera came into fairly general use in the 1850's, and after the Civil War the new techniques of photolithography gradually supplanted the artist in his traditional role of illustrator. Fortunately for this study the decrease in important architectural prints is partially compensated by the extraordinary number and variety of the drawings made by David J. Kennedy, a Scot, who settled in Philadelphia in 1835. *The Pennsylvania Magazine* for 1936 also credits Kennedy with the invention of the Busybody, a device of three mirrors which when mounted outside the window permitted the occupants of the house to see up and down the street without themselves being seen. Although much in use in Philadelphia prior to World War I, the Busybody has now been largely forgotten, and its originator is remembered instead for the hundreds of water colors of Philadelphia streets and buildings which he made between his arrival in the city and his death in 1898. The Kennedy drawings are somewhat uneven in quality, but from the more than one thousand examples preserved in the Historical Society of Pennsylvania five of the best views have been selected for illustration here (Figs, 16, 45, 65, 66, 80).

Supplementing the drawings of Kennedy are those of B. Ridgway Evans, an artist about whom very little seems to be known. The New-York Historical Society's *Dictionary of Artists in America* notes only that he was the delineator of a Philadelphia street scene in 1851. Scarcely less numerous than the Kennedy scenes that may have helped to inspire them but to which they are usually technically inferior, the wash drawings of Evans often supply useful architectural evidence for buildings which were standing in the period 1850 to 1890 (Figs. 26, 29, 32).

In spite of the inroads made by photography, the tradition of distinguished architectural prints and drawings begun by the Birches was never entirely neglected in the twentieth century. From about 1912 date many of the prints of Joseph Pennell which take Philadelphia and Philadelphia buildings as their subjects (Fig. 18), and from the 20's and 30's we have the etchings of Ernest David Roth (Fig. 127) and the lithographs of Theo. B. White (Fig. 132). Since the camera had relieved these later printmakers from the need for accuracy of architectural detail, they were free to record their impressions of the mood of the city, which had been rapidly changing since World War II and perhaps cannot be recalled as readily from any other source.

The tradition of Breton, Kennedy, and Evans was also continued in the mid-20's by Frank Hamilton Taylor, as evidenced by the view of the Jayne mansion that formerly stood on Chestnut Street (Fig. 115). Since many of Taylor's wash drawings are based on the work of earlier artists, they cannot in every case be used as evidence of the artist's own observation (Fig. 64). But unlike most earlier views, those of Taylor are usually accompanied by brief historical notes which, although not always completely accurate, often supply helpful leads.

To the late Joseph Sims we owe drawings of a number of buildings such as the Racquet Club of Philadelphia (Fig. 130) or the Pennsylvania Academy of the Fine Arts (Fig. 118), in their own way as handsome as those produced in the preceding periods. More recently, the efforts of the National Park Service to preserve the older parts of the city have also called for a new type of architectural drawing. Based on the findings of historians and archaeologists, and represented here by the work of Penelope Hartshorne (Fig. 14) and William Campbell (Fig. 15), this type of architectural rendering deserves a special place in any comprehensive survey of prints and drawings of Philadelphia buildings.

Falling somewhere between the product of the usual printmaker and that of the architectural historian, are the contemporary lithographs of Grant M. Simon (Fig. 20), Chairman of the Philadelphia Historical Commission, which in an unusual way combine the historian's interest in the past with the lithographer's concern for artistic effect.

NOTES TO ILLUSTRATIONS

The figures given below represent the approximate size of the print or drawing exclusive of the margins or any descriptive material. Measurements are in inches, with the vertical dimension being given first. When applied to Philadelphia, the designations "north" and "south" assume Market Street as the pont of reference; "above" and "below" mean north or west and south or east, respectively. Publications for which no date and place of publication are given are listed in the Bibliography.

Title-page
CHESTNUT STREET AT FIFTH, LOOKING EAST

Water color, unsigned, but probably by William Strickland (1788-1854). 14 by 18. Courtesy of the Atwater Kent Museum.

The building with the classical portico is the Second Bank of the United States and that beside it on the east, at the corner of Fourth Street, is the Philadelphia Bank, both designed by Strickland. The structure just visible at the left is the United States Hotel.

End Papers
EAST PROSPECT OF THE CITY OF PHILADELPHIA FROM THE JERSEY SHORE

Engraving, c.1754, from a drawing by George Heap (c.1715-1752) under the direction of Nicholas Scull (d.1762), Surveyor-General of Pennsylvania. Published in London, 1754.

Second state. Four sections, each 21¼ by 20⅛. Courtesy of the Historical Society of Pennsylvania.

Panoramas of this kind were made in the eighteenth century of a number of the most important American cities, including Boston, New York, and Charleston. The "East Prospect," as it is usually known, is the earliest engraved view of Philadelphia and by any standard one of the largest and most important prints of the city ever to appear. Joseph Jackson has called it "the most ambitious effort at picturing an American city, made before the Revolution." Nicholas Scull was a native Pennsylvanian who became surveyor-general of the province in 1748, and c.1750 cooperated with his friend George Heap in the production of the first important map of the Philadelphia area since that of Thomas Holme. About 1750 Heap undertook to draw a view of Philadelphia such as that Thomas Penn had requested be sent him as the basis for the engravings he planned to give his friends in London. It is not clear to what extent Scull's "direction" influenced the final form of the "East Prospect." Unfortunately Heap died before he could take his drawing to England, but the rights to the project were purchased from his widow by Nicholas Scull. The first state of the "East Prospect" was subsequently engraved by Gerard Vandergucht (1696-1776) and appeared in London in 1754 in an edition of 500 copies. For the second printing of 250 copies the word Calvinist, which had been spelled "Calvern" in the first edition, was corrected, and Scull's name was correctly spelled with a "c" instead of a "k." In 1756

Thomas Jeffery engraved and published in London a smaller version of Heap's original drawing, which also included as insets small views of the Battery and State House, as well as a map of the city. Although this is the version best known today, it does not seem to have been especially popular when it was first brought out. A number of the facts cited here are taken from Nicholas B. Wainwright's article on "Scull and Heap's East Prospect of Philadelphia," which appeared in *The Pennsylvania Magazine* for 1949.

1

MAP OF THE CITY AND ENVIRONS OF PHILADELPHIA WITH A VIEW OF THE STATE HOUSE

Engraving, 1777, by William Faden from a map by Nicholas Scull (d.1762) and George Heap (*c*.1715-1752). Reprinted by Thomas Fisher, Philadelphia, 1857. 24⅝ by 17⅛. Courtesy of the Library Company of Philadelphia.

The Fisher reprint of the Scull and Heap map does not differ essentially from the first state except for the shaded area at the west of the plan of the city, described at the bottom of the map as the forest of oak, elm, and hickory trees known as "Penn's Woods," the last remnant of which was cut down by the British in the winter of 1777 for fuel and to prevent its affording cover for the colonial troops. The view of the State House that appears on a number of the Scull and Heap maps, beginning about 1750, is usually considered the earliest known representation of that building. A summary of the evidence for considering Edmund Woolley the "architect" of the State House is given by Charles E. Peterson in the *Journal of the Society of Architectural Historians* for October, 1952.

2

PLAN OF PHILADELPHIA
1682

Engraving, *c*.1683, from the plan of Thomas Holme (1624-1695), Surveyor-General of Pennsylvania. 11¾ by 17⁹⁄₁₆. Courtesy of the Library Company of Philadelphia.

A copy of this map accompanied Penn's letter of 1683 to the Committee of the Free Society of Traders in London. Although the city blocks appear to be more or less uniform in size, measured plans of the eighteenth century indicate that they varied in some cases by as much as 100 feet. Holme erred in representing the west boundary of Philadelphia as nearly straight whereas in fact the bend of the Schuylkill River cuts into the plan of the city rather sharply at this point, as shown on the Scull and Heap map of 1777 (Fig. 1). The name "Schuylkill" is said to be Dutch for "Hidden River." The early history of Philadelphia is complicated by the frequency with which the names of streets were changed. By the first years of the eighteenth century Wynne Street had become Chestnut, and Songhurst was more generally known as Sassafras. Until the Revolution, Locust Street was called Prune, and Walnut, Pool. Toward the end of the eighteenth century the name of Holmes Street was changed to Mulberry. Before the renumbering of the streets running north and south, the word "Schuylkill" was prefixed to those west of Broad Street in order to distinguish them from those on the east. The career of Thomas Holme and his plan for Philadelphia is discussed by Oliver Hough in *The Pennsylvania Magazine* for 1895 and 1896. The date for John Brockett's plan for New Haven is taken from *Architecture and Town Planning in Colonial Connecticut* by Anthony N. B. Garvan (Yale University Press, 1951). The date given here for the plan of Charleston is based on the article "Charleston and Savannah" by Frederic R. Stevenson and Carl Feiss in the *Journal of the Society of Architectural Historians* for December, 1951. A map showing the prncipal buildings of early Philadelphia has been drawn by Grant M. Simon and published in *Historic Philadelphia*.

3
JOSHUA CARPENTER'S HOUSE
North side of Chestnut Street between Sixth and Seventh. Built prior to 1722; demolished 1826.

Water color, *c*.1826, by W. L. Breton (*c*.1773-1855). 5⅛ by 7¹⁄₁₆. Courtesy of the Historical Society of Pennsylvania.

Joshua Carpenter (d.1722) is known to have purchased land in Philadelphia as early as 1701. Later tenants of the house on Chestnut Street included Doctor Graeme, Governor Thomas, and John Dickinson. During the Revolution the house served as a military hospital and later as the home of the French ambassador. It was torn down about 1826, shortly after it was sold by Judge William H. Tilghman. Haviland's Arcade (Fig. 63) was later built on the site.

4
SLATE ROOF HOUSE
Southeast corner of Second and Norris' Alley (now Sansom). Built between 1687 and 1699 from designs of James Porteus (d.1737); demolished 1867.

Water color, *c*.1830, by W. L. Breton (*c*.1773-1855). 5 by 7⅛. Courtesy of the Historical Society of Pennsylvania.

The Slate Roof House was certainly finished by 1699, and Morrison, following Bridenbaugh, has suggested that it may have been built shortly after Samuel Carpenter acquired the necessary land, possibly as early as 1687. James Porteus (Portis, Portues) was a trained architect or master builder whom Penn brought to Philadelphia and who later helped to organize the Carpenters' Company. Joseph Jackson mentions Porteus as a native of Dumfries, Scotland, who had spent some time in London before coming to Philadelphia. The Charter of Privileges that Penn composed in the Slate Roof House may properly be thought of as a forerunner of the American Bill of Rights. It was to commemorate the fiftieth anniversary of the Charter that the so-called Liberty Bell was cast and hung in the State House in order that it might, in the words of the inscription, proclaim liberty "throughout all the land unto the inhabitants thereof." The Slate Roof House is described by E. and L. H. Carpenter in *Samuel Carpenter* (Philadelphia, 1912).

5
DETAIL OF THE HOUSE OF COUNT VALERIO CHIERICATO, VICENZA, ITALY
Design by Andrea Palladio (1518-1580).

Engraving, published by Isaac Ware, *The Four Books of Andrea Palladio's Architecture*, Bk. II, Pl. 3, London, 1738. 10⁵⁄₁₆ by 7. Courtesy of the Library Company of Philadelphia.

Although it is convenient to use the term "Palladian" to describe architecture based on the style of the Italian Renaissance, that word should be understood to include not only the work of the great Italian architect but also that of his numerous English imitators: such men as Isaac Ware (d.1766), William Halfpenny (d.1755), Batty Langley (1696-1751), and Abraham Swan (fl.1745-1765). The Palladian tradition in England is well summarized by John Summerson in *Architecture in Britain, 1530 to 1830* (Baltimore, 1954).

6

LETITIA STREET HOUSE
Now in Fairmount Park.
Built between 1703 and 1715; moved to Fairmount Park 1883.

Water color, *c.*1828, by W. L. Breton (*c.*1773-1855). 5³⁄₁₆ by 7⅛. Courtesy of the Historical Society of Pennsylvania.

Letitia Street, where the house originally stood, runs from Market to Chestnut between Front and Second. Old photographs of the house before its removal to Fairmount Park serve as a reminder that the present hood above the door is a restoration, but one apparently based upon such visual evidence as the drawing reproduced here. When it was moved to the Park, the house was believed to have been built in 1682 by William Penn as the first brick house in Philadelphia. Subsequent investigation has shown, however, that it was not standing at the close of the seventeenth century and there now seems no good reason to associate it with either Penn or his daughter Letitia. The dates given here are those proposed by Eberlein and Hubbard in *Portrait of a Colonial City.* In the view of some students of American architecture the plan of the Letitia Street House reflects the building practices of the Swedish settlers in Pennsylvania, a point discussed very fully by Thomas T. Waterman in *The Dwellings of Colonial America.*

7

BENEZET (OR BREINTNALL) HOUSE
North side of Chestnut Street between Third and Fourth.
Built *c.*1700; demolished 1818.

Engraving from a drawing by William Strickland (1788-1854) for Roberts Vaux, Mar. 4, 1818. Published in *The Port Folio*, October, 1818. 5¹⁵⁄₁₆ by 4⅝. Courtesy of the Free Library of Philadelphia.

As one of the first substantial dwellings in Philadelphia, this house, which stood on Chestnut Street near the bridge across Dock Creek, seemed to some too pretentious for a plain Quaker. At least that is the reason Watson gives to explain why David Breintnall (d.1731) let his new house to the Governor of the Barbadoes, then in Philadelphia for his health. Watson also relates that the house served for a time as a tavern under the sign of the Hen and Chickens before it came into the hands of Anthony Benezet. Born a French Huguenot, Benezet (1713-1784) became a Quaker and a champion of the rights of Negroes, writing tracts against slavery and establishing a free school for Negro children. Survey 173 at the Philadelphia Contributionship, dated Dec. 24, 1753, describes the Benezet house as 18½ ft. front, 26 ft. back, two stories, with a one-story kitchen at the rear, 12 ft. by 14 ft. A later survey of Dec. 25, 1762, mentions a new back building 42 ft. by 12 ft. Roberts Vaux, for whom the drawing was made, wrote the *Memoirs of the Life of Anthony Benezet* (Philadelphia, 1817). *The Port Folio* speaks of the Benezet house as "one of the oldest, if not the first brick house erected in Philadelphia."

8

GREATER MEETING HOUSE AND TOWN HALL
Southwest corner of Second and High (Market) streets.
Greater Meeting House built 1755; demol-

ished early in the nineteenth century. Town Hall built 1707-10; demolished 1837.

Water color, c.1830, by W. L. Breton (c.1773-1855). 8 by 10⅞. Courtesy of the Historical Society of Pennsylvania.

The stairs that led up to the second floor of the Town Hall (or Court House) were early used by Philadelphians when casting their votes. These were later removed, leaving only the balcony for public addresses and proclamations. The prototypes for buildings of this kind may still be seen in many English towns and other American examples still stand at New Castle, Delaware, and Newport, Rhode Island. The deep plaster cove cornices such as those on the Town Hall and the Greater Meeting House, nearby, seem characteristic, so far as America is concerned, of the Philadelphia region. Similar examples may be seen on the Letitia Street House (Fig. 6) and the Joshua Carpenter House (Fig. 3). Other Quaker meeting houses built before the Revolution include that on Society Hill on the south side of Pine between Front and Second (1753-1832) and the Fourth Street Meeting House (1763-1859) erected on the east side near Chestnut next to the Friends' School, which preceded it on that site. Quaker buildings in Philadelphia are discussed by Edwin B. Bronner in *Historic Philadelphia*, and in the same volume Agnes Addison Gilchrist gives the history of the market houses on High Street.

9
OLD SWEDES' CHURCH (GLORIA DEI)
Swanson Street near Christian.
Built 1698-1700.

Engraving by Cephas Grier Childs (1793-1871) from a drawing of Thomas Sully (1783-1872). Published by C. G. Childs in *Views in Philadelphia and its Environs, from original Drawings taken in 1827-30*, Philadelphia. 3⅜ by 4¹³⁄₁₆. Courtesy of the Free Library of Philadelphia.

In the same year in which the cornerstone was laid for the Philadelphia church, the Swedish community at Wilmington, Delaware, also began the construction of Christiana Church (Holy Trinity), which in some respects Old Swedes' resembles. A number of the craftsmen who worked on Gloria Dei appear to have come from Wilmington. Joseph Jackson names John Smart and John Brett as the carpenters and therefore possibly the designers of Old Swedes'. The pipes shown projecting through the roof in Sully's view of Old Swedes' are a reminder that in the late eighteenth and early nineteenth centuries even the more pretentious Georgian buildings were regularly heated by stoves.

10
SOUTHEAST PROSPECT OF THE CITY OF PHILADELPHIA

Oil on canvas, c.1720, by Peter Cooper. 27 by 94. Courtesy of the Library Company of Philadelphia.

The Cooper View was found in London and purchased by the Library Company in 1857. Its previous history is unknown. Cooper is identified on the "label" of the Southeast Prospect as a "painter," but in view of the character of his work and the fact that nothing else by him has been found, it is thought that he was probably a painter of houses or signs. Among the more imaginative details that he seems to have introduced into his panorama are the large round and pear-shaped finials that surmount a number of the taller structures. The line of buildings at the far left has sometimes been identified as "Budd's Row," a group of dwellings built by English settlers as early as 1691 and perhaps before. The photograph reproduced here was taken in July, 1960, shortly after the Cooper View had been cleaned.

11

CHRIST CHURCH
West Side of Second Street above Market.
Built 1727-44; steeple completed 1754 by Robert Smith (c.1722-1777) and others, possibly from design of [John?] Harrison (d.1760).

Oil on canvas, 1811, by William Strickland (1788-1854). Signed and dated on back. 48 by 52. Courtesy of the Historical Society of Pennsylvania.

The steeple of Christ Church was repaired by Robert Smith in 1771 and rebuilt after the fire of 1908. On July 5, 1736, Dr. Kearsley was paid for wooden urns he had ordered from England, the shape of which is preserved by the cast-iron replicas now on the roof. In 1834 Thomas U. Walter altered the interior. The dimensions of Christ Church, approximately 118 ft. by 61 ft., make it one of the largest Georgian churches in America. The steeple surmounting the square tower (28 ft. by 28 ft.) rises to a height of 196 ft. and must therefore have been one of the tallest structures in the British Colonies when it was built. Morrison gives the following heights for other comparable examples: Old North, Boston (1723), 191 ft.; First Baptist Meeting House, Providence, Rhode Island (1774-75), 185 ft.; St. Michael's, Charleston (1752-61), 185 ft. St. Andrew-by-the-Wardrobe and Gibb's St. Martin's-in-the-Fields are the English churches most frequently cited as possible sources for portions of the design of Christ Church. The handsome wineglass pul-

pit dates from 1769 and is the work of John Folwell. Thomas Lester and Thomas Pack cast the bells at the Whitechapel foundry in London, also the source of the Liberty Bell in the State House. Many of the signers of the Declaration of Independence worshiped at Christ Church and seven of them are buried in the churchyard. The comment concerning the bells quoted in the text was made by Johann D. Schöpf and is taken from the article by Robert W. Shoemaker in *Historic Philadelphia*.

12

ST. PETER'S CHURCH FROM THE NORTHEAST
Southwest corner of Third and Pine streets.
Built 1758-61 from designs of Robert Smith (c.1722-1777).

Lithograph, 1829, drawn on stone by W. L. Breton (c.1773-1855). Published by Kennedy & Lucas. 8 1/16 by 11 9/16. Courtesy of the Library Company of Philadelphia.

By the middle of the eighteenth century the Penn family had become members of the Church of England and the ground for St. Peter's was the gift of Thomas and Richard Penn, Proprietaries of the Province of Pennsylvania. The Choir School for which St. Peter's is famous is descended from the Parish Day School that Bishop White founded in 1834 as one of the first parochial schools of the Episcopal Church in America. In the churchyard are buried not only a number of persons important in early American history (including Charles Willson Peale, the painter), but also several Indian chieftains who died in Philadelphia while the city served as the national capital. The wooden figures of Prayer and Praise that now adorn the organ case are believed to be the work of William Rush and to have come from St. Paul's as did also the sounding board above the pulpit. The very full building specifications for St. Peter's are still preserved in the records of Christ Church. Insurance surveys exist at the Mutual Assurance Company for St. Paul's, both before and after Strickland's alterations.

13
ZION LUTHERAN CHURCH
Corner of Cherry and Fourth streets.
Built 1766-69 from designs of Robert Smith (c.1722-1777); rebuilt 1794-96; demolished 1869.

Engraving, 1799, by William (1755-1834) and Thomas (1779-1851) Birch. Published by W. Birch in *The City of Philadelphia, in the State of Pennsylvania North America; as it appeared in the Year 1800*, 1st ed., 1800. 8⁵⁄₁₆ by 11¹⁄₁₆. Courtesy of the Kean Archives.

Insurance surveys at the Philadelphia Contributionship give the dimensions of St. Michael's as 44 ft. 6 in. by 80 ft., and those of Zion Church as 109 ft. on Fourth Street and 70 ft. on Cherry. In 1870 the congregation of Zion Church moved to the church that still stands on Franklin Street above Race. Previously, in 1808, the English-speaking elements of Zion and St. Michael's had built St. John's Lutheran Church on Race Street east of Sixth, destroyed in 1924 to make way for the Delaware River (now the Benjamin Franklin) Bridge. The same Robert Smith who designed Zion Church was also "appointed architect" of the Third Presbyterian Church on Pine Street west of Fourth, built in 1767, remodeled 1837, 1857, 1867, and restored 1955.

14
SAMUEL NEAVE AND JAMES ABERCROMBIE HOUSES

272-274 and 268-270 South Second Street. Built c.1759.

Pencil drawing, 1960, by Penelope Hartshorne (b.1928). 15½ by 20. Courtesy of the artist.

The view of the Neave and Abercrombie houses reproduced here is based on careful research by the staff of the National Park Service but nevertheless conjectural in some details. Capt. James Abercrombie was a Scottish merchant who went down with his ship in the Baltic Sea the year after his house was finished. His widow later married Charles Stedman, who built the Powel House, and his son James, Jr., served for many years as Assistant Rector of Christ Church and St. Peter's. Later occupants included John Ross (who afterwards built the big house still standing on the southeast corner of Second and Pine streets) and William Cramond, for whom Benjamin Latrobe designed Sedgeley (Fig. 71). Samuel Neave was an English merchant who arrived in Philadelphia about 1735. His house on South Second Street was built about the same time as the Abercrombie House with which it shares a party wall. Neave followed the practice of many Philadelphia merchants of having his living quarters behind and above his store. It is possible that there was a separate front door to the store, not shown in Miss Hartshorne's drawing. There was a fine garden on the south side where Tucker's Tavern later stood. Other owners included Thomas C. Wharton of Walnut Grove and Owen Jones, Jr., a Quaker merchant who was exiled to Virginia during the Revolution.

15
CONJECTURAL RESTORATION OF THE ENTRANCE TO FRANKLIN COURT
South side of Market Street between Third and Fourth.

Franklin's house built 1764-65; demolished 1812. Houses on Market Street built 1787-88 and now much altered.

Pen and crayon, 1959, by William M. Campbell (b.1887). 11¾ by 15½. Courtesy of the Independence National Historical Park.

With the aid of old insurance surveys and the architectural fragments of the original buildings that can still be identified, it is possible to form a fairly complete picture of the probable appearance of the houses on Market Street. The trap doors that appear on the roofs were put there at Franklin's instructions to enable the occupants to wet the shingles in case of a nearby fire. As a further deterrent to the spread of fire, Franklin saw to it that the wooden parts of one room did not touch the wooden members of any other part of the house. When Franklin died in 1790 he left his houses on Market Street to his daughter Sarah and her husband Richard Bache. For a time the offices of the *Aurora,* published by William Duane, Sr., and his wife Margaret (formerly Mrs. Benjamin Franklin Bache) were housed in 322 and 316. In 1812 Franklin's descendants had his house torn down when they cut a street through to the southern border of the property. Franklin Court was opened through to Chestnut Street in 1852; the present Orianna Street runs through the middle of Franklin's lawn. Edward M. Riley gives additional details about Franklin's house in *Historic Philadelphia.*

16
MOUNT PLEASANT
East Fairmount Park, overlooking the Schuylkill.
Built 1761.

Water color, Aug. 4, 1871, by David J. Kennedy (1817-1898). 4½ by 7½. Courtesy of the Historical Society of Pennsylvania.

Capt. John MacPherson (Macpherson) had made his fortune as a privateer during the 1750's when England was at war with France and Spain. In 1779 General Benedict Arnold bought Mount Pleasant in preparation for his coming marriage to Peggy Shippen, but because of the Revolution, and his own treason, he was never able to live there. The origins of the design for Mount Pleasant have never been determined. As one possible source Thomas Waterman has pointed out similarities between it and the published work of Daniel Marot, and certainly the roofs of the lateral pavilions have a very French appearance.

17
CLIVEDEN
Germantown Avenue and Johnson Street (Germantown).
Built 1764.

Oil on paper, c.1870, by Edward Lamson Henry (1841-1919). 17 by 31½. Courtesy of Mr. and Mrs. Samuel Chew.

The date of Cliveden is sometimes given as 1761, but Benjamin Chew did not acquire title to the land on which the house is built until July 14, 1763 (Harry M. and Margaret B. Tinkcom, Grant M. Simon, *Historic Germantown*). Since it was probably painted nearly a century after the event, Henry's painting is not very good evidence of the Battle of Germantown, but it appears to be a good portrait of the house, which still looks much as he represented it. The emphasis of Renaissance designers upon the façades of their buildings is seen here in the use of gray ashlar for the front but stucco for the sides and back. The outbuilding at the left of the painting, which is connected with the main house by a curving passageway, still stands and originally served as the kitchen. Benjamin Chew (1722-1810) for whom the house was built was a distinguished jurist who before the Revolution served briefly as Chief Justice of the Supreme Court of Pennsylvania and from 1791 to 1808 as judge and president of the High Court of Errors and Appeals of Pennsylvania. Named for an estate in England owned by the royal family, Cliveden, like most of the large Georgian homes located beyond the limits of the old city, was intended as a summer residence. The present owners are Mr. and Mrs. Samuel Chew. A fuller description of the house, including its furnishings, is given by Alice Winchester in the article in *Antiques* (December, 1959) for which the photograph of Henry's painting reproduced here was originally made.

18
FRONT HALL OF CLIVEDEN
See Note 17.

Lithograph, July 2, 1912, by Joseph Pennell (1857-1926). 16¼ by 21. Courtesy of the Historical of Pennsylvania.

The front hall at Cliveden is in the form of a T. On the right is a sitting room and on the left a study. Two larger rooms flank the stair hall at the rear. Thomas Waterman has called Cliveden "the finest of American Palladian houses to remain complete with its interiors."

19
STENTON
Eighteenth and Courtland streets (Germantown).
Built 1728-34.

Water color, 1888, by E. Castello. 8¾ by 11⅛. Courtesy of the Historical Society of Pennsylvania.

James Logan (1674-1751) came to Pennsylvania in 1699 as William Penn's secretary, and when the Proprietary returned to England, Logan remained as his agent. Stenton served as Washington's headquarters before the Battle of Brandywine and later as the headquarters of General Howe, the British Commander, at the time of the Battle of Germantown. The house is now owned by the city, but is under the custody and control of the National Society of Colonial Dames of America in the Commonwealth of Pennsylvania.

20
CARPENTERS' HALL
South side of Chestnut Street between Third and Fourth.
Built 1770-75 from the designs of Robert Smith (c.1722-1777).

Lithograph, 1951, by Grant Miles Simon (b. 1887). Published by the artist in *The Beginnings of Philadelphia in the Province of Pennsylvania*. 6⅞ by 9⁹⁄₁₆. Courtesy of the artist.

The building at the northwest corner of Carpenters' Hall in the lithograph is New Hall, built in 1791 as the headquarters of the Company after the Bank of the United States had rented the original hall. A history of Carpenters' Hall will be found in the article in *Historic Philadelphia* by Charles E. Peterson who also includes a list of building projects with which Robert Smith is known to have been associated. On the basis of such a preliminary list, Peterson suggests that Smith should certainly "be known as one of the most successful architects of eighteen-century America."

21
WALNUT STREET JAIL
South side of Walnut Street between Fifth and Sixth.
Built 1773-76 from designs of Robert Smith (c.1722-1777); demolished c.1835.

Engraving by John Bower (fl.1809-1819). Published for Thomas Condie, bookseller. 13¼ by 7⅜. Courtesy of the Historical Society of Pennsylvania.

Before the construction of the Walnut Street Jail, prisoners were lodged in the Old Stone Prison (c.1723) on the corner of Third and High. The new jail was not finished in 1777 when the British took it over for use as a military prison. Here during the British occupation of Philadelphia over 275 American soldiers are said to have died or been executed. On July 17, 1784, the first balloon ascension in America took place from the courtyard of the jail. Talbot Hamlin in his monograph on Latrobe has called the Walnut Street Prison "the first large masonry-vaulted building in the country." Today part of the site of the Walnut Street Jail is occupied by the Penn Mutual Life Insurance Co. Facts concerning the Philadelphia prisons are taken from Thorsten Sellin's article in *Historic Philadelphia* and from Negley K. Teeters' monograph, *The Cradle of the Penitentiary; the Walnut Street Jail at Philadelphia, 1773-1835* (Pennsylvania Prison Society, 1955).

22
STATE HOUSE WITH SUPREME COURT BUILDING ON THE EAST AND CONGRESS HALL ON THE WEST
Chestnut Street between Fifth and Sixth.

State House erected c.1730-48; County Court Building (Congress Hall) added 1787-89; City Hall (Supreme Court Building) added 1790-91.

Engraving, c.1803, by William Birch (1755-1834). Published by W. Birch in *The City of Philadelphia, in the State of Pennsylvania North America; as it appeared in the Year 1800*, 2d ed., 1804. 8⁷⁄₁₆ by 11. Courtesy of the Atwater Kent Museum.

The finial just visible is that on the apex of the hipped roof which in 1781 was put on the brick tower when the original steeple was removed. At the west end of the State House may be seen the clock face mounted on a masonry base made to resemble the familiar tall-case clocks of the period. A dial was similarly mounted on the east end of the building, and rods that moved the hands ran from the mechanism located in the attic of the State House. The present stone clock case against the west wall is part of the restoration carried out by the Daughters of the American Revolution in 1896-98 when for a time it was planned to move the clock back to the position it had occupied in the eighteenth century. Under the auspices of the Philadelphia Chapter of the American Institute of Architects the city restored Congress Hall in 1912-13 and the Supreme Court Building in the years immediately before and after the First World War.

23
FIRST PRESBYTERIAN CHURCH
Southeast corner of Market (High) and Bank (White Horse Alley) streets.
Built 1793-94, possibly from designs of John Trumbull (1756-1843); demolished c.1822.

Engraving, 1799, by Thomas (1779-1851) and William (1755-1834) Birch. Published by W.

Birch in *The City of Philadelphia, in the State of Pennsylvania North America; as it appeared in the Year 1800,* 1st ed., 1800. 8½ by 11⅜16. Courtesy of the Kean Archives.

The name "Old Buttonwood" given to the first building of the Market Street Presbyterian Church was derived from the grove of sycamore trees that surrounded it. Although a few paths may have been surfaced by 1725, paved streets such as that represented in the Birches' engraving did not become common until after 1761 when a lottery was held to raise the necessary funds. Curbstones such as those shown here were not widely used before the end of the eighteenth century. Evidence for the attribution of the design of the First Presbyterian Church to John Trumbull is given by Theodore Sizer in the *Journal of the Society of Architectural Historians* for October, 1950. The building of St. Philip's is discussed by Anna Wells Rutledge in the *Journal* for October, 1959.

24

THE WOODLANDS
West bank of the Schuylkill at Fortieth and Woodland Avenue.
Built *c.*1742; enlarged 1788.

Engraving by George Murray (d.1822) after a drawing by William Strickland (1788-1854). 4¼16 by 6⅞16. Courtesy of the Free Library of Philadelphia.

From the name of the owners of The Woodlands comes the designation "Hamilton Village" formerly applied to the area of Philadelphia east of Fortieth Street and south of Market. Today the grounds of The Woodlands are used for burials, and the mansion is occupied by a superintendent in the employ of the cemetery company to which the estate

was sold in 1845. William Hamilton is credited with introducing into the United States a variety of important trees and shrubs, including the ginkgo tree and the Lombardy poplar. At one time poplars were plentiful in Philadelphia but most of them were cut down because of the damage done to the sidewalks by their roots and because of worms with which they were frequently infested.

25

LANSDOWNE
West Fairmount Park overlooking the Schuylkill.
Built *c.*1773; burned 1854.

Water color, *c.*1825, by George Lehman (d. 1870). 10⅞ by 16⅞. Courtesy of the Historical Society of Pennsylvania.

John Penn was the son of Richard Penn and the grandson of William Penn. He was governor of Pennsylvania from 1763 to 1771 and from 1773 to 1776. Lansdowne (Lansdown, Landsdown) was one of the estates selected by William Birch for inclusion in his *Country Seats of the United States,* but it does not seem to have interested other printmakers particularly. Willis P. Hazard gives the history of the house in his *Annals of Philadelphia and Pennsylvania in the Olden Time.*

26

THE LIBRARY COMPANY OF PHILADELPHIA
Northeast corner of Fifth and Library streets.
Built 1789-90 from designs of Dr. William Thornton (1759-1828); demolished 1884.

Wash drawing, 1884, by B. Ridgway Evans (fl. *c.*1850-*c.*1890) 5⅝16 by 6¼. Courtesy of the Historical Society of Pennsylvania.

161

From its foundation by Benjamin Franklin and his friends, the Library Company continued to grow with the city throughout the eighteenth century. By 1850 its collections totaled more than 55,000 volumes, making it second only to Harvard among the major libraries in America. The suggestion concerning the specific source of Thornton's design was made by Charles E. Peterson in his article on that subject, which appeared in *Historic Philadelphia*. To the south of Library Hall stood the Mercantile Library (Fig. 69) and beyond that the Philadelphia Dispensary (1801-1925) which, as the out-patient department of an organization devoted to the relief of the poor, Peterson has elsewhere referred to as the first "professional building" in the city and perhaps in the country. In 1956 the Drexel Building (Fig. 123), which in 1885 had superseded Library Hall on the site on Fifth Street, was torn down to make way for the new library of the American Philosophical Society, designed by Martin, Stewart & Noble and reproducing the façade of Thornton's building.

27
HOUSE OF WILLIAM BINGHAM
West side of Third Street north of Spruce.
Built *c.*1788; turned into a hotel 1806-7; burned Mar. 17, 1823.

Engraving, *c.*1798, by Thomas (1779-1851) and William (1755-1834) Birch. Published by W. Birch in the *City of Philadelphia, in the State of Pennsylvania North America; as it appeared in the Year 1800*, 1st ed., 1800. 8⅜ by 11. Courtesy of the Kean Archives.

A short distance north of William Bingham's mansion was that of his father-in-law Thomas Willing. Together with the houses of Samuel Powel and Mrs. Powel's brother-in-law, Col. William Byrd, these made the area of Third Street between Spruce and Willing's Alley one of the most fasionable in the city. The quotation from the letter of Charles Bulfinch to his parents is from the biography by Charles A. Place, *Charles Bulfinch, Architect and Citizen* (Boston, 1925). After the death of its owners, the Bingham house became a public hotel under the name Mansion House. Badly damaged in 1823 by the fire that destroyed Washington Hall (Fig. 53), it was later repaired and according to Scharf and Westcott continued to be used as a hotel until it again burned in 1847. It was finally razed about 1850.

28
COOKE'S BUILDING
Southeast corner of Third and Market streets.
Built *c.*1792; demolished *c.*1838.

Engraving, 1799, by Thomas (1779-1851) and William (1755-1834) Birch. Published by W. Birch in *The City of Philadelphia, in the State of Pennsylvania North America; as it appeared in the Year 1800*, 1st ed., 1800. 8¼ by 10⅞. Courtesy of the Historical Society of Pennsylvania.

The facts concerning "Cooke's Folly" given here are based on the brief account in Scharf and Westcott. It is discussed also in Westcott's *History of Philadelphia* and by Thomas Porter in his *Picture of Philadelphia*.

29
LEMON HILL
East Fairmount Park overlooking the Schuylkill.
Built *c.*1770; repaired after the Revolution *c.*1785-*c.*1788; remodeled (or rebuilt) *c.*1799?; restored *c.*1934 by Fiske Kimball.

Wash drawing, 1854, by B. Ridgway Evans (fl. c.1850-c.1890). Courtesy of the Historical Society of Pennsylvania.

Called "hokey pokey men," sellers of ice cream in Philadelphia pushed large cans of their product along the street in wheelbarrows, crying: "Hokey Pokey, find a cake; Hokey Pokey on the lake." In addition to ice cream, oysters, pies, crabs, and soup (Pepper Pot) were among the other products sold on the street. Today the pretzel men are among the last of the peripatetic vendors. The exterior walls of Lemon Hill are stucco over stone, ruled to resemble ashlar and painted white. The "Chinese" motif of the porch railings was made popular by Chippendale in the mid-eighteenth century, but in America, Jefferson and others continued its use until well into the nineteenth century. Lemon Hill is now cared for by the Colonial Dames of America, Chapter Two.

30
HOUSE FOR ROBERT MORRIS
South side of Chestnut Street between Seventh and Eighth.
Begun c.1794 from designs of Major Pierre Charles L'Enfant (1754-1825); demolished c. 1800.

Water color, c.1798, by Thomas (1779-1851) or William (1755-1834) Birch. Presumably the original sketch for the engraving published by W. Birch in The City of Philadelphia, in the State of Pennsylvania North America; as it appeared in the Year 1800, 1st ed., 1800. 8⅛ by 10⅞. Courtesy of the Library Company of Philadelphia.

According to H. Paul Caemmerer (The Life of Pierre Charles L'Enfant Planner of the City Beautiful, Washington, 1950) his mansion

cost Morris $30,000, in addition to $9,000 paid the architect. In order to raise the funds to pay for his new house, Morris sold several other properties in Philadelphia including No. 190 High Street, then occupied by President and Mrs. Washington. Later converted to commercial use, the house on High Street was torn down in 1832. Its history, with an account of those who lived in it, is related by Harold Donaldson Eberlein in Historic Philadelphia. Morris died May 7, 1806, and was buried in the yard of Christ Church.

31
PRESIDENT'S HOUSE
West side of Ninth Street south of Market.
Built 1792-97; demolished c.1829.

Wash drawing by William Strickland (1788-1854). 3 by 8¼. Courtesy of the Historical Society of Pennsylvania.

Dennis C. Kurjack, in the Journal of the Society of Architectural Historians for May, 1953, points out that credit for the construction of the President's House belongs to four master carpenters: Col. William Williams, John Rakestraw, John Smith, and Robert Allison, all of whom were members of the Carpenters' Company. Of these Williams (d. 1794) seems to have been the most important. A view of the President's House, after alterations by the University of Pennsylvania and very similar to that produced here, was also published in 1828 by C. G. Childs after a drawing by George Strickland (1797-1851), a brother of William Strickland, the architect. Insurance surveys at the Mutual Assurance Company indicate the plan of the President's House after it was altered by the University of Pennsylvania.

32

HEADHOUSE, NEW MARKET
Second Street below Pine.
Built *c*.1805.

Water color, 1870, by B. Ridgway Evans (fl.
c.1850-*c*.1890). 4⅛ by 4⅞. Courtesy of the
Historical Society of Pennsylvania.

A map of 1820 shows that at that date the
Fellowship and Hope hose companies had
their headquarters in the north or Pine Street
headhouse, and the Southwark Hose was
quartered at the south or Cedar Street end.
This and other facts concerning the New
Market are taken from the article by Dr.
Margaret Tinkcom in *The Pennsylvania Magazine* for October, 1958. Cedar is now called
South Street.

33

PLAN AND ELEVATION OF ROW HOUSES
South side of Sansom between Seventh and
Eighth streets.
Built *c*.1801-3 by Thomas Carstairs (1759-
1830) for William Sansom.

Architectural rendering (water color), c.1800,
by Thomas Carstairs, designer and builder.
17⅞ by 27¹³⁄₁₆. Courtesy of the Library Company of Philadelphia.

Carstairs seems to have arrived in Philadelphia about 1784. He later received second
place in the competition for the design of
Library Hall, won by William Thornton (Fig.
26), and in 1804 was admitted to the Carpenters' Company. The houses on Walnut
Street appear to have been begun before
those on Sansom. The two rows were identical
in plan but varied somewhat in exterior details. The following description of a house
on Sansom Street is taken from insurance
survey No. 3515 dated Apr. 14, 1812, and

published with the permission of the Philadelphia Contributionship for the Insurance
of Houses from Loss by Fire (punctuation
added): "I have Surveyed a House belonging
to Lydia P. Harris Situate on the South side
of Sansom Street about midway between 7 &
8th Streets; 18 feet front by 40 feet deep,
three stories high; 14 & 9 in. walls; two rooms
& short passage in the lower story; the floor
of yellow pine; narrow boards; base and subbase round; single Architraves, mantles with
reeded pilasters, fluted dentil & tablets, marble
hearths & jambs; glass 10 by 16; an arch in
the passage with reeded pilasters & soffit; the
2nd story in two rooms, yellow pine floor; base
& subbase & architraves same as below; breast
clossets [*sic*] in back chamber; mantles with
pilasters, the 3rd story floor of common yellow
pine base only & subbase under the windows;
single architraves & mouldings; plain mantles,
breast clossets in both rooms. Garret in two
rooms, plaistered [*sic*]; one circular & one
plain ridged dormer window; trap door &
skylight in the roof; stairs between the rooms,
open newel, plain string & ramped mahogany
rail leading from the lower story into the
garret. Kitchen in the cellar finished as common. Outside shutters to the first and second
stories; frontispiece to the street door with
reeded columns; flat pediment & circular sash
over the door; painting old; built about 8
years; a safe place for ashes. [Signed] John C.
Evans. [and below the figures] $1800 at 2½.
. . . $45."

34

THE PERMANENT BRIDGE
Schuylkill River at Market Street (Middle
Ferry).
Caisson work (1798-1800) from plans of
William Weston; superstructure (1800-5) by
Timothy Palmer; wooden cover erected (1805-
6) by Owen Biddle (1774-1806) from design

164

of Judge Richard Peters assisted by Adam Traquair and John Dorsey; enlarged *c.*1850 to accommodate the tracks of the City Railroad; burned Nov. 20, 1875.

Aquatint by M. Dubourg from a drawing by C. A. Busby, architect. Published by J. Taylor, London, 1823. 9¾ by 22⅜. Courtesy of the New York Public Library.

The Schuylkill Bridge Company was formed Mar. 16, 1798. Originally it had been hoped to build a stone bridge, but this proved too expensive. Even when constructed of white pine, the Permanent Bridge is said to have cost nearly $300,000. The purpose of the wooden cover was of course to protect the main beams from the weather and thereby prevent them from rotting. Not everyone was convinced this was a wise plan, however; in *An Essay on Building Wooden Bridges* Charles Willson Peale was one of those who came out against covering wooden bridges. While the paint of the Permanent Bridge was still wet, it was dashed with sand and stone dust "thrown on with a common tin dust pan," the joints of ashlar masonry also being imitated. The bridge was 550 ft. long (1300 ft. if the abutments and wingwalls are included) and 42 ft. wide. The middle arch measured 194 ft. 10 in. When the bridge was opened to the public Jan. 1, 1805, the wooden cover had not been completed. Until recent years, an obelisk giving the history of the bridge stood on Market Street at the eastern approach. Richard Sanders Allen discusses the relationship of the Permanent Bridge to other American bridges in his *Covered Bridges of the Middle Atlantic States* (Brattleboro, Vermont, 1959), and a complete account of the circumstances surrounding its construction is given by Judge Richard Peters in *A Statistical Account of the Schuylkill Permanent Bridge* (Philadelphia, 1807). The nationalism im-

plied by the title of Biddle's *Carpenter's Assistant* and its relationship to the work of Asher Benjamin were pointed out by Henry-Russell Hitchcock in *American Architectural Books.*

35
THE PENNSYLVANIA HOSPITAL FROM THE SOUTHEAST
Block bounded by Eighth, Ninth, Spruce, and Pine streets.
East wing built *c.*1755 from designs made in 1751 by Samuel Rhoads; west wing built *c.*1796; center section built 1794-1805 from designs of David Evans, Jr.

Engraving, 1814, by John G. Exilious (fl.1810-1814). 11⅜ by 18. Courtesy of the Historical Society of Pennsylvania.

The center section of the Pennsylvania Hospital was attributed to David Evans, Jr., by Charles E. Peterson in *Philadelphia Architecture in the Nineteenth Century. The Casket* for October, 1830, gives John Dorsey as the author of the central pavilion, but it is difficult to see this accomplished design as an early work of even so ingenious an amateur. Possibly Dorsey suggested the substitution of the surgical amphitheatre for the dome originally planned. Samuel Rhoads was a member of the Carpenters' Company, the Philosophical Society, and the Board of Managers of the Hospital. His earlier design for the central section may be seen in the engraving by Robert Kennedy (1755) published by Edward B. Krumbhaar in his article on the Pennsylvania Hospital that appeared in *Historic Philadelphia.* The cornerstone for the east wing was laid May 28, 1755, and the first patient transferred to the unfinished building on Dec. 17, 1756. On the staff of the Pennsylvania Hospital were a number of the physicians and surgeons important for the early history of American medicine, including Thomas Bond, Thomas Cadwalader, Philip Syng Physick, and of course Benjamin Rush, recognized as "the most eminent American physician of his day." More than $25,000 was raised for the hospital by exhibiting the painting of Christ Healing the Sick in the Temple, sent by Benjamin West to the Board of Managers for that purpose and still hanging in the Administration Building. Details concerning West's picture and other early events connected with the hospital are given by Thomas G. Morton and Frank Woodbury in *The History of the Pennsylvania Hospital 1751-1895* (Philadelphia, 1897).

36
VIEW OF PHILADELPHIA FROM THE NEW JERSEY SHORE

Water color, c.1810, by J. L. Boqueta De (Bouquet de) Woiseri. 22½ by 35¼. Courtesy of the New York Public Library.

Boqueta De Woiseri made similar views of a number of other American cities, including Baltimore, Boston, Richmond, Charleston, New York, and New Orleans. Paul Beck's shot tower had a daily capacity of five tons. It was taken down in 1828.

37
THE PENNSYLVANIA ACADEMY OF THE FINE ARTS
North side of Chestnut between Tenth and Eleventh streets.
Erected 1805-6 from designs of John Dorsey (c.1759-1821); burned June 11, 1845.

Water color, c.1812, by Pavel Petrovitch Svinin (1787-1839). 5⅜ by 7¾. Courtesy of the Metropolitan Museum of Art, Rogers Fund, 1942.

The files of the Academy contain a letter from Dorsey to Col. Jonathan Williams in Elizabethtown, New Jersey, Aug. 1, 1805, in which appears a rough sketch of the new building, and Dorsey is spoken of as the designer in a letter from Charles Willson Peale to his son Raphael, dated Sept. 7, 1805. The records of the Academy also make it clear that Owen Biddle served as builder. The appearance of the new building shortly after its erection is described in *The Port Folio* for 1809. In 1820 a sculpture gallery was constructed on the east side of Dorsey's building, and in 1823 a Director's Room was added. These may have been designed by William Strickland, who is known to have been a member of the building committee. In 1822 new steps without parapets were added and presumably the order was changed from Ionic to Tuscan, as shown in Strickland's drawing, now in the Historical Society of Pennsylvania and reproduced in *Philadelphia Architecture in the Nineteenth Century* (Theo. B. White, ed.). For a view of the Academy as rebuilt after the fire of 1845, see Figure 38. The letter from Latrobe to Isaac Hazlehurst is cited by Talbot Hamlin in his monograph on Latrobe.

38
THE PENNSYLVANIA ACADEMY OF THE FINE ARTS
North side of Chestnut between Tenth and Eleventh streets.
Restored and enlarged 1846-47 from designs of Richard A. Gilpin; demolished 1870.

Mezzotint by John Sartain (1808-1897) from a drawing by James Hamilton (1819-1878). 4⅛ by 8⅞. Courtesy of the Free Library of Philadelphia.

The two wings added by Gilpin were each 50 ft. by 25 ft. The galleries were 16 ft. in height with coved ceilings springing from cornices and rising to skylights. The painting galleries had the corners cut off to avoid areas that would be hard to light. The Academy decided suddenly to sell the building on Chestnut Street after the skylights had been severely damaged by a storm in the spring of 1870. After the demolition of the Academy, Fox's American Theater stood on the site until it burned Feb. 25, 1877. Sartain's engraving appeared at the top of membership certificates of the Academy. The early events connected with the Academy are discussed by Helen W. Henderson in *The Pennsylvania Academy of the Fine Arts* (Boston, 1911).

39
ORPHAN ASYLUM
Northeast corner of Eighteenth and Cherry streets.
Built 1817; burned 1822.

Engraving. Published in *The Port Folio* for 1820. 3^{11}⁄$_{16}$ by 3½. Courtesy of the Free Library of Philadelphia.

Thomas Porter in his supplement to Dr. Mease's *Picture of Philadelphia* gives a very full account of the first building of the Orphan Asylum, described as of brick and measuring 50 ft. by 53 ft. The Philadelphia Orphan Society was established by the women of the Second Presbyterian Church, Third and Arch streets, and only women were eligible for membership. The Maria Dorsey who served as Secretary of the founding group does not seem to have been John Dorsey's wife, but she may have been a daughter. After the fire the Orphan Asylum was rebuilt from the designs of William Strickland, John Dorsey (if he were the designer of the first building) having

died the previous year. Childs published a view of the second building, which is also reproduced by Agnes Addison Gilchrist in *William Strickland: Architect and Engineer, 1788-1854*. In 1872 Strickland's building was sold, and the Orphanage moved to Sixty-fourth and Haverford Avenue.

40
PUMP HOUSE, PHILADELPHIA WATERWORKS
Center (Penn) Square.
Built 1799-1801 from designs of Benjamin Henry Latrobe (1764-1820); in use to c.1815; demolished 1827-28.

Colored drawing, c.1828, by Frederick C. Graff (1774-1847). 15½ by 20. Courtesy of the Historical Society of Pennsylvania.

Graff was chief draftsman during the construction of the waterworks. Built of white marble on the exterior, the Pump House was 60 ft. square, with offices in the corners. The columns were monoliths, 16 ft. high (Costen Fitz-Gibbon, *The Architectural Record*, July, 1927). In the early 1700's Center Square was used for public hangings, and during the Revolution the militia drilled there.

41
VIEW OF CENTER (PENN) SQUARE
Pump House erected 1799-1801 from designs of Benjamin Henry Latrobe (1764-1820). Nymph and Bittern fountain carved c.1809 by William Rush (1756-1833).

Water color, c.1812, by Pavel Petrovich Svinin (1787-1839). 6¼ by 8. Courtesy of the Metropolitan Museum of Art, Rogers Fund, 1942.

Rush's figure is better known as the Nymph of the Schuylkill. The title used here is that proposed by Henri Marceau in his catalogue for the exhibition of Rush's work held at the Philadelphia Museum of Art in 1937, which has also been followed in most other matters relating to Rush. In his well-known painting of "William Rush Carving the Allegorical Figure of the Schuylkill" Thomas Eakins shows the nude model posing in the presence of a chaperone who sits knitting near by.

42
BANK OF PENNSYLVANIA
West side of Second Street above Walnut. Built 1798-1801 from designs of Benjamin Henry Latrobe (1764-1820); demolished 1871 (?).

Water color, May, 1826, by Alexander Jackson Davis (1803-1892) from a geometrical elevation of Josiah R. Brady (c.1760-1832). 11⁹⁄₁₆ by 16¹¹⁄₁₆. Courtesy of the Historical Society of Pennsylvania.

Davis gives the dimensions of the Bank as 50 ft. by 120 ft. (including the portico). After serving as a federal prison during the Civil War, Latrobe's building was demolished by the government in "the 1860's," according to Talbot Hamlin, or in 1871, according to Frank H. Taylor. In the notes that accompany his drawings, Taylor further identifies as the United States Appraisers' Warehouse the building erected on the site of the former bank, but this has not been verified. Nor is it clear what, if anything, Davis intended to represent by the ornate building at the right of his drawing.

43
IONIC CAPITAL OF THE BANK OF PENNSYLVANIA
See note 42.

Wash drawing, 1800, by Frederick C. Graff (1774-1847) 20 by 26¼. Courtesy of the Library of the Franklin Institute.

In the inscription at the left corner of the drawing, Graff notes that he is representing the capital at half size and "under direction of the architect, B. H. Latrobe."

44
IONIC CAPITAL FROM THE NORTH PORCH OF THE ERECTHEUM
Acropolis, Athens, Greece.
Built c.420-410 B.C.; architect unknown.

Engraving, published by James Stuart and Nicholas Revett, *The Antiquities of Athens*, Vol. II, Chap. II, Pl. VIII, Fig. 1 (detail), London, 1787. 3¼ by 4½. Courtesy of the University of Pennsylvania.

45
HOUSE FOR EDWARD SHIPPEN BURD
Southwest corner of Chestnut Street at Ninth. Built 1801-2 from designs of Benjamin Henry Latrobe (1764-1820); demolished c.1865.

Water color, 1836, by David J. Kennedy (1817-1898). 6¹³⁄₁₆ by 11⅛. Courtesy of the Historical Society of Pennsylvania.

Of this example of Latrobe's work Talbot Hamlin has written: "The Burd house is a strong chord of simple, clearly related notes struck with convincing authority. This is the most London of all Latrobe's houses. . . ." In view of John Dorsey's apparent dependence upon the designs of Latrobe, the use of large inset arches on the Burd house may help to explain the importance given that motif on the Orphan Asylum (Fig. 39), assuming that Dorsey was the designer.

46
FIRST CHESTNUT STREET THEATER
North side of Chestnut Street above Sixth.

Built 1791-94; remodeled 1801 from the designs of Benjamin Henry Latrobe (1764-1820); burned Apr. 2, 1820.

Etching, c.1804, by Gilbert Fox (1776-c.1806) from a drawing by William Birch (1755-1834). Published by W. Birch in *The City of Philadelphia, in the State of Pennsylvania North America; as it appeared in the Year 1800*, 2d ed., 1804. 7⅞ by 11. Courtesy of the Historical Society of Pennsylvania.

Thomas Wignell and Alexander Reinagle (1756-1809) were co-managers of the Chestnut Street Theater, and Joseph Jackson and others have assumed that the plans for the building, based on the theater at Bath, were probably prepared by Wignell's brother-in-law, John Inigo Richards, a scene painter in England. More recently Richard D. Stine *(The Philadelphia Theater, 1682-1829; Its Growth as a Cultural Institution*, Ph.D. Dissertation, University of Pennsylvania, 1951) has suggested that L'Enfant may have had a hand in the design. The exterior dimensions of the first Chestnut Street Theater are given as 90 ft. by 134 ft.; total seating capacity was 1,165. Hamlin states that the auditorium was designed by scene painters on the staff of the theater, rather than by Latrobe. Jardella's reliefs were last heard of as being in a house at 2014 Delancey Place. In 1795 "The Art Pantheon," or "Rickett's Amphitheater," as it was also known, was opened on the southwest corner of Sixth and Chestnut streets. Built like a large circular tent of wood, this was primarily a circus, although plays were presented occasionally. In December, 1799, the Pantheon burned. M. Antonia Lynch discusses the history of the early theater in Philadelphia in "The Old District of Southwark," *Publications of the City History Society of Philadelphia* (Philadelphia, 1909). For additional bibliography on Philadelphia theaters, see Note 49.

47
SECOND CHESTNUT STREET THEATER ("NEW THEATER")
North side of Chestnut Street above Sixth.
Built 1820-22, to replace "Old Drury" (Fig. 46), from designs of William Strickland (1788-1854); demolished 1856.

Engraving by Fenner, Sears & Co. from a drawing by R. Goodacre. Published May 15, 1831, by J. T. Hinton & Simpkin & Marshall, London. 4⅛ by 5¾. Courtesy of the Free Library of Philadelphia.

The exterior measurements of the second Chestnut Street Theater are given as 92 ft. by 150 feet. The three tiers of boxes were supported by cast-iron columns. A fuller description of the second Chestnut Street Theater is given by Agnes Addison Gilchrist in *William Strickland: Architect and Engineer, 1778-1854*.

48
ARCH STREET THEATER
North side of Arch Street west of Sixth.
Built 1826-28 from designs of William Strickland (1788-1854); remodeled 1863; demolished 1936.

Engraving by Joseph Yeager (c.1792-1859). 6⅛ by 8. Courtesy of the Free Library of Philadelphia.

Built of stone and brick, the Arch Street Theater measured 70 ft. by 155 ft. and had a capacity of 1,500 persons. After Mrs. John Drew retired as manager in 1892, it became a variety and later a foreign language theater; from 1902 to 1907 it was known as Blaney's Theater *(100 Years in Philadelphia: The Evening Bulletin's Anniversary Book, 1847-1947)*.

49
WALNUT STREET THEATER
Northeast corner of Ninth and Walnut streets.
Built 1809; remodeled 1828 from designs of
John Haviland (1792-1852).

Engraving by Fenner, Sears & Co. from a
drawing by Charles Burton (fl.1819-1842).
Published July 15, 1831, by J. T. Hinton &
Simpkin & Marshall, London. 4 by 6. Courtesy
of the Free Library of Philadelphia.

The Walnut Street Theater measures approximately 90 ft. by 146 ft. Arthur Hobson
Quinn gives a brief history of the early Philadelphia theaters in *Historic Philadelphia*.
Longer studies are those of Thomas C. Pollack
(*The Philadelphia Theatre in the Eighteenth
Century*, Philadelphia, 1933) and T. F. Marshall (*A History of the Philadelphia Theatre,
1878-1890*, Philadelphia, 1943).

50
FAIRMOUNT BRIDGE (THE COLOSSUS)
Schuylkill River, at the Upper Ferry.
Built 1809-12 from designs of Louis Wernwag
(1769-1843), engineer, and Robert Mills
(1781-1855), architect; burned Sept. 1, 1838.

Aquatint by [Carl Fredrik] Akrel (1779-1868)
from drawing by Axel Leonhard Klinckow-
ström. Published in *Atlas til Friherre Klin-
kowströms Bref om de Förente Staterne*
[Stockholm, 1824]. 9¹³⁄₁₆ by 16½. Courtesy
of the Library of Congress.

The over-all length of the bridge was 400
ft.; the rise of the arch 20 ft., and its elevation
above the water 30 ft. Joseph Johnson assisted
Wernwag as engineer. The Colossus made
Wernwag famous and soon he was commissioned to build bridges over the Schuylkill,
Susquehanna, and Delaware for a variety of

other cities and companies. Elizabeth B. Mock
(*The Architecture of Bridges*, New York,
1949) calls the Colossus "the greatest span ever
achieved in wood or stone." The third great
covered bridge across the Schuylkill was constructed in 1831 by John Babb of Wilkes-
Barre for the state-owned Philadelphia and
Columbia (now the Pennsylvania) Railroad.
Known as the Columbia Bridge, this enormous structure of seven spans, totaling 1,018
ft., crossed the Schuylkill at Belmont Avenue.
In 1886 it was replaced by an iron bridge.
In his *Encyclopedia of Philadelphia* Joseph
Jackson calls the Columbia Bridge the
first railroad bridge constructed in America.
Canal boats like those in the print carried
cargo between Philadelphia and points along
the Schuylkill, including Reading and Pottsville.

51
WIRE SUSPENSION BRIDGE
Schuylkill River, near Fairmount.
Opened Jan. 2, 1842; designed by Col. Charles
Ellet, Jr.; demolished 1874.

Lithograph, *c*.1842, by George Lehman (d.
1870). Printed by P. S. Duval. 13 by 20⅜.
Courtesy of the Atwater Kent Museum.

About 1808 a chain bridge was erected at
the Falls of the Schuylkill. When this fell
from the weight of snow in January, 1816,
it was replaced by the footbridge built by
White & Hazard, wire manufacturers, which
has been called the "first wire suspension
bridge ever built." White & Hazard's bridge
was 408 ft. long but only 16 feet above the
river. Ellet's bridge was 343 ft. between abutments and 27 ft. wide. It was financed by the
city of Philadelphia. The early bridges of
Philadelphia are discussed by Fred Perry
Powers in Vol. I of the *Publications of the*

City History Society of Phiadelphia (Philadelphia, 1914) and other useful information on the subject is supplied by Vol. 6, No. 1, of the *Bulletin* of the Atwater Kent Museum.

52
FAIRMOUNT (SCHUYLKILL) WATERWORKS FROM THE MOUNT
Fairmount on the Schuylkill River.
Built 1812-22 from the designs of Frederick C. Graff (1774-1847).

Lithograph, printed and published by J. T. Bowen, Philadelphia. 13½ by 21¾. Courtesy of the Atwater Kent Museum.

Wainwright gives 1838 as the date of this print. The waterworks was also one of the few Philadelphia subjects selected for reproduction by Currier & Ives. Visible at the foot of the hill is the "forebay," a rectangular area blasted out of the rock to provide a basin in which the water was gathered prior to passing into the wheelhouse and the turbines. In modern times the forebay was filled in to provide a foundation for the present roadway. The year following his death, Frederick Graff was honored at the direction of City Councils by having his sculptured bust set up in the little Gothic monument still standing in the overgrown park at the south of the old engine house. Harold Donaldson Eberlein gives a brief history of the waterworks in *The Architectural Record* for July, 1927.

53
WASHINGTON HALL
West side of Third Street above Spruce.
Completed 1816 from designs of Robert Mills (1781-1855); burned 1823.

Aquatint from a drawing by George Strickland (1797-1851). Published in *The Port*

Folio for February, 1817. 9¹¹⁄₁₆ by 15½. Courtesy of the Library Company of Philadelphia.

Washington Hall was opened Oct. 1, 1816, with religious services conducted by Bishop White. The building measured approximately 73 ft. by 138 ft. and provided accommodations for nearly 6,000 persons in the auditorium— possibly the largest in the country at the time —for which Philip Justus supplied a roof so designed that there was no need for interior columns. The connection between Mills's design for Washington Hall and the work of Ledoux was pointed out by Rich Bornemann in "Some Ledoux-Inspired Buildings in America," *Journal of the Society of Architectural Historians,* March, 1954. Bornemann would also see the influence of Ledoux in the design of Latrobe's Pump House in Center Square.

54
SECOND BANK OF THE UNITED STATES
South side of Chestnut between Fourth and Fifth streets.
Built 1818-24 from designs of William Strickland (1788-1854).

Lithograph, *c.*1848, by Deroy from a drawing by Augustus Koellner (1812-1906). Printed by Cattier and published by Goupil, Vibert & Co., New York and Paris, as No. 12 in *Views of American Cities,* 1848-51. 7½ by 11½. Courtesy of the Library of Congress.

Agnes Addison Gilchrist cites the most important documents relating to the Second Bank in the appendix to her monograph on Strickland. Following its purchase by the federal government, Strickland's building served from 1844 to 1932 as the Philadelphia Custom House, and in 1941, after restoration by the Works Project Administration, it was leased

to the Carl Schurz Memorial Foundation. Today it also houses the headquarters of the Independence National Historical Park of which
it is a part. A good brief history of the Second
Bank is that of Bray Hammond in *Historic
Philadelphia*. To the east of the Custom House
in Koellner's view is just visible the marble
façade of the Philadelphia Bank, erected on
the corner of Fourth and Chestnut streets in
1836 from Strickland's design. The Philadelphia Bank gave up these quarters in 1859,
but the building was not demolished until
1882.

55
THE PARTHENON
Akropolis, Athens, Greece.
Built 447-432 B.C. from the designs of Iktinus;
Kallikrates was the builder and Pheidias was
in charge of the sculpture.

Engraving, published by James Stuart and
Nicholas Revett, *The Antiquities of Athens*,
Vol. II, Chap. I, Pl. III, London, 1787. 8¹³⁄₁₆
by 15¼. Courtesy of the University of Pennsylvania.

56
NAVAL ASYLUM (U.S. NAVAL HOME, AFTER
1879).
Gray's Ferry Road at Twenty-fourth Street.
Built 1827-33 from designs of William Strick-
land (1788-1854).

Lithograph, 1838, by J. C. Wild (c.1804-1846);
printed by J. Collins. Published by J. C. Wild
& J. B. Chevalier in *Views of Philadelphia,
and its Vicinity*, Philadelphia, 1838. 4⅞
by 6¾. Courtesy of the Kean Archives.

According to Gilchrist, attic rooms were
added to the Naval Asylum in 1848, and dur-

ing the 1870's the roof was raised and dormer
windows were put on. Granite was used for
the basement and Pennsylvania marble for
the upper stories and portico. By the use of
brick floors and vaulted ceilings, Strickland
tried to make the building as fireproof as possible, although sashes, frames and doors were
of wood. A contemporary description of the
Asylum and the circumstances surrounding
its construction may be found in *The Casket*
for December, 1832.

57
FIRST CONGREGATIONAL UNITARIAN CHURCH
Tenth and Locust streets.
Built 1828 from the designs of William Strick-
land (1788-1854); demolished 1885.

Engraving, 1829, by Cephas Grier Childs (1793-
1871) from a drawing by Hugh Reinagle
(c.1788-1834). Published by C. G. Childs in
*Views in Philadelphia and its Environs, from
original Drawings taken in 1827-30*, Philadelphia. 3¹¹⁄₁₆ by 6¹⁄₁₆. Courtesy of the Free
Library of Philadelphia.

As the son of Alexander Reinagle, the
musical director of the "New Theater" on
Chestnut Street (Fig. 46), Hugh Reinagle was
trained primarily as a scene painter. Much of
his career was spent in New York City. The
First Unitarian Church had been founded in
Philadelphia in 1796, largely as a result of
the lectures of Joseph Priestley (d.1804). For
a number of years the congregation met
wherever space could be found, including for
a time Carpenters' Hall, before the lot at
Tenth and Locust streets was acquired and
the first church erected from the designs of
Robert Mills.

58
UNITED STATES MINT
Northwest corner of Chestnut and Juniper streets.
Built 1829-33 from designs of William Strickland (1788-1854); demolished 1902.

Engraving by William H. Hay from a drawing by the architect. Published by C. G. Childs in *Views in Philadelphia and its Environs, from original Drawings taken in 1827-30*, Philadelphia. 3¾ by 7¼. Courtesy of the Free Library of Philadelphia.

The Casket for October, 1831 gives the dimensions of the Mint as 123 ft. wide by 139 ft. long, not including the two porticoes, each 27 ft. by 60 ft. The central court measured 55 ft. by 84 ft. Assaying, melting, and refining was done in the basement; coining and printing on the main floor. Standards of weights and balances were in the attic. As early as 1806 steam power had been introduced into the building on Seventh Street for the heavier work. The Widener Building now occupies the site of Strickland's Mint.

59
PHILADELPHIA (MERCHANTS') EXCHANGE
Walnut, Third, and Dock streets.
Built 1832-34 from designs of William Strickland (1788-1854).

BANK OF THE UNITED STATES
South Third Street, near the head of Dock Street.
Built 1795-97 from designs of Samuel Blodgett (Blodget), Jr. (1757-1814).

Mezzotint by John Sartain (1808-1897) after a wash drawing by William Strickland, now in the Historical Society of Pennsylvania. 9 by 13⁷⁄₁₆. Courtesy of the New-York Historical Society.

In her article published in *Historic Philadelphia,* Agnes Addison Gilchrist describes the Exchange in detail and discusses several other structures for their possible influence on Strickland. Blodgett's design for the Bank of the United States is said to have been based on that of the Dublin Exchange. After the Bank's charter was not renewed in 1811, Stephen Girard acquired its building as the headquarters for his private bank. Later he refused to sell to the Second Bank of the United States, which then commissioned Strickland to design the classical temple on Chestnut Street (Fig. 54). Chartered by the State after Stephen Girard's death in 1831, the Girard Bank failed in 1842; later permitted to reopen, it and its successor, the Girard National Bank of Philadelphia, occupied Blodgett's building until 1926. The present domed banking room was added by James H. Windrim about 1900. The history of the bank on Third Street and its occupants is told by James O. Wettereau in *Historic Philadelphia.* Both the Philadelphia Exchange and the Bank of the United States are now part of the Independence National Historical Park.

60
UNIVERSITY OF PENNSYLVANIA
Ninth Street between Market and Chestnut.
Built 1829 from designs of William Strickland (1788-1854); demolished *c.*1874.

Lithograph, 1838, by J. C. Wild (*c.*1804-1846). Published by J. C. Wild & J. B. Chevalier in *Views of Philadelphia, and its Vicinity*, Philadelphia, 1838. 4¹³⁄₁₆ by 6⅝. Courtesy of the Kean Archives.

The new buildings of the University of Pennsylvania, like their predecessors, were insured by the Mutual Assurance Company and the Philadelphia Contributionship, which have preserved the surveys describing in considerable detail the interiors of both Medical Hall and Collegiate Hall.

61
FIRST PRESBYTERIAN CHURCH
Washington Square at the southeast corner of Seventh and Locust streets.
Built 1820-22 from designs of John Haviland (1792-1852); demolished 1939.

Engraving by John Boyd (fl.1810-1825) from a drawing by the architect. Published by S. C. Atkinson in *The Casket*, April, 1829. 4½ by 7³⁄₁₆. Courtesy of the New York Public Library.

R. A. Smith gives the dimensions of the Washington Square Presbyterian Church as 88 ft. by 71 ft. *The Port Folio* for October, 1822, includes a full description of the church and mentions James Clark as the builder and John Struthers as the stone cutter. An apartment house is scheduled to rise on the site of Haviland's building, now occupied by a parking lot. In 1828 Haviland seems also to have designed a tower for St. Andrew's, but this was never built.

62
PENNSYLVANIA INSTITUTION FOR THE DEAF AND DUMB (NOW PHILADELPHIA MUSEUM COLLEGE OF ART)
Northwest corner Broad and Pine streets.
Built 1824-25 from designs of John Haviland (1792-1852).

Aquatint. Published in *The Port Folio* for November, 1824. 3¾ by 8⅜. Courtesy of the Historical Society of Pennsylvania.

When founded in 1820 the Pennsylvania Institution for the Deaf and Dumb was first located at Eleventh and Market streets. In the early 1890's it moved to Mt. Airy, and in 1893 the Museum School took over the building at Broad and Pine streets. Haviland's building originally had a front of approximately 96 ft. on Broad Street and a depth of 92 ft. The inscriptions in the manual alphabet identify the statue on the left as that of Charles Michel, Abbé de l'Epée (1712-1789), a French Jansenist who developed this system of communication for deaf-mutes, and that on the right as Roch-Ambroise Cucurron, Abbé Sicard (1742-1822), who carried on the work of de l'Epée. The system of de l'Epée and Sicard was that used by the Pennsylvania Institution for the Deaf and Dumb in Philadelphia. No evidence has been found that the statues intended for the niches were ever put in place.

63
PHILADELPHIA ARCADE
North side of Chestnut Street between Sixth and Seventh.
Built 1826-27 from designs of John Haviland (1792-1852); demolished 1863.

Lithograph, 1833, by George Lehman (d. 1870). Printed by Childs & Inman. 6¾ by 10⁵⁄₁₆. Courtesy of the Free Library of Philadelphia.

The date of the print is that given by Wainwright. Contemporary descriptions of the Arcade appeared in Atkinson's *Casket* for December, 1828, and December, 1832. Although the Arcade in Providence, Rhode Island, built by Russell Warren (1783-1860) in 1827-29, seems similar to that in Philadelphia, Robert Alexander considers that Haviland's New York Arcade had the most

174

direct influence on Warren (*Journal of the Society of Architectural Historians,* October, 1953). The story of Peale's Museum prior to its removal to the Arcade is told by Charles Coleman Sellers in *Historic Philadelphia.*

64
COLONNADE ROW
South side of Chestnut between Fifteenth and Sixteenth streets.
Built 1830 from designs of John Haviland (1792-1852); partially destroyed 1868 to make way for the Colonnade Hotel (1869-1925).

Wash drawing by Frank Hamilton Taylor (1846-1927). 7⁷⁄₁₆ by 10. Courtesy of the Library Company of Philadelphia.

Across the street from Colonnade Row stood T. U. Walter's Church of the Epiphany (Episcopal), consecrated 1834 and demolished shortly after 1900. The quotation from Hazard's *Register* is taken from William Murtagh's article on the Philadelphia row house, the best treatment of the subject to appear.

65
RESIDENCE OF CHARLES BLIGHT
Southeast corner of Chestnut at Sixteenth Street.
Built 1828 from designs of John Haviland (1792-1852); no longer standing.

Water color, 1836, by David J. Kennedy (1817-1898). 8¼ by 13⁹⁄₁₆. Courtesy of the Historical Society of Pennsylvania.

The scale of the Blight mansion is suggested by the fact that the façade is said to have been 80 ft. long and the porch 12 ft. deep. No date has been found for the demoli-

tion of the house, but it may have been shortly after 1867 when the property changed hands. The evidence presently available suggests that Haviland was engaged to design only the façade of the Blight residence.

66
POWELTON
Northwest corner of Thirty-second and Race streets.
Built *c.*1830(?); demolished 1885.

Water color by David J. Kennedy (1817-1898). 8 by 13¹¹⁄₁₆. Courtesy of the Historical Society of Pennsylvania.

The Powel estate extended to the bank of the Schuylkill River. It was later the property of E. Spencer Miller. Robert C. Smith in *Historic Philadelphia* points out since William Johnston made the drawings for Phil-Ellena, he may also have been responsible, at least in part, for the design.

67
GIRARD COLLEGE
Corinthian and Girard avenues.
Built 1833-47 from designs of Thomas U. Walter (1804-1887).

Engraving by A. W. Graham (fl.1830-1870) from a drawing by the architect. 11¾ by 19⅛. Courtesy of the Metropolitan Museum of Art, Dick Fund, 1924.

Many of the competition drawings for Girard College, found in recent years and deposited by the College in the Historical Society of Pennsylvania for safe keeping, are discussed by Agnes Addison Gilchrist in the *Journal of the Society of Architectural Historians* for May, 1957. Although best known

175

for his public buildings, Walter also designed a number of important private residences. Among the most impressive of those in the Philadelphia area were the Dundas-Lippincott House, erected about 1840 on the site now occupied by the Fidelity-Philadelphia Trust Building, and the Matthew Newkirk House (after 1876 St. George's Hall), built in 1836 at the southwest corner of Thirteenth and Arch streets and demolished about 1903.

68
LONGITUDINAL SECTION, FOUNDER'S HALL, GIRARD COLLEGE
Corinthian and Girard avenues.
Built 1833-47 from the designs of Thomas U. Walter (1804-1887).

Architectural rendering (water color), 1834. 8¼ by 20¼. Courtesy of the Historical Society of Pennsylvania.

The scale of the drawing is shown as 14 ft. to 1 in. R. A. Smith gives the following dimensions for Founder's Hall: columns 6 ft. in diameter and 55 ft. in height; total height of entablature 16 ft. 4 in.; body of the building 111 ft. by 169 ft. Each capital was carved in 12 pieces, which were then doweled together. The roof was covered with marble tiles, 4½ ft. long, 4 ft. wide, and ¾ in. thick in the center, having a total weight of 906 tons.

69
MERCANTILE LIBRARY
Fifth south of Library Street.
Built 1844-45 from designs of William L. Johnston (1811-1849); demolished c.1925.

Engraving by William E. Tucker (1801-1857) from a drawing by Langenheim. 5¹³⁄₁₆ by

6⅜. Courtesy of the Free Library of Philadelphia.

A William Johnson appears as "architect and builder" on prints of the First Methodist Protestant Chapel at the corner of Eleventh and Wood streets (1840). This was presumably the same man who served as architect for the important Jayne Building (Fig. 84), but aside from a few facts of this kind, little is known of Johnston's professional activities. The Mercantile Library was founded in 1820 for the benefit of persons employed in the various commercial establishments of the city. It occupied the building on Fifth Street until 1868, when it moved to the Franklin Market Building on Tenth Street below Market. Built in 1860 from the designs of John McArthur, Jr., and never a financial success, the Franklin Market had been sold to the Pennsylvania Railroad in 1867, and from it acquired the following year by the Mercantile Library. In 1953 the Library moved to its new quarters on Chestnut Street (Fig. 138).

70
FIRST REFORMED DUTCH CHURCH
Northwest corner of Seventh and Spring Garden streets.
Built 1853-55 from designs of Stephen D. Button (1803-1897); no longer standing.

Lithograph by John Frampton Watson (fl. c.1833-c.1860). Printed by L. N. Rosenthal. 19¼ by 27½. Courtesy of the Library of Congress.

Wainwright does not list this print. Scharf and Wescott give the dimensions of the First Reformed Dutch Church as 71 ft. by 115 ft.; today the site is occupied by a gas station. Button was also the architect for the Tabernacle Methodist Episcopal Church at Eleventh above Jefferson Street (*Public Ledger*, Aug. 13, 1856; lithograph at the Library Company).

71

SEDGELEY (SEDGLEY)
East bank of the Schuylkill River, north of Lemon Hill.
Built 1799 from designs of Benjamin Henry Latrobe (1764-1820); demolished 1857.

Engraving by Cephas Grier Childs (1793-1871) from a drawing by Edward Williams Clay (1799-1857). Published by C. G. Childs in *Views in Philadelphia and its Environs, from original Drawings taken in 1827-30*, Philadelphia. 3⅛ by 4¹³⁄₁₆. Courtesy of the Free Library of Philadelphia.

Sedgeley was occupied by William Cramond until his bankruptcy in 1806, when it was bought by Samuel Mifflin. James Cowles Fisher used it for a summer home from about 1812 until 1836, when it was purchased by Isaac S. Loyd for a real estate development that proved unsuccessful. Shortly after the estate passed into the possession of the city in 1857 the house was demolished. The stone gate house still stands, but for stylistic reasons it would appear in its present form to date from a period after that of the main house. Other early examples of the Gothic Revival in America are listed by Theodore Bolton in the *American Collector* for April and May, 1948.

72

DORSEY'S GOTHIC MANSION
North side of Chestnut between Eleventh and Twelfth streets.
Built *c.*1810 from designs of John Dorsey (*c.*1759-1821); remodeled 1853.

Engraving by Benjamin Tanner (1775-1848) from a drawing by Robert Mills (1781-1855). Published in *The Port Folio*, February, 1811. 5¹⁵⁄₁₆ by 5½. Courtesy of the Free Library of Philadelphia.

In *The Casket* for October, 1830, Dorsey's mansion is described as having a front of 60 ft. and a depth of 26 ft. The subsequent history of the house was scarcely less unusual than its appearance. As part of the movement to promote native manufacturing, which had brought into being the Philadelphia shot towers, mentioned earlier, Dorsey proposed to manufacture "floor-cloths and carpets" at his Chestnut Street mansion. This enterprise cannot have been very long-lived, if it ever began, for Survey No. 3483 at the Philadelphia Contributionship, dated Nov. 28, 1811, lists as the owner of the Gothic Mansion the Philadelphia merchant Godfrey Haga, who had been associated with Dorsey in the building of the Permanent Bridge and who seems to have owned the Gothic Mansion until his death in 1825. Haga, in turn, rented the house to a Mrs. Rivardi who proposed making alterations on the north side in order to adapt it for use as a boarding school and academy. As the commercial elements on Chestnut Street moved westward, the Gothic Mansion was turned first into stores and later, about 1853, transformed into a music hall by George W. Watson, a carriage maker, who had his showrooms on the ground floor (Philadelphia Contributionship, Survey No. 9114, Jan. 25, 1853). After the burning of the Temple Theater, the Gothic Mansion came to be known first as Temple Hall, and then as Egyptian Hall when it was taken over by a magician named Keller. From 1894 to 1911 the Free Library occupied the premises, and when at the end of that time the building was finally demolished, it is said that fragments of Dorsey's house were still visible (*Public Ledger*, Mar. 5, 1911).

177

PENN'S GREAT TOWN

73
THE PHILADELPHIA BANK
Southwest corner of Fourth and Chestnut streets.
Built 1807-8 from designs of Benjamin Henry Latrobe (1764-1820); demolished 1836.

Engraving, c.1828, by William Birch (1755-1834). 5⁹⁄₁₆ by 7¼. Courtesy of the Free Library of Philadelphia.

The Casket (November, 1829) gives the dimensions of the Philadelphia Bank as 65 ft. front on Fourth Street and 50 ft. in depth on Chestnut Street. Contemporary with the bank is Latrobe's Christ Church in Washington, D.C., also in the Gothic style, and still standing on G Street near Sixth Southeast. Formed in 1803 and incorporated by charter the following year, the Philadelphia Bank was the predecessor of the present-day Philadelphia National Bank. The dates and a number of the other facts cited here are those given by Nicholas B. Wainwright in *The Philadelphia National Bank* (Philadelphia, 1953).

74
BURNING OF THE MASONIC HALL
North side of Chestnut Street between Seventh and Eighth.
Built 1808-11 from designs of William Strickland (1788-1854). Tower and interior burned Mar. 9, 1819; demolished 1853.

Aquatint by John Hill (1770-1850) after a painting by S. Jones. Figures by John Lewis Krimmel (1789-1821). Published by William Smith, Philadelphia, 1819. 21⅛ by 17⅜. Courtesy of the New-York Historical Society.

The Masonic Hall measured 82 ft. on the front by 169 ft. on the side; the tower was 180 ft. high. The cornerstone was laid Apr. 17,

1809, and the building dedicated June 24, 1811. The interior of the Masonic Hall is shown in Duval's lithograph of "Naylor's Grand Fancy Dress Party" (Wainwright No. 308). Strickland does not seem to have cared particularly for the Gothic style, but he did employ pointed arches (combined, however, with a dome) for the Temple of the New Jerusalem (1816), later (1826) the Academy of Natural Sciences, Twelfth and Sansom streets; he also used labels and similar motifs for the "Parsonage" built for the Rev. Courtland Van Rensselaer at the corner of River Bank and Talbot Street, Burlington, New Jersey (1835). Nicholas B. Wainwright has written the full history of the Philadelphia Contributionship (*A Philadelphia Story: The Philadelphia Contributionship for the Insurance of Houses from Loss by Fire,* Philadelphia, 1952) and has contributed to *Historic Philadelphia* a short essay summarizing the part played by eighteenth-century fire insurance companies in Philadelphia. From 1827 to 1933 the headquarters of the Franklin Institute was in Haviland's building on Seventh Street, and the Masonic Hall was apparently used only for exhibitions. Plans to have Strickland remodel the Hall as a permanent home for the Institute had to be abandoned because of the depression of 1837.

75
NEW MASONIC HALL
North side of Chestnut Street between Seventh and Eighth.
Built 1853-55 from designs of Sloan & Stewart; burned 1886.

Lithograph, c.1855, by Tholey. Printed by Friend & Aub. Published by J. G. Simpson. 23 by 19. Courtesy of the Library of Congress.

S. K. Hoxie was the builder of the new Masonic Hall, dedicated Sept. 26, 1855. Sloan

178

and Stewart seem to have practiced in partnership from about 1852 until shortly after the Panic of 1857. The Masons moved to their new building on Broad and Filbert streets in 1873, and in 1885 the Hall on Chestnut Street became the Temple Theater and Egyptian Museum.

76
GRAND LODGE ROOM, NEW MASONIC HALL
See Note 75.

Lithograph, 1855, by Max Rosenthal (1833-1918) from a drawing by Collins & Autenrieth. 21 by 26⅞. Courtesy of the Library of Congress.

Edward Collins and C. M. Autenrieth (1833-1908) were architects in their own right, and it seems possible, therefore, that since they prepared the drawing of the Grand Lodge Room from which Rosenthal worked, they may also have designed its furnishings and decoration.

77
EASTERN STATE PENITENTIARY
Fairmount Avenue at Twenty-first Street.
Built 1823-36 from designs of John Haviland (1792-1852).

Engraving by Cephas Grier Childs (1793-1871) from a drawing by the architect. Published by R. Desilver. 13⅜ by 25⅞. Courtesy of the Historical Society of Pennsylvania.

In 1821 Haviland won the competition for the new prison authorized by the State of Pennsylvania, but he was not appointed architect and the entire plan approved until 1823. Construction continued until 1836, although the first prisoners were admitted as early as

1829. The history of the prison and the origins and influence of the idea it embodies is discussed by Norman B. Johnston in *Pioneers in Criminology*, ed. by Herman Mannheim (Chicago, 1960).

78
PHILADELPHIA COUNTY PRISON
Tenth and Reed streets, Moyamensing.
Built 1832-35 from designs of Thomas U. Walter (1804-1887); scheduled for demolition c.1963.

Architectural rendering (wash), presumably from the office of the architect. 4⁹⁄₁₆ by 15½. Courtesy of the Historical Society of Pennsylvania.

Walter won the competition for the new Philadelphia County Prison in 1831, and the cornerstone was laid Apr. 2, 1832. Sometimes considered the first full-fledged example of the Egyptian Revival in America, the Debtor's Wing (not shown in the drawing) was added on the east in 1836, but never used for that purpose, since the law providing imprisonment for debt was repealed before it was completed. The Women's Department on the west side was added in 1837-38. The central tower was taken down in the twentieth century. A painting of the prison by the architect is owned by the Historical Society of Pennsylvania. Walter also used the Gothic style for the Fourth Universalist Church, Locust above Thirteenth Street, and the Pennsylvania College (c.1850), Ninth below Locust Street, neither now standing.

79
SECTION OF CELLS, PHILADELPHIA COUNTY PRISON
See Note 78.

179

Architectural rendering (water color), 1841, by Joseph D. Koecker. 7¼ by 17. Courtesy of the Historical Society of Pennsylvania.

The scale of the drawing is given as 8 ft. to 1 in. Koecker appears to have been Walter's principal delineator.

80
RESIDENCE OF TURNER CAMAC
Northeast corner of Eleventh Street and Montgomery Avenue.
Built c.1825; demolished 1870.

Water color by David J. Kennedy (1817-1898). 7⅜ by 12⅜. Courtesy of the Historical Society of Pennsylvania.

The quotation from Downing in the text is from the introduction to his *Cottage Residences* (New York, 1842). A brief discussion of Downing's career and his influence on American taste may be found in the author's article "The Beautiful and the Picturesque," which appeared in the spring issue of the *American Quarterly* for 1951. On the bottom of the water color that he made in 1838, D. J. Kennedy notes concerning the residence of Turner Camac: " . . . it was [in] a beautiful spot surrounded by old forest trees with a sloping lawn to the north, the entrance to it was by Camac's Lane from Broad Street north of Monument Cemetery; the lane was bordered by rows of fir trees, and from Girard Avenue north, and as far east as Fifth Street, it was open country, fields of grain, cattle pasture etc."

81
ST. STEPHEN'S EPISCOPAL CHURCH
East side of Tenth Street between Market and Chestnut.

Built 1822-23 from designs of William Strickland (1788-1854).

Engraving, 1829, by Cephas Grier Childs (1793-1871) from a drawing by George Strickland (1797-1851). Published by C. G. Childs in *Views in Philadelphia and its Environs, from original Drawings taken in 1827-30*, Philadelphia. 4⁹⁄₁₆ by 3¹⁵⁄₁₆. Courtesy of the Free Library of Philadelphia.

According to Gilchrist, St. Stephen's measures on the exterior 102 ft. by 61 ft., including the towers, which are 86 ft. high. The church was enlarged on the north side in 1878, and in 1918 the south gallery was taken down to conform to the north side.

82
ST. MARK'S CHURCH
North side of Locust at Sixteenth Street.
Built 1848-51 from plans sent over from England by the Ecclesiological Society and executed with modifications by John Notman (1810-1865).

Architectural rendering (water color), Sept. 18, 1847, by John Notman. 15 by 15¾. Courtesy of the Historical Society of Pennsylvania.

The cornerstone of the church was laid on the Feast of St. Mark, 1848; the first service was held Oct. 21, 1849, although the building was not consecrated until May, 1850, and the spire and tower were not completed until 1851. The Clergy House was added in 1893, and the Lady Chapel erected 1899-1902 from the designs of Cope & Stewardson (The Rev. Alfred Mortimer, *St. Mark's Church, Philadelphia, and Its Lady Chapel*, privately printed, 1909). The tenets of the Ecclesiological Society are discussed by Kenneth Clark in *The Gothic Revival* (London, 1928).

83

FLOATING CHURCH OF THE REDEEMER
Anchored in the Delaware River at the foot of Dock Street.
Built 1849 by Clement L. Dennington; burned 1868.

Lithographed and printed by William Endicott & Co., New York. 17 3/16 by 15 3/8. Courtesy of the Library Company of Philadelphia.

The Floating Church was ordered by the Churchmen's Missionary Association for Seamen of the Port of Philadelphia and built by Dennington at Bordentown, New Jersey. It measured 90 ft. by 34 ft. and seated 500 persons. H. and O. Filolet, father and son of New York, decorated the interior. Reconsecrated to St. John in 1853, the Church of the Redeemer was set on brick foundations on Lower Broadway in Camden, New Jersey, where it burned on Christmas morning, 1868. Floating churches were also to be found on the North and East rivers in New York City.

84

JAYNE BUILDING
84 Chestnut Street.
Built 1849-50 from the designs of William L. Johnston (1811-1849); completed by Thomas U. Walter (1804-1887); demolished 1958.

Engraving by John M. Butler. 21 1/2 by 15 1/8. Courtesy of the Library Company of Philadelphia.

Jayne's new granite building is described in the *Public Ledger* for November, 1850, as the "most extensive as well as expensive" (over

half a million dollars) in the United States. It had a front on Chestnut Street of 42 ft. and a depth of 137 ft. Side walls were of brick, and there was an underground tunnel connecting Jayne's building with the Post Office on Dock Street. Iron columns supported the wooden floor joists. At first, water collected by the tin roof and stored in five iron tanks on the eighth floor (capacity 5,000 gals.) provided a measure of fire protection as well as supplied the "spring seat closet" located on each floor; later, city water was used. The above facts are taken from the notice published by Charles E. Peterson in "American Notes," *Journal of the Society of Architectural Historians,* October, 1950. The architect of the Jayne Building was identified by Robert C. Smith (*JSAH*, March, 1951).

85

STANDPIPE OF THE WEST PHILADELPHIA WATERWORKS
West side of the Schuylkill River, near Thirty-fifth and Sycamore streets.
Built *c.*1855 by Birkinbine & Trotter, engineers; demolished *c.*1870.

Lithograph, c. 1853, by [William H.] Rease (fl.*c.*1844-1860) & [Francis H.] Schell (1834-1909). 16 1/4 by 7 3/4. Courtesy of the Library Company of Philadelphia.

The West Philadelphia Waterworks adjoined the grounds of Solitude, where the Zoo now stands. Intended to take the place of a reservoir, at least for a time, the standpipe went into operation in August, 1855, according to Wainwright. In publishing Birkinbine & Trotter's design, *Gleason's Pictorial Drawing-Room Companion* (Mar. 26, 1853) speaks of it as "about" to be erected, and it is not clear how closely the standpipe as finally constructed conformed to Rease &

Schell's lithograph. The figure of Washington on the top was to be 16 ft. high; that of Henry Clay, to which it was compared in the text, is illustrated in *Gleason's* for Jan. 8, 1853. There is reason to believe, however, that at least this part of the design of the standpipe was never carried out, the place of the figure being taken by a flagpole. Information on the factory of Robert Wood & Co. comes from *Godey's Lady's Book* (July, 1853) and R. A. Smith's *Illustrated Guide to and through Laurel Hill Cemetery* (Philadelphia, 1852). Ezra Coleman seems to have been Robert Wood's principal competitor in Philadelphia. The whole question of "Philadelphia's Ornamental Cast Iron" is discussed by Frances Lichten in *Antiques* for August, 1952.

86
Northern Liberties and Spring Garden Waterworks
East bank of the Schuylkill, above Fairmount. Built 1845; no longer standing.

Lithograph by Charles Conrad Kuchel from a drawing by Thomas M. Scott. Printed by P. S. Duval & Co., 1852. 17¼ by 25⅛. Courtesy of the Library Company of Philadelphia.

The engines housed in this granite building pumped water into a reservoir near Girard College. A number of Philadelphia's buildings are discussed in articles on the Egyptian Revival by Frank J. Roos, Jr. (The Egyptian Style, Notes on Early American Taste," *Magazine of Art,* 1940), Claire Whittler Eckels ("The Egyptian Revival in America," *Archaeology,* Autumn, 1950), and William S. Rusk ("Egyptian Echoes in American Architecture," *Americana,* July, 1934). Richard G. Carrott is understood to be completing a

much-needed study of the Egyptian buildings in the United States as a doctoral dissertation for the Department of the History of Art at Yale University. The Odd Fellows' Hall on Brown Street is described at length in the *Public Ledger* for Nov. 5, 1847, and the issue of June 10 mentions an iron-front store in the Egyptian manner, then in the process of erection on Walnut below Second for Isaac P. Morris & Co. (now demolished). The evidence for assigning the Crown Street Synagogue to Walter is given by Rachel Wischnitzer in the *Journal of the Society of Architectural Historians* for December, 1954, and under a grant from the American Philosophical Society Alfred Bendiner has prepared a set of drawings of Mikveh Israel "showing the plans, elevations, and sections of what [that] building may have looked like." These are now on file in the library of the Society (*Year Book of the American Philosophical Society,* 1959). The presumed basis of the selection of the Egyptian manner for the Pennsylvania Fire Insurance Company suggests the use of the style by Robert Cary Long, Jr (1810-1849), for the design (1836) of a fireproof record office in Baltimore (Richard H. Howland and Eleanor P. Spencer, *The Architecture of Baltimore,* Baltimore, 1953). According to Moses King, the addition to the Pennsylvania Fire Insurance Company was made in 1902 from the designs of Theophilus Parsons Chandler. Until it burned in 1959, an excellent example of a commercial building in the Egyptian style was that at 138 South Front Street in what is now the wool district of Philadelphia.

87
Laurel Hill Cemetery
Between the Schuylkill River and Ridge Avenue above Thirty-fifth Street.
Designed in 1836 by John Notman (1810-1865).

Lithograph by Deroy from a drawing by Augustus Koellner (1812-1906). Printed by Cattier and published by Goupil, Vibert & Co., New York and Paris, as No. 10 in *Views of American Cities,* 1848-51. 7½ by 11⅛. Courtesy of the Kean Archives.

Because it was not printed in Philadelphia, this view of Laurel Hill is not listed by Wainwright. The architect's drawing for the Gothic mortuary chapel, built 1838, appears in *Philadelphia Architecture in the Nineteenth Century* (ed. Theo. B. White), together with a plan of the grounds of the cemetery. Two guide books offer the best evidence for the early appearance of Laurel Hill: *Guide to Laurel Hill Cemetery near Philadelphia* (Philadelphia, 1844) and R. A. Smith *Illustrated Guide to and through Laurel Hill Cemetery* (Philadelphia, 1852). Pevsner emphasizes the association of the English style of gardening with liberal political views in his article on "The Genesis of the Picturesque" (*The Architectural Review,* November, 1944). A good, brief history of the English garden—and one that has influenced considerably the thinking of the author—is that of H. F. Clark (*The English Landscape Garden,* London, 1948). Christopher Hussey's *The Picturesque* (London, 1927) is the classic study of this aspect of Romantic aesthetic.

88

PLAN OF PROPOSED DESIGN OF FAIRMOUNT PARK
East and west banks of the Schuylkill River between Fairmount and Thirty-fifth Street.

Lithograph, 1859, by Louis Napoleon Rosenthal from a drawing by Andrew Palles, civil engineer. 28¹³⁄₁₆ by 20⁵⁄₁₆. Courtesy of the Library Company of Philadelphia.

Not listed by Wainwright because essentially a map, this is one of the earliest plans of Fairmount Park to come to the attention of the author. As usual in such cases, a number of the proposals embodied in the design, even if "adopted by City Councils," were never carried out. No detailed history of the Park exists, but a good, brief account was published by Agnes Martin in *The School Bank* for October, 1935. On the site of John Penn's estate called Solitude, later the location of the West Philadelphia Waterworks, was opened in July, 1874, the first zoological garden in America, incorporated 1859.

89

PAGODA AND LABYRINTH GARDEN
Northeast of Fairmount on south side of Coates Street (Fairmount Avenue).
Built 1828 from designs of John Haviland (1792-1852); demolished shortly thereafter.

Lithograph by Hugh Bridport (1794-*c*.1868). Printed by William B. Lucas. 12³⁄₁₆ by 17⅜. Courtesy of the Atwater Kent Museum.

Wainwright calls this the "earliest known Philadelphia scene issued as a lithograph." Atkinson's *Casket* (November, 1828) describes in some detail the opening of the Pagoda and Labyrinth Garden, which probably closed the following year. On the basis of old maps, the Pagoda does not seem to have been standing after 1834. Haviland's Pagoda and other "Oriental Forms in American Architecture 1800-1870" are discussed by Clay Lancaster in *The Art Bulletin* for 1947, and the American pleasure garden is the subject of an article by Harold Donaldson Eberlein and Cortlandt Van Dyke Hubbard in *The Pennsylvania Magazine* ("The American 'Vauxhall' of the Federal Era," April, 1944).

90
INTERIOR OF THE CHINESE MUSEUM
Northeast corner of Ninth and Sansom streets.
Built *c.*1836-1838 from designs of Isaac Holden (d.1884); burned 1854.

Water color, 1852, by David J. Kennedy (1817-1898). 7¼ by 11⅞. Courtesy of the Historical Society of Pennsylvania.

The long room pictured in Kennedy's water color appears to be that on the second floor of the Sansom Street building, extending the entire length of the structure and originally occupied by Peale's Museum. Kennedy notes that it would accommodate 15,000 people, but probably 4,000 is a more realistic figure. Although the order of the columns of the gallery is certainly not Classic, or even Western, neither is there anything specifically "Chinese" about the building except its name. The front of the museum on Sansom Street was approximately 235 ft. long and the side on Ninth Street about 67 ft. On the first floor, in addition to the room occupied originally by Dunn's Chinese collections, there was a "lecture room" with a separate entrance and ticket office on Sansom Street. Burton's National Theater, which adjoined the Chestnut Street side of the museum, was also known as General Welch's Circus (Kennedy) or Cook's Circus (Scharf and Westcott). Oberholtzer devotes several pages of his history to the Chinese Museum, and Holden is mentioned as its designer by H. S. Tanner. Of English birth, Holden had come to Philadelphia in 1826 and there practiced architecture in association with his brother until 1838, when both men returned to Manchester. B. Sprague Allen gives a good account of the influence of the Orient on Western art and life in *Tides in English Taste* (Cambridge, Massachusetts, 1937), from which several of the examples cited in the text are taken.

91
THE ATHENAEUM OF PHILADELPHIA
East side of Washington Square.
Built 1845-47 from designs of John Notman (1810-1865).

Wood engraving by Samuel E. Brown (fl. *c.*1840-*c.*1860) from a drawing by Nicholson B. Devereux. Published in *Gleason's Pictorial Drawing-Room Companion,* August, 1854. 5⅝ by 9¾. Courtesy of the Athenaeum of Philadelphia.

A brief history of the Athenaeum as an institution, from its founding in 1814 to 1850, is given by Arthur M. Kennedy in *Historic Philadelphia.* The two competitions and the final selection of John Notman as the architect of the new building was the subject of the address by Robert C. Smith at the 136th annual meeting of the Athenaeum, Feb. 5, 1951 (later printed and distributed to the stockholders and invited guests). At exactly the same time that Notman was designing the building on Washington Square, Robert Cary Long, Jr., was also providing a new building for the Baltimore Athenaeum in a similar *palazzo* style. Old photographs of the Ingersoll and McKean villas appear in Francis James Dallett's article on "John Notman, Architect" (*The Princeton University Library Chronicle,* Spring, 1959).

92
A SYMMETRICAL ITALIAN VILLA
Designed *c.*1850, by Samuel Sloan (1815-1884).

Lithograph, presumably by the architect. Printed by P. S. Duval & Co., Philadelphia. Published by Samuel Sloan in *The Model Architect,* Philadelphia [1852]. 5⅜ by 8.

A thorough study of the Italian villa style in the United States has yet to be published, but an introduction to the topic is provided by C. L. V. Meeks' "Henry Austin and the Italian Villa" (*The Art Bulletin*, June, 1948). Of the architectural books published in Philadelphia during the nineteenth century, none was of more importance or had greater influence than those of Sloan. *The Model Architect*, noted above, was followed by *City and Suburban Architecture* (1859), *Sloan's Constructive Architecture* (1859), *American Houses* (1861), and *Sloan's Homestead Architecture* (1861). Of particular importance was *The Architectural Review* (1868-1870), largely written as well as edited by Sloan, and usually considered to have been the first periodical limited exclusively to architecture published in the United States.

Bartram Association. Survey No. 9118, July 18, 1854, in the files of the Philadelphia Contributionship gives the approximate measurements of the Eastwick villa as 66 ft. by 73 ft. The roofs were of slate except for that of the tower which was shingled. Two furnaces warmed the mansion; the kitchen was in the basement. Guardian lions removed from the southern gate of Bartram Hall were later set up in Fairmount Park at the entrance to Memorial Hall. Eastwick died in 1879 and the city bought the old part of the estate with Bartram's house in 1890. Later, the remainder of the property was acquired and the Norman villa, then damaged by vandals, was torn down. Mrs. Andrew M. Eastwick describes Bartram Hall in Vol. II of the *Publications of the City History Society of Philadelphia* (Philadelphia, 1930).

93
BARTRAM HALL, RESIDENCE OF ANDREW M. EASTWICK
Bartram estate, west side of the Schuylkill River below Gray's Ferry.
Built 1851 from designs of Sloan & Stewart; demolished c.1895.

Lithograph, presumably by the architects. Printed by P. S. Duval & Co., Philadelphia. Published by Samuel Sloan in *The Model Architect*, Philadelphia [1852]. 7¹³⁄₁₆ by 11⅝.

The new mansion was erected not far from the stone house built with his own hands about 1730 by John Bartram (1699-1777), famous for having created on his farm the earliest botanical garden in America. His son William (1739-1823) is remembered also as America's first ornithologist of importance. Today Bartram's house and garden are open to the public as part of the Philadelphia park system, but under the supervision of the John

94
JOSEPH HARRISON HOUSE
Rittenhouse Square at the northeast corner of Eighteenth and Locust streets.
Built 1855-57 from designs of Samuel Sloan (1815-1884); demolished 1925.

Lithograph by Louis Napoleon Rosenthal, presumably from a drawing by the architect. 7⅞ by 12. Courtesy of the Historical Society of Pennsylvania.

Wainwright lists John Frampton Watson as the artist of this print, which also appeared in Sloan's *City and Suburban Architecture* (Philadelphia, 1859). Harold N. Cooledge, Jr., gives 1855 as the date of the Harrison mansion in the check list of buildings by Samuel Sloan, published in the *Journal of the Society of Architectural Historians* for March, 1960, and old photographs of the house show the figures "1856" in the gable of the pavilion on the left. Harrison is said to have patterned his home on one he had seen in St. Petersburg (Charles J. Cohen, *Rittenhouse Square Past and Present*, privately printed, 1922).

95
ROMAN CATHOLIC CATHEDRAL OF SS. PETER AND PAUL
East side of Logan Square.
Built 1846-64 from designs of Fathers Maller and J. B. Tornatore, Napoleon LeBrun (1821-1901), and John Notman (1810-1865).

Lithograph by Edward Schnabel from a drawing by John Notman. Printed by P. S. Duval, *c.*1854. 24 by 19¾. Courtesy of the Historical Society of Pennsylvania.

John T. Mahoney, architect of several other Roman Catholic buildings in Philadelphia, was associated with Notman in the design of the façade (*Philadelphia Architecture in the Nineteenth Century*, Theo. B. White, ed.). An inscription on the print gives the length of the Cathedral as 216 ft. and the width as 130 ft. Most of the frescoes on the interior are the work of Constantino Brumidi (1805-1880), best known as the decorator of the dome of the Capitol in Washington, D.C. When the number of Roman Catholics increased after the Revolution, St. Augustine's had been built on Fourth Street near Vine (1799-1801), for which William Strickland designed a cupola in 1829 (Agnes Addison Gilchrist, Documentary Supplement to *JSAH*). Burned in the anti-Catholic riots of 1844, St. Augustine's was rebuilt in 1848. Although the gilt cross was raised to the top of the dome in September, 1859, the Cathedral was not dedicated until Nov. 20, 1864.

96
ACADEMY OF MUSIC
Southwest corner, Broad and Locust streets.

Built 1855-57 from designs of Napoleon LeBrun (1821-1901) and Gustav Runge (1822-1900).

Architectural rendering (water color), presumably by the architects. 18 by 19¼. Courtesy of the Academy of Music.

In accordance with a resolution adopted at the meeting of Sept. 22, 1854, the Building Committee of the Academy advertised in two daily papers for the design of a new opera house. The specifications required (in part) that the building "be of simple but imposing style of architecture, the material of brick, with single or double walls. The lower story on Broad Street and Locust Street and the dressings of the entire building to be of granite, brownstone or iron. The front and Locust Street flank of pressed brick; the south front and rear of good front stretchers. There being streets on front and flanks, public exits must be provided on all. The house to be arranged as to comfortably seat 4,000 persons in not more than three tiers of boxes, a balcony and parquet. To have proper saloons, wide passages and stairways, the latter to be of iron or stone. Particular attention must be given to the comfort of the audience—freedom of exit—perfection of ventilation, heating, lighting, decoration and acoustic properties; and for the prevention of fire provision must be made to heat the entire house by fires under the footways." At the request of the competitors the time for receiving the designs was extended to Dec. 15, 1854. Subject "to certain alterations and modifications," the committee recommended that the first premium go to LeBrun & Runge and the second to S. D. Button. The committee mentions receiving designs from 12 architects but does not name them. Among the drawings in the possession of the Academy, however, is one showing for purposes of comparison the plans submitted by a number of the competitors, including: [Stephen D.] Button, [James Eliot?] Cabot, [Edward] Collins & Co., [John T.] Mahoney, and an otherwise unidentified architect named Trimble. On the recommendation of LeBrun & Runge, the seating capacity of the projected opera house was reduced to 3,000, and before finally deciding on a plan, LeBrun is said to have visited Europe to inspect the great opera houses there, especially La Scala in Milan. The cornerstone for the new Academy was laid July 25, 1855, and the opening performance was given Jan. 26, 1857. Prior to the erection of the Academy, most of the musical activities of the city had been sponsored by the Musical Fund Society, organized in 1820 and incorporated three years later. In 1824 the Society purchased the Fifth Presbyterian Church on the south side of Locust between Eighth and Ninth streets and engaged William Strickland to make the necessary alterations. In 1847 the Musical Fund Society Hall was enlarged by LeBrun and again remodeled in 1891. Here in 1856 the Republican party came into being. In 1942 the Society sold the Hall for use as a warehouse and office building (Agnes Addison Gilchrist, *William Strickland*). According to R. A. Smith, other buildings in Philadelphia by LeBrun included: Seventh, or Penn Square, Presbyterian Church, corner of Broad and Olive streets (1842-c.1884); St. Peter's Church, Franklin Avenue and Fifth Street (1843); Church of the Nativity, Eleventh and Washington streets; and Jefferson Medical College (enlargement), Tenth Street between Chestnut and Walnut (1845). The later work of N. LeBrun & Sons in New York City is the subject of an article in *The Architectural Record* for May, 1910.

97
LONGITUDINAL SECTION, ACADEMY OF MUSIC
See Note 96.

Engraving by L. Ritter. Printed by Ernst & Korn, Berlin. Published by G. Runge in *Das Neue Opernhous Academy of Music in Philadelphia,* Berlin, 1860.

The architects' drawings give the dimensions of the square space under the stage as 48 ft. by 53 ft. "dug down 24 ft. below curb" and that of the circular well under the auditorium as 20 ft. in diameter "20 ft. below N. E. curb." Provision was made for 8 smaller wells, each 8 ft. in diameter. On a lithograph in the Historical Society, G. Runge appears as the architect of the elaborate store of M. L. Hallowell & Co. (1854) at 147 Market Street, but nothing else by him has come to the author's notice. He habitually used only the initial of his first name, variously identified as "Gustavus" (Academy of Music: Centennial Program), "George" (Withey), or Gustav (Thieme-Becker).

98
WEST ARCH STREET PRESBYTERIAN CHURCH
Southeast corner of Arch and Eighteenth streets.
Built 1850-55 from designs of Joseph C. Hoxie (1814-1870).

Lithograph. Artist unknown (print trimmed). $29\frac{11}{16}$ by $25\frac{9}{16}$. Courtesy of the Arch Street Presbyterian Church.

This view of the Arch Street Church is not in Wainwright's list. *Ballou's Pictorial Drawing-Room Companion* for July, 1855, gives the following exterior dimensions for Hoxie's building: length, 150 ft.; width, 75 ft.; projection of transepts, 6 ft. with width of 48 ft.; height of bell towers, 115 ft.; height of center tower, 170 ft.; diameter of dome, 54 ft. Other churches by Hoxie in Philadelphia included: the Eleventh Presbyterian Church, southwest corner of Fifth and Arch streets; the Fourth Baptist Church, northwest corner of Fifth and Buttonwood streets, and the Methodist Episcopal Church at Eight and Buttonwood. It is not known what, if any, was Joseph C. Hoxie's relationship to the Solomon K. Hoxie who served as builder for Sloan & Stewart's Masonic Hall (Fig. 75) and Johnston's Jayne Building (Fig. 84).

99
DEPARTMENT FOR MALES, PENNSYLVANIA HOSPITAL FOR THE INSANE
North side of Market at Forty-fourth Street. Built 1856-59 from designs of Samuel Sloan (1815-1884); demolished 1959.

Engraving by John M. Butler (fl.1840-1860). $3^{15}\!/_{16}$ by $7\frac{1}{2}$. Courtesy of the Kean Archives.

Under the Quakers, Philadelphia had a long and outstanding record for the care of the poor, the homeless, and the ill. In their Almshouse (1713-1841) on the south side of Walnut between Third and Fourth streets the Society of Friends created Philadelphia's first charitable enterprise. The Philadelphia General Hospital is also considered to be one of the nation's earliest public hospitals. The first use of the ideas of Pinel and Tuke was the Friends' Asylum near Philadelphia, designed by William Strickland in 1815 (Agnes Addison Gilchrist, Documentary Supplement to *JSAH*). Sloan seems to have come to Philadelphia from Lancaster County about 1833 and first to have served as a carpenter at the Eastern State Penitentiary before becoming foreman under Isaac Holden for the construction of the Female Department for the Insane.

100
STORE OF DALE, ROSS & WITHERS
219 Market Street.

Built *c.*1857 from designs of Stephen D. Button (1803-1897); demolished *c.*1955(?).

Lithograph by John Frampton Watson (fl. *c.*1833-*c.*1860). 35 by $22\frac{1}{2}$. Courtesy of the Library Company of Philadelphia.

Wainwright notes that the number of Dale, Ross & Withers was later changed to 521; in that case whatever remained of Button's building was demolished to make way for the Independence Mall. Unlike most iron "front" buildings of the period, the Penn Mutual Life Insurance Building was an all-iron structure, the importance of which Charles E. Peterson first pointed out in the *Journal of the Society of Architectural Historians* for December, 1950. In addition to the Penn Mutual Building, R. A. Smith mentions G. Parker Cummings (fl.1845-1865) as the architect of Swaim's Building on the southeast corner of Chestnut and Seventh streets ("in the Italian or Palladian style of architecture, with a red sandstone front") and the Sansom Street Hall, Sansom Street west of Sixth, erected 1848, as a Public Bathhouse and Lyceum ("a mixture of Greek and Italian" forms, the order of the first story being based on the Baths of Diocletian in Rome). The role of Bogardus in the development of the iron building is discussed by Turpin Bannister in "Bogardus Revisited," *Journal of the Society of Architectural Historians*, December, 1956.

101
CHARLES OAKFORD'S MODEL HAT STORE
158 Chestnut Street.
Occupied by Oakford from 1854 to 1860.

Lithograph. Printed by P. S. Duval. $15\frac{1}{8}$ by $23^{13}\!/_{16}$. Courtesy of the Library Company of Philadelphia.

Oakford seems to have taken great pride in his hat business. By way of advertisement, he had lithographs issued depicting three of the four successive locations of his store and another showing the workroom (Wainwright Nos. 55, 56, 57, 58). Wainwright also reproduces the lithograph representing the interior of the store after its move to the Continental Hotel and identifies the portly man in the foreground of our Figure 101 as the proprietor himself. Together with that of Rockhill & Wilson, Tailors, and L. J. Levy & Co.'s Dry Goods Store (designed by John Fraser c.1855), the lithographs of Oakford's various stores represent the most important views of the interiors of commercial establishments in Philadelphia at this period.

102
CONTINENTAL HOTEL
Southeast corner of Ninth and Chestnut streets.
Built 1857-60 from designs of John McArthur, Jr. (1823-1890); demolished 1923-24.

Engraving by Robert Whitechurch (1814-c.1880). Published by W. Syckelmoore. 4⅞ by 7⅝. Courtesy of the Free Library of Philadelphia.

The Continental was opened Feb. 13, 1860, on the site now occupied by the Benjamin Franklin Hotel, which had become available in 1854 with the burning of Burton's National Theater (previously Cook's Circus) and the Chinese Museum (Fig. 90). A full description of the hotel appears in the anonymous pamphlet *A Traveler's Sketch: Continental Hotel* (Philadelphia, 1861). Good monographs are also available on the Tremont House (W. H. Eliot, Boston, 1830) and the Parker House (J. W. Spring, Boston, 1927). In the *Journal of Southern History* for May, 1957, Doris Elizabeth King discusses "The First Class

Hotel and the Age of the Common Man." The London Coffee House (c.1702-1884), opened 1754 on the southwest corner of Market and Front streets, was one of the most important of the early taverns in Philadelphia that were the forerunners of the hotels of the nineteenth century (Robert Earle Graham, "The Taverns of Colonial Philadelphia," *Historic Philadelphia*). Among the Georgian mansions later converted into hotels was the Burd residence on the north side of Chestnut Street near Eighth, leased in 1798 to Robert Morris and in 1883 remodeled to serve as Green's Hotel.

103
BUSINESS EXCHANGE AND LOBBY OF THE CONTINENTAL HOTEL
See Note 102.

Wood engraving from hotel stationery. 7 by 9½. Courtesy of the Free Library of Philadelphia.

Claimed by its builders to be one of the four major American hotels, the Continental contained approximately 700 rooms and was operated on the American plan. Lincoln stayed here Feb. 21, 1861, and showed himself to the citizens of Philadelphia from the balcony. The quotation from *Putnam's Magazine* concerning the bridal suite in the St. Nicholas is from Jefferson Williamson, *The American Hotel; An Anecdotal History* (New York, 1930). The Continental was said to have had the largest bar in the country. Russell Lynes has a delightful chapter on "Palaces for the People" in *The Tastemakers* (New York [1954]).

104
SECTIONAL FLOATING DRY DOCK
Delaware River, foot of Christian Street.
c.1855.

Lithograph by [William H.] Rease (fl.c.1844-1860) & [Francis H.] Schell (1834-1909). Published by T. Sinclair. 13 by 21⁹⁄₁₆. Courtesy of the Atwater Kent Museum.

J. Simpson & Neill are listed on the print as the shipwrights and proprietors of the sectional floating dry dock. The Atwater Kent Museum identifies the three-masted square-rigged ship being worked on as the Messenger, and the ferry at the left as the Peytona. R. A. Smith notes that floating dry docks of this kind were first tried out in the harbor of New York. The U. S. Dry Dock in Philadelphia was built in 1849-51, according to Smith, at a cost of $813,742, including the basin, two railways, and other equipment.

105
PANORAMIC VIEW OF PHILADELPHIA
c.1855.

Lithograph by Asselineau from a water color by John Bachman (fl.1850-1877). Printed by Lemercier. Published by Wild, Paris. 15³⁄₈ by 22¹¹⁄₁₆. Courtesy of the Historical Society of Pennsylvania.

The print reproduced here is apparently a pirated edition of that of P. S. Duval, listed by Wainwright and described by him as "perhaps the most valuable lithograph of Philadelphia from an iconographic standpoint." Like most prints, however, it must be used with some caution, since such details as the dome and western towers of the Roman Catholic Cathedral make it clear that in some respects, at least, Bachman was representing Philadelphia as he thought it would be, rather than as it was. At the bottom of the print appears a strip of the west bank of the Schuylkill with the grounds of Powelton, the scene of the agricultural fairs, and in

the lower right-hand corner the new Almshouse of Blockley Township, built 1830-34 from the designs of William Strickland (last buildings demolished c.1955). Bachman's original water color now hangs in the Rare Book Department of the Free Library of Philadelphia.

106
RODEPH SHALOM SYNAGOGUE
Southeast corner of Broad and Green streets. Built 1869 from designs of Fraser, Furness & Hewitt; demolished 1925.

Lithograph, 1869, by Ben Lirfont (?). 20⁵⁄₁₆ by 14⁵⁄₈. Courtesy of the Historical Society of Pennsylvania.

Organized in 1755, Rodeph Shalom is the oldest Ashkenazic (Germanic) congregation in the occidental world. In 1926 a new synagogue was erected at Broad and Green streets from the designs of Edward P. and Grant M. Simon. "The History of the Jews in Philadelphia from Colonial Times to the Age of Jackson" is the subject of a recent book by Edwin Wolf, 2nd (Philadelphia, 1957).

107
COLLEGE HALL, UNIVERSITY OF PENNSYLVANIA
Spruce Street between Thirty-fourth and Thirty-sixth.
Built 1870-72 from designs of Thomas W. Richards.

Engraving by John McGoffin (1813-after 1883). 4¹¹⁄₁₆ by 7⁷⁄₁₆. Courtesy of the Historical Society of Pennsylvania.

The cornerstone of College Hall was laid Jan. 15, 1871, and the completed building was opened with appropriate ceremonies Oct. 11, 1872 (Edward Potts Cheyney, *History of the University of Pennsylvania, 1740-1940,* Philadelphia, 1940). The other three buildings erected from Richards' designs were the Medical Building (now Logan Hall), the Dental Building (now the Hare Building) and the University Hospital (now concealed on the exterior by later remodeling and additions).

108

INDEPENDENCE HALL IN 1876
Chestnut between Fifth and Sixth streets. See Note 22.

Lithograph by Thomas Hunter from a drawing by Theodore Poleni. 14⅝ by 20⅝. Courtesy of the Library of Congress.

In the background is John McArthur's Public Ledger Building (1867). On the far left is the Philosophical Society, founded in 1743 by Benjamin Franklin and others and usually considered the oldest learned society in America. After many difficulties, in 1789 the Society succeeded in completing as its permanent home this simple but well-proportioned brick building in the late Georgian style that still stands in Independence Square adjacent to the south side of the Supreme Court Building (City Hall). An awkward third story added in 1890 was fortunately removed in 1949. The interesting history of Philosophical Hall, which numbered among its various tenants the University of Pennsylvania and the museum specimens and numerous progeny of Charles Willson Peale, is told by William E. Lingelbach in *Historic Philadelphia.*

109

INTERIOR OF THE EAST (ASSEMBLY) ROOM OF INDEPENDENCE HALL
1856.

Water color, 1856, by Max Rosenthal (1833-1918). 12¹³⁄₁₆ by 18⅜. Courtesy of the Historical Society of Pennsylvania.

This water color was lithographed in color by Louis N. Rosenthal and published by Stayman & Brother (Wainwright No. 185). The events connected with the use of the Assembly Room mentioned here are based on Edward M. Riley's account of "The Independence Hall Group," which appeared in *Historic Philadelphia.*

110

GIRARD AVENUE BRIDGE
Erected 1872-74 from designs of Thomas C. Clark, engineer, and Henry A. (1832-1875) and James P. (1849-1882) Sims, architects.

Lithograph by Currier & Ives. 8⅜ by 12⅜. Courtesy of the Atwater Kent Museum.

Its designers are commemorated by a plaque underneath the Girard Avenue Bridge, beside the East River Drive. Replacing a wooden bridge at the same site, built in 1855, the new iron bridge was 865 ft. long and 100 ft. wide. The lower level, intended primarily for pedestrians, seems never to have been very popular, and in recent years the Schuylkill Expressway has destroyed its usefulness altogether.

111

BALLOON VIEW OF THE CENTENNIAL GROUNDS
1876.

Wood engraving, 1876, from photographs by R. Newell & Sons and sketches by Theo. R. Davis. Published in the *Supplement to Harper's Weekly,* Sept. 30 1876. 19¾ by 30⅝.

Courtesy of the Historical Society of Pennsylvania.

Of the many books describing the Centennial, that of Thompson Westcott is probably the best known and the most useful (*Centennial Portfolio: A Souvenir of the International Exhibition at Philadelphia*, Philadelphia, 1876). The account of the Centennial in the text is based upon the introduction written by the author for *A Plan for the Adaptation of Memorial Hall*, prepared for the Fairmount Park Commission, August, 1958, by Hatfield, Martin & White, architects, and used here with their permission.

112
MASONIC TEMPLE
Northeast corner of Broad and Filbert streets. Built 1868-73 from designs of James H. Windrim (1840-1919).

Water color, 1908, by P. F. Goist. 23½ by 17½. Courtesy of the Grand Lodge, Free and Accepted Masons of Pennsylvania.

The lot on Broad Street was purchased in 1866; the cornerstone was laid June 24, 1868, and the new building dedicated Sept. 26, 1873. When built, the Temple in Philadelphia was considered "the wonder of the Masonic World" and it is still one of the most elaborate structures of its kind in the country. Its apartments include halls decorated in the Egyptian, Gothic, Moorish, Ionic, Corinthian, and Norman styles, dating for the most part from the 1890's (*The Masonic Temple, Philadelphia*, privately printed by the Grand Lodge, Free and Accepted Masons of Pennsylvania, Philadelphia, 1947). The role of the Masons in Philadelphia is discussed by Norris S. Barratt and Julius F. Sachse in *Freemasonry in Pennsylvania, 1727-1907* (Philadelphia, 1908).

113
HORTICULTURAL HALL
West Fairmount Park.
Built 1875 from designs of Herman Joseph Schwarzmann (1843-1891); demolished 1955.

Lithograph, 1875, by Julius Bien, New York Published by G. Meyer, Philadelphia. 12¼ by 21. Courtesy of the Library of the Franklin Institute.

The notice of copyright on the print lists "Schwarzmann and Pohl" as the architects of Horticultural Hall. On this site originally stood Lansdowne (Fig. 25), the last fire-blackened ruins of which were cleared away at the time of the Centennial. Schwarzmann is usually credited also with having laid out the Philadelphia Zoological Garden at Thirty-fourth and Girard Avenue.

114
WANAMAKER'S GRAND DEPOT
Thirteenth and Market streets.
Remodeled 1876; demolished 1902.

Wood engraving by Vaningen-Snyder from a drawing by A. Blanc. 6⅛ by 9⅛. Courtesy of the Free Library of Philadelphia.

In 1861 John Wanamaker and Nathan Brown had opened "Oak Hall" as a Men's & Boys' Clothing Store on the first floor of the McNeille Building, southeast corner of Sixth and Market streets (*Golden Book of the Wanamaker Stores*, Philadelphia, 1911). Sigfried Giedion (*Space, Time and Architecture*,

192

Cambridge, Massachusetts, 1954) points out that Wanamaker's was unusual in departing from the prevailing "warehouse pattern" and that its opening in Philadelphia coincided with that of Eiffel and Boileau's Magasin au Bon Marché in Paris. Contemporary with Wanamaker's and also of vaguely Moorish inspiration was Kiralfy's Alhambra Palace (later the South Broad Street Theater), opened in 1876 as an attraction for the crowds attending the Centennial (demolished *c.*1937). A plaque in the John Wanamaker store commemorates the fact that it stands on the site of Central High School, opened in 1838 as one of the first schools in the country to give a free education beyond the lower grades.

115
DAVID JAYNE RESIDENCE
Southeast corner of Chestnut and Nineteenth streets.
Built 1865-66 from designs of John McArthur, Jr. (1823-1890); demolished 1922.

Wash drawing by Frank Hamilton Taylor (1846-1927). 7⅜ by 11. Courtesy of the Library Company of Philadelphia.

The Aldine Theater is now called the Viking. John McArthur, Jr., was born in Scotland and came to the United States about 1833. He was apprenticed to his uncle, who, like his father, was a carpenter. In 1848 he was awarded first place in a competition for the design of a new "House of Refuge." Among the important private residences in the city for which McArthur was also the architect is the Childs mansion, still standing on the corner of Twenty-second and Walnut streets. George W. Childs was the publisher of the *Public Ledger*. If part of the original house, one of the earliest mansard roofs in the Philadelphia area must have been

that on Medary, the residence designed in 1847 for Harry Ingersoll by John Notman (Francis James Dallet in *The Princeton University Library Chronicle,* Spring, 1959, and the *Journal of the Society of Architectural Historians* for May, 1960). Of Jayne's house Moses King wrote in 1902: "This great white marble mansion—still unsurpassed—has been one of Philadelphia's most noticeable structures for a generation."

116
UNITED STATES POST OFFICE AND FEDERAL BUILDING
West side of Ninth Street between Chestnut and Market.
Built 1873-84 from designs of Alfred B. Mullett (1834-1890) under supervision of John McArthur, Jr. (1823-1890); demolished c.1935.

Wood engraving from a drawing by F. B. Schell. Probably originally published in *Harper's Weekly.* 8⅞ by 13³⁄₁₆. Courtesy of the Free Library of Philadelphia.

Philadelphia's new post office measured 425 ft. on Ninth Street and 175 ft. on Chestnut. French's sculptured group over the pediment was moved to Fairmount Park when the Post Office was demolished (*Philadelphia Architecture in the Nineteenth Century,* Theo. B. White, ed.). John Maass includes a chapter on the Mansardic Era in his entertaining book on *The Gingerbread Age* (New York [1957]). The structure on the west of the Post Office is the Record Building (1881), no longer standing.

117
PHILADELPHIA CITY HALL
Penn Square, Broad and Market streets.
Built 1871-81 from designs of John McArthur,

Jr. (1823-1890), assisted by Thomas U. Walter (1804-1887).

Architectural rendering, 1884, by E. Eldon Deane. 19⅝ by 20. Courtesy of the Atwater Kent Museum.

The Philadelphia City Hall covers 4½ acres and has over 600 rooms; the height of the tower is 547 ft. and that of the statue of William Penn on the top 37 ft. Although the City Hall was occupied in 1881, the decoration was not complete nor the statue of William Penn put in place until the 90's. Alexander Calder (1846-1923) was in charge of the sculpture. In 1919 ornaments weighing more than twenty tons are said to have been removed from the exterior of the City Hall to prevent their falling on passers-by. Visible on the right of the view reproduced here is the Wilson Brothers' Broad Street Station and on the left Strickland's U.S. Mint. Wayne Andrews devotes a chapter to "The Age of Elegance" in *Architecture, Ambition and Americans.*

118
THE PENNSYLVANIA ACADEMY OF THE FINE ARTS
Southwest corner of Broad and Cherry streets. Built 1872-76 from designs of Frank Furness (1839-1912).

Colored drawing by Joseph P. Sims (1890-1953). 10 by 13⅛. Courtesy of the Pennsylvania Academy of the Fine Arts.

The cornerstone of the Academy was laid Dec. 7, 1872. Of Furness and the new building on Broad Street, *The American Architect and Building News* (Oct. 14, 1876) had this to say: ". . . By far the most important element in the recent building of Philadelphia is Mr. Furness's work. Nobody would think of calling it commonplace; and it is so far from being scholastic that a good deal of it is hard to classify. . . . The Fine Arts Building, in particular, considering its size, its site, and the elaborateness of its decoration, must be pronounced an architectural failure. Its lines are 'pestered,' instead of accentuated, by its ornament. . . . Whatever else Mr. Furness's work is, it is full of life; and the life of it would atone for much worse faults than it shows. . . . It is the work of an architect full of spirit and invention, who has not yet reached the prime of his powers. . . ." For the galleries of the Academy, Furness used rooms of various sizes so arranged that there is a vista through them and the spectator is never at a loss as to the direction he is to take. Mansardic roofs were also used on the Guarantee Safe Deposit and Trust Co. (later Tradesmen's National Bank & Trust Co.) at 320 Chestnut Street, built from Furness' designs in 1875 and now demolished. These and other of Furness' buildings are discussed by William Campbell in his article in *The Architectural Review* ("Frank Furness: An American Pioneer," November, 1951) for which Nikolaus Pevsner provided the notes to the illustrations comparing Furness' designs to those of Viollet-le-Duc. Among the rapidly diminishing number of buildings by Furness that remain standing are the First Unitarian Church (1884) at Twenty-second and Chestnut streets and the entrance pavilions at the Philadelphia Zoo (1873-1875). The Baltimore and Ohio Railroad Station (*c.*1886) is scheduled for demolition in the near future.

119
"BANK ROW," NORTH SIDE OF CHESTNUT BETWEEN FOURTH AND FIFTH STREETS

409—Provident Life and Trust Co.
    Built 1879 from designs of Frank Furness (1839-1912); demolished 1960.

194

415—Philadelphia Trust, Safe Deposit and Insurance Co.

Built 1874 from designs of James H. Windrim (1840-1919); demolished 1959

421—Bank of Pennsylvania (building later owned by the Philadelphia Bank, now the Philadelphia National Bank).

Built 1857-59 from designs of John M. Gries (1827-1862).

427—Farmers' and Mechanics' Bank (building now owned by the Philadelphia National Bank).

Built 1855 from designs of John M. Gries (1827-1862).

431—The Pennsylvania Company (building now owned by the Philadelphia National Bank).

Built 1873.

435—Peoples Bank (Girard Building).

Built c.1874 from designs of James H. Windrim (1840-1919); demolished c.1907 and replaced with the Lafayette Building, still standing.

Drawing (pen and ink), presumably the original for *Baxter's Panoramic Business Directory of Philadelphia*. 7⅜ by 33¾. Courtesy of the Historical Society of Pennsylvania.

The buildings at both ends of the "Bank Row" block were of cast iron; that at the Fourth Street corner with the large windows was the "Crystal Building" (1853), replaced in 1890 by a building for the Provident Trust Co., also designed by Furness and now demolished. At the Fifth Street corner stood the five-story "Brown's Iron Building," destroyed with the Girard Building about 1907 to make way for the Lafayette Building, now standing on the site. Good details of the Provident Life and Trust Co. appeared in the *Architectural Forum* for June, 1960 ("Fearless Frank Furness"), and the original design was published by James C. Massey in the *Journal of the Society of Architectural*

Historians for May, 1960. Massey also made the study of "Bank Row" that resulted in the information on the various buildings included here. The work of William Butterfield is discussed and illustrated by John Summerson in his volume of essays entitled *Heavenly Mansions* (London [1949]).

120

THE LIBRARY COMPANY OF PHILADELPHIA
Northwest corner of Locust and Juniper streets.
Built 1878-80 from designs of Frank Furness (1839-1912); demolished 1940.

Drawing (pen and ink), presumably by the architect. 11½ by 15. Courtesy of the Library Company of Philadelphia.

The minutes of the Library Company show that on Nov. 27, 1878, the Directors expressed themselves as favoring a new building that would be "as far as possible a reproduction in its exterior" of Thornton's Library Hall on Fifth Street in the belief that this "would gratify the feelings of the members." On Dec. 31, however, James S. Biddle moved to reconsider "so much of the report of the committee on the fireproof building as recommended that the new building should to some extent resemble the [old] building." Biddle's motion carried, and the design finally adopted seems to have been a compromise in that it suggests the earlier building without being a copy of it. The interior of the new building is said to have followed closely the lines of Library Hall (*Philadelphia Architecture in the Nineteenth Century*, Theo. B. White, ed.). When the Library Company moved from Library Hall on Fifth Street, it was into two new buildings, that on South Broad Street, designed by Addison Hutton, and that on Locust and Juniper streets, for which Furness was the architect.

121

BROAD STREET STATION
Unexecuted design by Furness, Evans & Co.
for addition to earlier building (opened
1882) by Wilson Bros. & Co.

Architectural rendering (water color), c.1892,
presumably from the office of the architects.
17¾ by 25¾. Courtesy of the Atwater Kent
Museum.

Arthur Truscott is credited with having
produced the Gothic details for Wilson Bros.
& Co. (*Philadelphia Architecture in the Nineteenth Century*, Theo. B. White, ed.) Truscott was later made the head of the Department of Architecture at Drexel Institute. The
Philadelphia stations are discussed by Carroll
L. V. Meeks in *The Railroad Station: An
Architectural History* (New Haven, 1956),
and the Wilson Brothers describe their part
of the building in the catalogue of the firm's
work, published in 1885. When remodeled,
the Pennsylvania Station measured 306 ft. on
Broad Street, facing Penn Square, and 212
on Market. The large terra cotta relief,
"Progress of Transportation," made by Karl
Bitter for the waiting-room of the Broad
Street Station, has been moved to the new
building at Thirtieth Street. Furness, Evans
& Co. also designed the Arcade Building
(completed 1902) still standing at Fifteenth
and Broad streets and originally connected
with the Station by a covered bridge across
Market Street (Edwin P. Alexander, *The
Pennsylvania Railroad: A Pictorial History*,
New York, 1947). The Broad Street Station
was demolished in 1953.

122

THE GIRARD LIFE INSURANCE, ANNUITY AND
TRUST COMPANY OF PHILADELPHIA
Northeast corner of Broad and Chestnut
streets.

Built 1888-89 from designs of Addison Hutton
(1834-1916); demolished 1926.

Architectural rendering (pen and ink). Pub-
lished in the *Supplement to the Builder &
Decorator* for March, 1888. 12½ by 7¾.
Courtesy of the Free Library of Philadelphia.

The Builder & Decorator describes the
Girard Building as being 180 ft. high and
speaks of an open court in the center. About
1857, Hutton entered the architectural office
of Samuel Sloan as a draftsman and in 1864
became a partner. Before the dissolution of
the partnership in 1868, the firm of Sloan &
Hutton designed a number of important
buildings, including: Swarthmore College
(1857-68), Theological Seminary of St. Charles
Borromeo in Overbrook (1866) and the main
office of the Philadelphia Saving Fund Society on the southwest corner of Seventh and
Walnut streets (1868-69; western addition,
1900, by Furness, Evans & Co.). Hutton was
a Fellow of the American Institute of Architects as well as a lecturer on architecture at
the University of Pennsylvania. In a booklet
published in 1890 on the occasion of the opening of its new building, the Girard Trust Co.
noted: "The Romanesque style of architecture is now regarded as the national style
of the United States and is most distinctly de-
serving of that title. In its ready adaptability
to modern buildings, it has assumed new
beauties, without losing those more ancient.
The severest simplicity is permitted in it and
the most elaborate and faithful carving. It
is eminently practical in construction and its
resistance to weather is ample." The best
treatment of the career and style of H. H.
Richardson, who did more than anyone else
to popularize the Romanesque style in
America, is that of Henry-Russell Hitchcock
(*The Architecture of H. H. Richardson and*

His Times, New York, 1936). The original eight stories of the Girard Building were later increased to fourteen, and after its sale about 1908 it became known as the Liberty Building. It seems to have formed a unit with the Lincoln Building on the north (the former Betz Building), and with it to have been known as the Lincoln & Liberty Building. Will H. Decker, the architect of the Betz Building (1891), which has been called "the first Philadelphia skyscraper," had perhaps more feeling for bizarre design than any other architect active in Philadelphia. According to John Harbeson ("Philadelphia's Victorian Architecture"), Decker was also the designer of the Manhattan Building at Fourth and Walnut streets (demolished 1960).

123
DREXEL BUILDING
Southeast corner of Fifth and Chestnut streets.
Built 1885 and enlarged *c*.1887-89 from designs of Wilson Bros. & Co.; demolished 1955.

Drawing (pen and ink) by John J. Dull. From a brochure describing their new building put out by Drexel & Co. 7 by 8⅞. Courtesy of the Independence National Historical Park.

The exterior of the Drexel Building was of marble and white enameled brick; each of the two wings measured 220 ft. by 56 ft. The northern part of the east wing (on the site of the old post office and balancing Drexel's Bank) was occupied on the first floor by the Tradesmen's National Bank, and on the second by the Philadelphia Stock Exchange. On the right in the drawing is the building constructed by the Mercantile Library (Fig. 69) and on the left that of the Second Bank of the United States (Fig. 54).

124
DREXEL BUILDING
See Note 123.

Working drawing from the office of Wilson Bros. & Co. 22½ by 15. Courtesy of the Independence National Historical Park.

The floors throughout the building were made of hollow terra cotta blocks, forming flat arches between I-beams carried by girders and columns. The blocks entirely concealed the beams, so that no metal was exposed to possible damage by fire. Since the partitions were also made of hollow terra cotta blocks and the floors were strong enough to support them at any point, interior walls could be moved or omitted entirely, as the tenant desired. Ventilation was provided by four electrically driven fans on the roof that sucked air from each of the 400 rooms. Both gas and electricity were used for illumination. When completed, the Drexel Building was considered by its owners to compare "favorably with the largest of the new buildings in New York and Chicago." For details of the development of the tall building in Chicago, see Carl W. Condit, *The Rise of the Skyscraper* (Chicago, 1952) and Frank A. Randall, *The History of the Development of Building Construction in Chicago* (Urbana, Illinois, 1949).

125
BINGHAM HOUSE
Southeast corner of Eleventh and Market streets.
Built *c*.1876; altered 1890 from designs of Willis Gaylord Hale (d.1907); demolished 1926.

Drawing (pen and ink), 1890, by C. F. Sherborne. 4⅝ by 6¾. Courtesy of the Historical Society of Pennsylvania.

The Bingham House was preceded on the same site by the Mansion House and followed by the Earle Theater. Old photographs indicate that the remodeling of the hotel conformed to the architect's design in most essentials. Hale seems to have been Will Decker's nearest rival in the pursuit of the unusual in architectural design (see Note 122). Other of his buildings in Philadelphia included: United Firemen's Insurance Co., 419 Walnut Street, c.1878 (demolished); Record Building, Ninth and Chestnut, 1881 (Fig. 116; demolished); Union Trust Co., 713-721 Chestnut Street, 1884 (partially demolished); Hale Building, Chestnut and Juniper streets, 1884 (John Harbeson, "Philadelphia's Victorian Architecture," *The Pennsylvania Magazine*). Hale also remodeled the Walnut Street Theater in 1903, and Moses King mentions as by him the H. Josephine Widener Library, Broad Street and Girard Avenue, the entrance to the Garrick Theater, and the Rittenhouse Hotel.

126

HORTICULTURAL HALL
South Broad and Lardner (now Manning) streets.
Built 1895-96 from designs of Frank Miles Day (1861-1918); demolished 1917.

Wash drawing, 1917, by Frank Hamilton Taylor (1846-1927). 7½ by 10. Courtesy of the Library Company of Philadelphia.

After graduating valedictorian from the University of Pennsylvania in 1883, Day worked in the London office of Basil Champneys (1842-1935) and attended the Royal Academy. He opened his Philadelphia practice in 1887, winning in that year the competition for the Art Club. The American Baptist Publication Society Building, com-

pleted in 1898, still stands. Horticultural Hall was designed for the Pennsylvania Horticultural Society in 1894; the cornerstone was laid Aug. 15, 1895, and the building opened in 1896. Founded 1827, the Society first used the site on Broad Street for its autumn show in 1865; its first building there, by Sloan & Hutton, opened in 1867, burned in 1881, and was rebuilt along the original lines (James Boyd, *A History of the Pennsylvania Horticultural Society*, Philadelphia, 1929). Day's design, the third on the site, was of Pompeian brick and stone. Ralph Adams Cram (*The Architectural Record*, April, 1904), mentions that the painting of the frieze, if not its entire execution, was the work of a Mr. Smith. When Horticultural Hall was razed in 1917, the lower run of its interior stair was incorporated into the Schubert Theater, which replaced it. Day's other works include residences and hospitals in New York, Philadelphia, and Washington, and academic buildings for Princeton, Cornell, Yale, Wellesley, and the University of Pennsylvania (Weightman Hall, 1904, in the Gothic style).

127

MEN'S DORMITORIES, UNIVERSITY OF PENNSYLVANIA
Thirty-seventh and Spruce streets.
Begun in 1895 from designs of Cope & Stewardson.

Etching, 1928, by Ernest David Roth (b. 1879). 10 by 6¹⁵⁄₁₆. Courtesy of the Faculty Club, University of Pennsylvania.

John Stewardson (1858-1896) entered Harvard in 1877; he was a member of the Atelier Pascal in Paris from 1879 to 1881 and attended the Ecole des Beaux Arts in Paris from then until his return to Philadelphia in 1882. Walter Cope (1860-1902) traveled in Europe from 1884 to 1886 when the firm of Cope & Stewardson was established. Both men were instrumental in the founding of the T-Square Club. Cope also served as chairman (1896-98) of the committee on the restoration of Independence Hall. Other buildings by the firm include the Harrison Building (1895, Fifteenth and Market), the Pennsylvania Institute for the Instruction of the Blind (1898, Sixty-fourth and Malvern, Overbrook), the Lady Chapel added to Notman's St. Mark's Church (Fig. 82) in 1902, houses at 1503, 1926 Spruce Street and 1631, 1633 Locust Street and the William Penn Charter School (1888; demolished 1926), Twelfth and Market (*The Architectural Record*, November, 1904). The Dormitories were begun at the western end and continued by Emlyn Lamar Stewardson (1863-1937), third partner in the firm, and George Bispham Page (1870-1948), a draftsman for the old firm until 1902. Their last work on the Dormitories dates from 1930; later additions in 1955 and 1959 are by Trautwein & Howard.

128
HOUSE FOR MESSRS. NEIL AND MAURAN
315-317 South Twenty-second Street.
Built 1890 from designs of Wilson Eyre, Jr. (1858-1944).

Architectural rendering (water color) by the architect. 11¾ by 13¾. Courtesy of the Fine Arts Library of the Universitity of Pennsylvania.

Examples of Eyre's architecture are to be found in New York, Michigan, Maryland, Louisiana, Maine, and Rhode Island. Buildings by him still standing in Philadelphia include: 242 and 245-247 South Seventeenth Street, the Moore House (now a restaurant) at 1321 Locust, the Leidy House at 1319

Locust Street (now the Poor Richard Club), and the T-Square and Mask and Wig Clubs at 206 and 310 South Quince Street, respectively. Examples of his country houses include those of A. J. Drexel in Lansdowne and J. W. Pepper in Jenkintown. All these were built between 1890 and 1903 (*The Architectural Record,* October, 1903).

129
THE UNIVERSITY MUSEUM, UNIVERSITY OF PENNSYLVANIA
Thirty-third and Spruce streets.
Begun 1893 from designs of Wilson Eyre, Jr., Frank Miles Day & Bro., and Cope & Stewardson.

Architectural rendering (water color) by Wilson Eyre, Jr. 8¼ by 24¼. Courtesy of the Fine Arts Library of the University of Pennsylvania.

Contemporary estimates of the University Museum appear in all the articles cited concerning Day, Eyre, and Cope & Stewardson as well as in Montgomery Schuyler's discussion of "The Architecture of American Colleges" (*The Architectural Record,* Sept. 1, 1910).

130
THE RACQUET CLUB OF PHILADELPHIA
215 South Sixteenth Street.
Built 1907 from designs of Horace Trumbauer (1868-1938).

Colored drawing by Joseph P. Sims (1890-1953). 10½ by 15. Courtesy of the Racquet Club of Philadelphia.

Trumbauer seems to have been the favorite of the Widener family; not only did he build their residence, "Lynwood Hall," in Elkins Park, but also the Widener Building on the site of the old Mint by Strickland and the Widener Memorial Library at Harvard University. He also achieved recognition as the architect of hotels; from his designs are: the St. James Hotel (Thirteenth and Walnut), the Adelphia Hotel (Thirteenth and Chestnut), the Benjamin Franklin Hotel (Ninth and Chestnut), the Ritz-Carlton Hotel (Broad and Walnut, altered in 1955 and now an office building), and the Château Crillon (west side of Rittenhouse Square). His also are the Public Ledger Building (Sixth and Chestnut), the addition to the Union League (Fifteenth and Sansom), the Jefferson Medical School and Hospital (Tenth and Walnut), the Hahnemann Medical School (Broad and Race) and the North Philadelphia Station of the Pennsylvania Railroad (Broad and Glenwood). In New York he designed the Evening Post and the Duveen and Wildenstein buildings. Duke University at Durham, North Carolina, has no less than twenty-six buildings by Trumbauer; in 1915 he was awarded an honorary M.A. degree by Harvard.

131
John Wanamaker Philadelphia Store
Thirteenth and Market streets.
Built 1902-10 from designs of Daniel Hudson Burnham (1846-1912).

Pencil drawing (1926) by Lester George Hornby (b.1882). 15½ by 21½. Courtesy of the John Wanamaker Philadelphia Store.

Burnham was born in Henderson, New York, and moved with his family to Chicago in 1855. Educated in Waltham, Massachusetts, he returned to Chicago in 1867 and worked there in the offices of several architectural firms, including Loring and Jenney. His

numerous works are scattered from London (Selfridge's Department Store, 1906) to the Philippine Islands (the plan of Baguio, the summer capital). The Wanamaker store was begun on Feb. 22, 1902, the Grand Depot being taken down and replaced a section at a time so that business could continue throughout the eight years required to erect the new structure. The first steel section of the new store was opened in March, 1906; the cornerstone laid in June, 1909; the building completed with appropriate ceremonies on June 11, 1910; and the entire store opened on Nov. 14, 1910. At that time it was said to be the largest building in the world devoted to retail merchandising (250 ft. by 480 ft., 247 ft. high above the sidewalk, and containing a floor area of 45 acres or 2 million square feet). The organ, brought from the Louisiana Purchase Exhibition of 1903 at St. Louis and then considered to be the largest in existence, was installed in 1911. On the Market Street side of the store is an "Egyptian Hall" with columns compared to Karnak, sphinxes, and other Egyptians motifs; and there is also a "Greek Room" with mahogany wainscot and peacock-pattern colored inlays in the pilasters (*Golden Book of the Wanamaker Stores,* Philadelphia, 1911).

132
Girard Trust Corn Exchange Bank
Northwest corner of Broad and Chestnut streets.
Built 1905-8 from designs of McKim, Mead & White.

Lithograph by Theo. B. White (b.1903). 17⅛ by 12½. Courtesy of the artist.

Charles Follen McKim (1847-1909) studied mining engineering at Harvard but was converted to architecture by Russell Sturgis with whom he began his apprenticeship. After having worked for a time in the office of H. H. Richardson, in 1878 he became a partner in the firm of McKim, Mead & Bigelow. McKim was always the leader of his firm, and to him are largely due the basic plans and structural designs of the buildings it produced. With Burnham he was a member of the McMillan Commission studying the plan of Washington, D.C., and one of the founders of the American Academy in Rome in 1895. William Rutherford Mead (1846-1928) graduated from Amherst in 1867, fell under the spell of Sturgis and spent a year traveling in Italy, before returning to New York and a career in architecture (Mead's contribution to the firm was mainly in the sphere of office management). Stanford White (1853-1906), after receiving an M.A. from New York University, traveled in Europe for two years, and later worked for Gambrill & Richardson. He replaced Bigelow in the firm in 1880 and twenty-six years later was shot by Harry K. Thaw while watching a play on the roof of Madison Square Garden. Important works of the firm include the Boston Public Library (1887), the Lowe Memorial Library at Columbia University (1895), and the Pennsylvania Railroad Station in New York (1910). Construction of the Girard Trust did not begin till 1905, although the bank's decision to build had been made in 1901. Allen Evans of the Philadelphia firm of Furness, Evans & Co. was supervisor in charge of construction. In 1922 the bank's expansion required an eight-story office structure adjacent on the north side, and to this, twenty-two more floors were added in 1930. This building is also the work of the firm of McKim, Mead & White, which continues to practice today under the same name.

Rendering, 1917, by Jacques Gréber. $4^{11}\!/_{16}$ by $22^{11}\!/_{16}$. Published by the Fairmount Park Art Association in *The Fairmount Parkway*, Philadelphia, 1919.

Also involved in the plans for the Parkway, besides Wilson Eyre, Paul P. Cret, and Jacques Gréber, were Albert Kelsey, Charles E. Dana, Clarence C. Zantzinger, Charles L. Borie, Jr., Horace Trumbauer, Milton B. Medary, Jr., George S. Webster, Benjamin A. Haldeman, and others. Information on the history of this design may be found in *The Proposed Parkway for Philadelphia* (Albert Kelsey [ed.], Philadelphia, 1902) and in the *Annual Reports* (1903 ff.) published by the Fairmount Park Art Association. Exhibited in the first municipal city planning exhibition in America at City Hall, May 15 to June 15, 1911, were studies of the Parkway by Horace Trumbauer, Clarence C. Zantzinger, and Paul P. Cret, studies of City Hall Plaza (now Reyburn Plaza) and designs for the Franklin Institute by John T. Windrim, and drawings of the museum by Brite and Bacon. A model of the Parkway design in one of its earlier stages was also exhibited in Leipzig, Germany, in 1913. Logan Square, which seems to have been among the knottiest problems in the history of the design, had previously been important as the site of the great fair held by the Sanitary Commission in the early summer of 1864 for the benefit of the soldiers and sailors of the Union forces. The proceeds of the fair exceeded a million dollars, and the temporary buildings were used for a short time thereafter as barracks for three thousand convalescent soldiers from military hospitals in the city.

133
PLAN OF THE BENJAMIN FRANKLIN PARKWAY
Begun 1917 from designs of Jacques Auguste Henri Gréber (b.1882).

134
FEDERAL RESERVE BANK OF PHILADELPHIA
Northeast corner of Tenth and Chestnut streets.

Built 1932-34 from the designs of Paul P. Cret (1876-1945).

Architectural rendering (pencil) by William H. Livingston (b.1898). 20⅝ by 32. Courtesy of Harbeson, Hough, Livingston & Larson.

The design of the Federal Reserve Bank was made in expectation of the addition of another floor, added in 1951. An older building to the east was to have remained intact, but with a new façade. In 1940 Cret demolished this and added a wing with a garden, immediately to the right of the elevation shown here. William H. Livingston was the partner in the firm of Paul P. Cret who was in charge of the design of the Federal Reserve Bank in Philadelphia. Two other buildings for the Federal Reserve by Cret are the Bank in Boston and the Federal Reserve Board building in Washington, D.C. (1935-37). The long list of Cret's works includes the Folger Memorial Shakespeare Library (Washington, D.C., 1930), the Detroit Institute of Arts (Detroit, Michigan, 1922, with Zantzinger, Borie & Medary), the Hall of Science at the Century of Progress (Chicago, 1933), Bancroft Hall and the Chapel at the Naval Academy (Annapolis, Maryland), and several battle monuments to the American dead of World War I in Europe and the United States. As a consultant for the University of Texas, he seems to have been responsible, at least in part, for as many as fourteen of the academic buildings there. Articles on Cret may be found in *Architecture* (May, 1931) and *Pencil Points* (October, 1938). In "Ten Years of Modernism" (*Architectural Forum*, August, 1933), Cret sets forth his own theories of architecture.

135
DELAWARE RIVER (NOW BENJAMIN FRANKLIN) BRIDGE

Approach beginning at Sixth Street between Race and Vine. Erected 1920-26 from designs of Paul P. Cret (1876-1945), architect, and Ralph Modjeski (1861-1940), chief engineer.

Architectural rendering by Paul P. Cret. 13¼ by 61⅛. Courtesy of the Delaware River Port Authority.

The study of the several sites proposed for the Delaware River Bridge entailed one of the first traffic surveys in America. The Bridge cost upwards of $25 million and has a total length of just under two miles; the foundations are sunk to bed rock 105 ft. below mean water level, and the towers stand 380 ft. above it (*Report to the Delaware River Bridge Joint Commission*, Philadelphia, 1921). The roadway, suspended 135 ft. above the water by 25,000 miles of steel wire, consisted originally of a pavement 57 ft. wide for vehicular traffic, four railway tracks, and two walkways, and measured a total of 128 ft.; granite and concrete masonry totaled 315,000 cu. yds. (Wilbur J. Watson, *Bridge Architecture*, New York, 1927). Widening of the pavement in 1948 eliminated two of the railway tracks and the flagpoles on pedestals, two of which stood at the beginning of either approach. These were topped by figures of alighting victories sculptured by Leon Hermant, now stored under the Philadelphia approach to the bridge. William J. H. Hough was the partner in the firm in charge of the design of the Delaware River Bridge. Other bridges by the firm of Paul P. Cret are the Henry Avenue Bridge over the Wissahickon in Philadelphia (1930), and the Klingle Valley (1931) and Calvert Street (1933) bridges in Washington, D.C. As a consultant for the office of the U.S. Army Engineer at Pittsburgh, Cret had a part in the design of the Emsworth and Montgomery dams on the Ohio River and the Tygart River Reservoir Dam in West Virginia.

136
PHILADELPHIA SAVING FUND SOCIETY BUILDING
Southwest corner of Twelfth and Market streets.
Built 1930-32 from designs of Howe & Lescaze.

Architectural rendering by George A. Newman. 21½ by 9½. Courtesy of the Philadelphia Saving Fund Society.

"With George Howe, dying a few weeks ago at Philadelphia, not only has gone the author of the finest skyscraper in America, the dean of the Yale University School of Architecture, the man who, directing the Public Federal Works Agency in 1942, has turned American official architecture toward the modern style; but with his death America loses much more—the only humanistic figure of the architectural scene"; these are the words of the Italian architect Bruno Zevi whose tribute to George Howe (1886-1955) was published in the *Journal of the American Institute of Architects* (October, 1955). Works of Howe before 1928 include houses, branch banks for PSFS, and the Memorial Chapel at Bony, France (1926), pictured in the *Monograph of the Works of Mellor, Meigs & Howe* (New York, 1923) and *U. S. A. Tomorrow* (October, 1954). Buildings by the firm of Howe & Lescaze (terminated in 1934) include the Oak Lane Country Day School (1929) and other schools and residences. During World War II, Howe was associated with Oskar Stonorov and Louis I. Kahn in the field of housing. One of Howe's last buildings, designed in collaboration with Robert Montgomery Brown (b.1908) was the WCAU Radio and TV Broadcasting Station (City Line Avenue, 1952). William Lescaze, born in Geneva, Switzerland,

in 1896, continues to practice in New York. In 1939 he won the Silver Medal of the A. I. A. for the Swiss Pavilion at the New York World's Fair, and more recent works include the Longfellow Building, Washington, D.C. (1941) the Calderone Theater, Hempstead, Long Island (1949), Temple University School of Fine Arts (1955), and 711 Third Ave., New York City (1956). The PSFS Building was one of the first large buildings in America to be air-conditioned throughout and was also one of the first to use the then relatively new material, stainless steel, on a large scale. Included in the contract for the PSFS Building was the three-level garage still standing at Twelfth and Filbert streets and intended for the use of the employees and tenants. The PSFS Building was first published in the *Architectural Forum* (December, 1932), and a "Re-Appraisal" by Frederick Gutheim appeared seventeen years later in the *Architectural Record* (October, 1949). The publication in connection with the architectural exhibition at the Museum of Modern Art referred to in the text was *The International Style: Architecture Since 1922* by Henry-Russell Hitchcock and Philip Johnson (New York, 1932).

137
CARL MACKLEY HOUSES
M and Bristol streets, Juniata Park.
Built 1933-34 from designs of Oskar Stonorov (b.1905) and Alfred Kastner; constructed under the direction of W. Pope Barney, architect.

Isometric drawing by the architects. 5⅝ by 5⅞. Courtesy of Oskar Stonorov.

Stonorov was born in Frankfurt, Germany, and while a student in Europe worked with the sculptor Aristide Maillol and the architect

André Lurçat. Active principally in the field of city planning and housing, Stonorov was an early member of C.I.A.M. and was associated with some of the first publications of Le Corbusier. He is currently occupied with a project for the redevelopment of downtown Newark, New Jersey, and another design, primarily residential in character, is soon to be built in the neighborhood of Fourth and Carpenter streets in Philadelphia. The Carl Mackley Houses contain 272 apartments: 80 of two and one-half rooms (living room, bedroom, kitchenette, and bath), 120 of four rooms (living room, two bedrooms, kitchen, and bath), and 72 of five rooms (living room, three bedrooms, kitchen, and bath). The apartments originally rented for $22.50, $36, and $45 per month. The development was authorized under Public Works Administration Housing Project Number One, 1933.

138
MERCANTILE LIBRARY
1021 Chestnut Street.
Built 1953 from designs of Martin, Stewart & Noble.

Architectural rendering (water color) by Earle D. Oakes (b.1923). 13½ by 22. Courtesy of the Free Library of Philadelphia.

The firm of Martin, Stewart & Noble is currently in charge of the renovation of the Academy of Music (work begun 1957) and in 1958 designed the new Psychiatric Unit for the Pennsylvania Hospital. In 1944 the trustees of the Mercantile Library elected to become a part of the Free Library of Philadelphia and in 1952 an agreement was made with the Philadelphia Parking Authority whereby the old Franklin Market Building (see Note 69) was exchanged for the Chestnut Street site (35 ft. by 163 ft.) and $350,000 wherewith to

erect a new branch library. Robert W. Noble was the partner in charge of the design of the Mercantile Branch of the Free Library. His building won the Bronze Medal of the Philadelphia Chapter of the A.I.A. for "outstanding attainment in architectural design" and the Award of Merit of the National Committee of Honor Awards of the A.I.A. It was published in the *Architectural Forum* for August, 1954. As a result of the success of the Mercantile Library, Martin, Stewart & Noble have built other branches in the areas of Kensington, West Oak Lane, and Wadsworth, based on the same theory of "selling" reading.

139
LANKENAU HOSPITAL AND HEALTH CENTER
Lancaster Avenue, Overbrook, Pennsylvania.
Built 1953-59 from designs of Vincent G. Kling (b.1916).

Architectural rendering (tempera) by Robert E. Schwarz. 16 by 42. Courtesy of the architect.

Lankenau Hospital won the A.I.A. Honor Award in Hospital Architecture in 1954. It has been published in the *Architectural Forum* (August, 1951), *Progressive Architecture* (December, 1954), and the *Bulletin of the American Institute of Architects* (July-August, 1954). Other works of Vincent Kling include the Kissam Lane Elementary School (Glen Head, New York, 1956), the Transportation Center Building on Penn Center Plaza (Philadelphia, 1957), Christ Chapel at the Episcopal Academy (1959), and the U.S. Embassy Office Building at Quito, Ecuador (1960). Kling's designs have been exhibited at the Museum of Modern Art (1944) and at the National Gallery (One Hundred Years of American Architecture [1957], sponsored by the A.I.A. in commemoration of its centennial).

140
PENNSYLVANIA STATE OFFICE BUILDING
Broad and Spring Garden streets.
Completed in 1958 from designs of Carroll, Grisdale & Van Alen; Harbeson, Hough, Livingston & Larson; and Nolen & Swinburne.

Architectural rendering (tempera) by Emil F. Kempa. 30 by 36. Courtesy of the architects.

The firm of Carroll, Grisdale & Van Alen is represented in Philadelphia by a number of buildings, including the Philadelphia International Airport Terminal (1952), the Youth Study Center on the Parkway at Twentieth Street (1949), and the Law School dormitories at the University of Pennsylvania (1958). Harbeson, Hough, Livingston & Larson continue the work associated with their names when they were the partners of Paul Cret, particularly in the field of government buildings (e.g., the House Office Building now under construction in Washington, D.C.) and the architectural treatment of major engineering works (e.g., the new Walt Whitman Bridge and the Turnpike Bridge over the Delaware northeast of Philadelphia). Theirs also is the new general plan of the Philadelphia Zoo and such structures there as the Lion and Tiger Grotto and the Pachyderm House. Nolen & Swinburne is most noted for its work in academic building, particularly the plan of Temple University, begun in 1955. The Dormitory there won an award for an outstanding proposed building from the Philadelphia Chapter of the A.I.A., as did the Gwynedd Junior College Library (1959). Nolen & Swinburne's most recent work is the La Salle College Science Building (1960).

141
GARDEN OF THE PENNSYLVANIA STATE OFFICE BUILDING
Broad and Spring Garden streets.
Executed in 1958 from designs of Ian L. McHarg (b.1920).

Architectural rendering (tempera) by Emil F. Kempa. 30 by 36. Courtesy of the architects.

McHarg, a native of Scotland who saw service in the British Army for seven years during World War II, was educated in landscape architecture and city planning at Harvard. After four years of teaching and government service in a planning capacity in Scotland, he returned to the United States in 1954 and has recently become an American citizen. He is the author of a number of articles published in such professional journals as the *Architectural Record* (September, 1957), *Landscape Architecture* (Fall, 1957), the *Journal of the Institute of Landscape Architects* (February, 1958), and *Architects' Year Book* (Nos. 6 and 8). Another major urban garden design by McHarg is to be found at the University of Pennsylvania adjacent to Dietrich Hall.

142
EXTENSION OF THE MOORE SCHOOL OF ELECTRICAL ENGINEERING, UNIVERSITY OF PENNSYLVANIA
Southwest corner of Thirty-third and Walnut streets.
Built 1958 from designs of Geddes, Brecher, Qualls & Cunningham.

Architectural rendering (tempera) by Emil F. Kempa. 20¼ by 37⅝. Courtesy of the architects.

Geddes, Brecher, Qualls & Cunningham, established within the past decade, is a firm of young men. Two of its members, Geddes and Qualls, are on the faculty of the Department of Architecture at the University of Pennsylvania. Although the firm has not as yet many constructed buildings to its credit, the outstanding quality of its architectural designs has been amply recognized by the twelve prizes already awarded it. The extension to the Moore School of Electrical Engineering has won not only the First Honor Award from the A.I.A. on the national level but also the Silver Medal from the Pennsylvania Society of Architects and the Gold Medal from the Philadelphia Chapter of the A.I.A. The design of the F. J. Cooper Jewelry Store at 1416 Chestnut St. (1959) has won the Benjamin Franklin Medal of the local chapter of the A.I.A.; and in the international competition for the design of the National Opera House at Sydney, Australia (1955), the firm (and its collaborators) took second prize. Currently under construction is the startling curvilinear design for the Police Administration Building at Eighth and Race streets.

143
SECTION, EXTENSION OF THE MOORE SCHOOL OF ELECTRICAL ENGINEERING
See Note 142.

Longitudinal section by the architects. Courtesy of the architects.

The extension of the Moore School has been published in the *Architectural Forum* (March, 1959) and the *Architectural Record* (August, 1957).

144
WASHINGTON SQUARE EAST URBAN RENEWAL, EASTERN SECTION
Apartment Houses to be located at Second and Dock streets.
Designed by I. M. Pei & Associates, 1958.

Architectural rendering (tempera) by Robert E. Schwarz. 18 by 35. Courtesy of the Philadelphia City Planning Commission.

Ieoh Ming Pei (b.1917) was born in Canton, China, the son of a Shanghai banker. He came to the United States in 1935 to study architecture at the Massachusetts Institute of Technology, from which he was graduated in 1939. He has taught at Harvard and been associated with William Zeckendorf's firm of Webb & Knapp. For Zeckendorf he designed the Mile High Center at Denver, Colorado, and buildings in Pittsburgh, Washington, Chicago, and New York. The most recent design of his own firm (established 1955) is the new Earth Sciences Building (to be completed in 1962) for M.I.T. The history of the efforts to preserve and restore the area around Independence Hall, which ultimately led to the creation of the Mall, the National Park, and the Society Hill development, is reviewed by Charles E. Peterson in the *Annual Report* of the Fairmount Park Art Association for 1952.

145
ALFRED NEWTON RICHARDS MEDICAL RESEARCH BUILDING
Hamilton Walk, University of Pennsylvania. Built 1959-60 from designs of Louis I. Kahn. (b.1901).

Drawing (pencil), 1960, by Louis I. Kahn. 14⅞ by 13⅝. Courtesy of the architect.

Born in Estonia, the son of a stained-glass worker, Kahn came to the United States in 1906. Although he showed great promise as a painter, he elected to study architecture at the University of Pennsylvania, graduating in 1924. One of his first commissions after grad-

206

uation was as chief designer of the Sesquicentennial Exposition held in Philadelphia in 1926 (*Greater Philadelphia Magazine,* September, 1960); later he worked in the offices of Paul P. Cret and Zantzinger, Borie & Medary. Having taught also at the Massachusetts Institute of Technology and at Yale, Kahn is now Professor of Architecture at the University of Pennsylvania. Among the more important buildings erected from his designs are the Yale Art Gallery at New Haven, Connecticut (1955), and the A. F. of L. Medical Center in Philadelphia (Broad and Vine streets, 1957-58). His work has been the subject of articles in *Perspecta* (Fall, 1957) and the Italian publication *Casa Bella* (July, 1960). The Richards Medical Research Building has been published in the *Architectural Record* (September, 1959, and August, 1960) as well as in the *Architectural Forum* (July, 1960). In May, 1960, Eero Saarinen presented to Kahn the Brunner Award of the National Institute of Arts and Letters, which cited him as "a man who has used his superior gifts to tread the hard path of discovery rather than the easy way to Success" (*Time,* June 6, 1960).

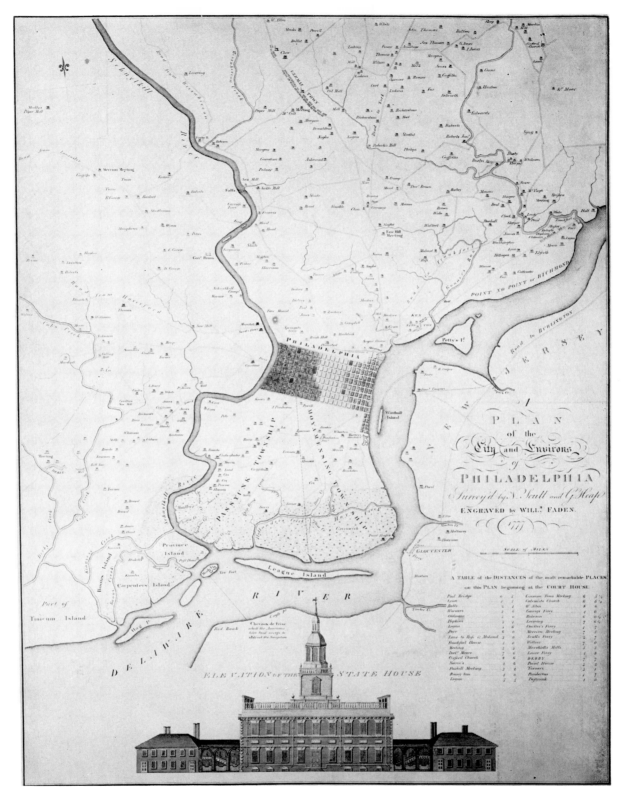

1. Map of the City and Environs of Philadelphia with a View of the State House. Scull and Heap. 1777.

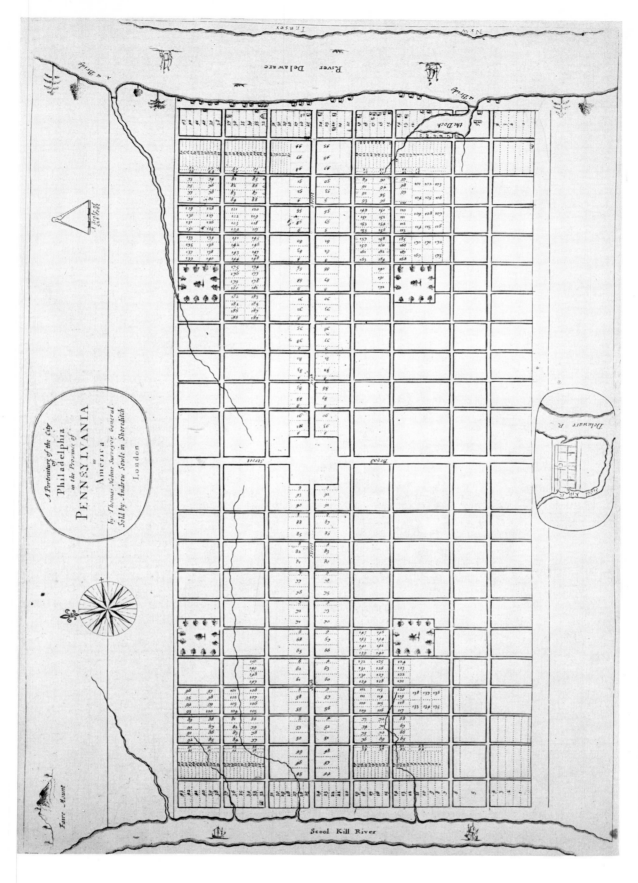

2. Plan of Philadelphia. Thomas Holme. 1682.

3. Joshua Carpenter's House. Built between 1701 and 1722; demolished 1826.

4. Slate Roof House. James Porteus. Built between 1687 and 1699; demolished 1867.

5. Detail of the House of Count Valerio Chiericato, Vicenza, Italy.
Andrea Palladio. Second half of the 16th century.

6. Letitia Street House, now in Fairmount Park. Built between 1703 and 1715.

7. Benezet (or Breintnall) House. Built *c*.1700; demolished 1818.

. Greater Meeting House and Town Hall. Southwest corner of Second and Market streets. Greater Meeting House (on left) built 1755; demolished in early 19th century; Town Hall (on right) built 1707-10; demolished 1837.

9. Old Swedes' Church (Gloria Dei). 1698-1700.

10. Southeast Prospect of the City of Philadelphia. Peter Cooper. *c.*1720.

11. Christ Church. 1727-44. Steeple 1754.

12. St. Peter's Church from the Northeast. Robert Smith. 1758-61.

13. Zion Lutheran Church. Robert Smith. Built 1766-69; demolished 1869.

14. Samuel Neave and James Abercrombie Houses. *c.*1759.

15. Conjectural Restoration of the Entrance to Franklin Court. Built 1788 and now much altered

16. Mount Pleasant, East Fairmount Park. 1761.

17. Cliveden, Germantown. 1764.

18. Front Hall of Cliveden, Germantown. 1764.

19. Stenton, Germantown. 1728-34.

20. Carpenters' Hall. Robert Smith. 1770-75.

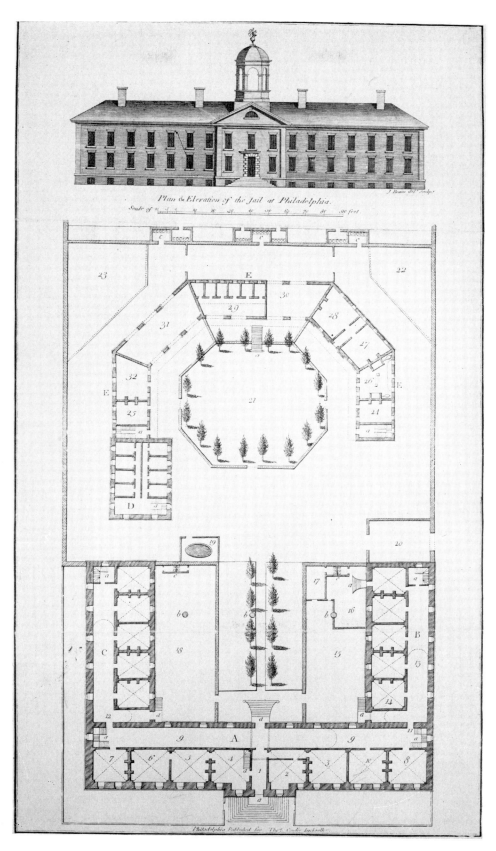

Plan & Elevation of the Jail at Philadelphia.

21. Walnut Street Jail. Robert Smith. Built 1773-76; demolished c.1835.

22. State House (*c.*1730-48) with Supreme Court Building (1790-91) on the East and Congress Hall (1787-89) on the West.

23. First Presbyterian Church. John Trumbull(?). Built 1793-94; demolished c.1822.

24. The Woodlands, West Philadelphia. Built *c*.1742; enlarged 1788.

25. Lansdowne, West Fairmount Park. Built *c.*1773: burned 1854.

26. Library Hall. William Thornton. Built 1789-90; demolished 1884.

27. House of William Bingham. Built *c.*1788; burned 1823.

28. Cooke's Building. Built *c*.1792; demolished *c*.1838.

29. Lemon Hill. Built *c.*1770; remodeled (or rebuilt) *c.*1799.

30. House of Robert Morris. Major Pierre Charles L'Enfant. Begun *c*.1794; demolished *c*.1800.

31. President's House. Built 1792-97; demolished *c*.1829.

32. Headhouse, New Market, *c*.1805.

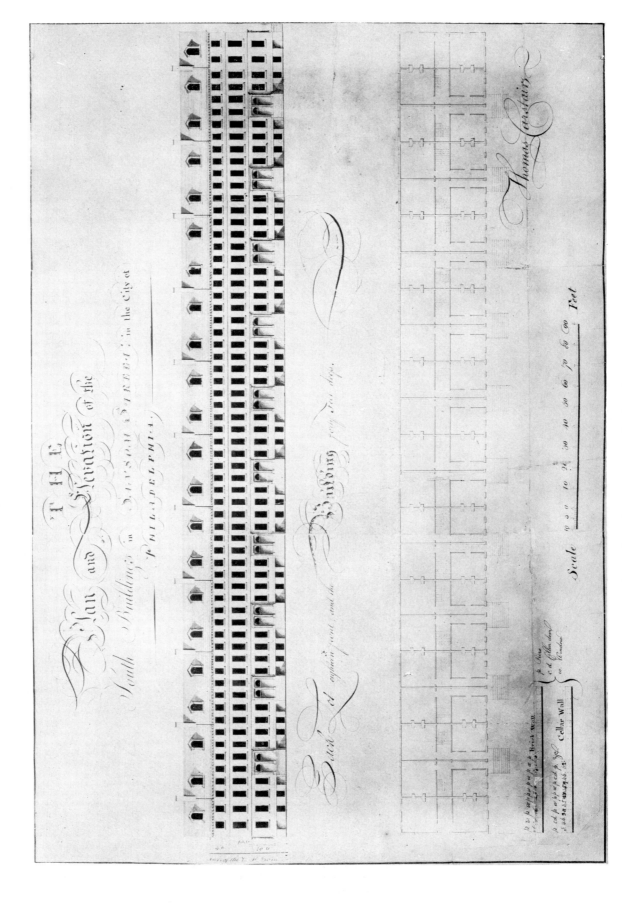

33. Plan and Elevation of Row Houses. Thomas Carstairs. Built c.1801-3; now greatly altered.

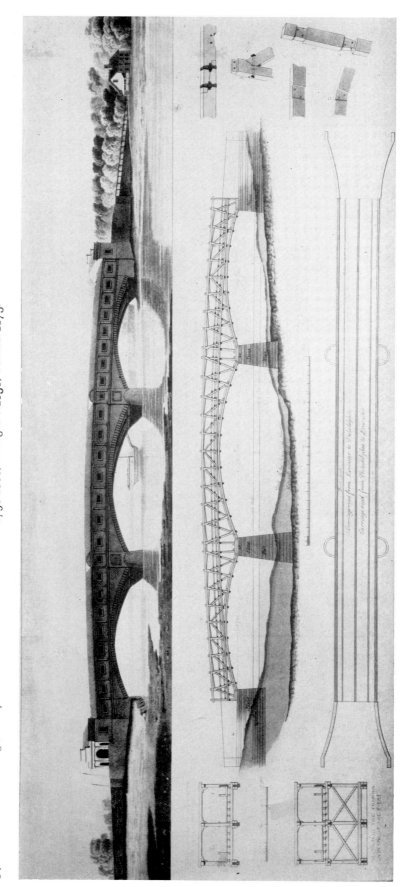

34. The Permanent Bridge, Schuylkill River at Market Street. Built 1798-1806; enlarged c.1850; burned 1875.

35. The Pennsylvania Hospital from the Southeast. East wing built *c.*1755 from designs of Samuel Rhoads; west wing built *c.*1796; center section added 1794-1805 from designs of David Evans, Jr.

36. View of Philadelphia from the New Jersey Shore. J. L. Boqueta De Woiseri; c.1810.

37. The Pennsylvania Academy of the Fine Arts. John Dorsey. Built 1805-6; burned 1845.

38. The Pennsylvania Academy of the Fine Arts. Richard A. Gilpin. Restored and enlarged 1846-47; demolished 1870.

39. Orphan Asylum. Built 1817; burned 1822.

40. Pump House, Center Square. Benjamin Henry Latrobe. Built 1799-1801; demolished 1827-28.

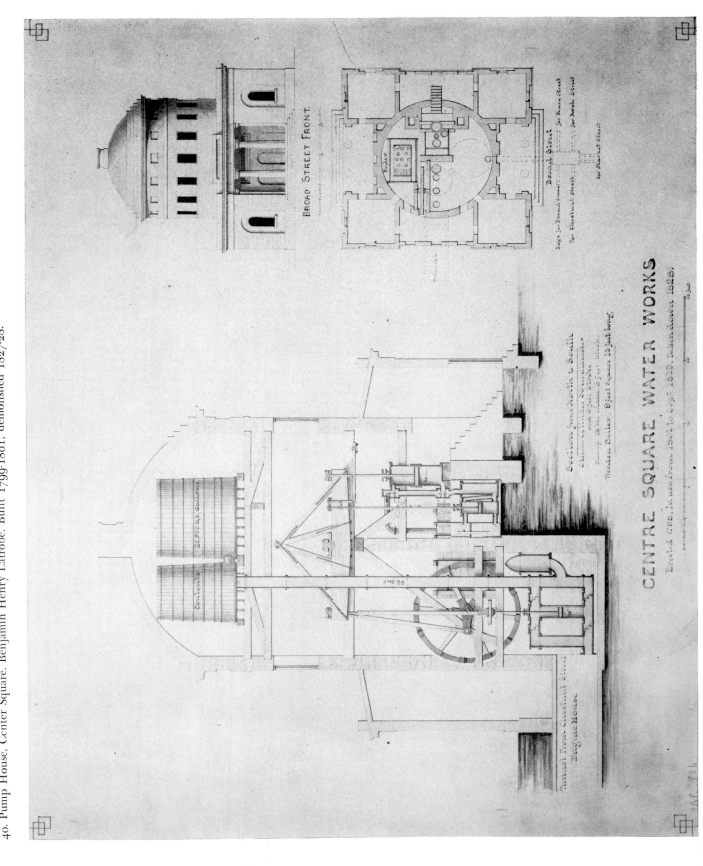

BROAD STREET FRONT.

CENTRE SQUARE WATER WORKS

Erected 1799, in use from 1801 to Sept. 1815. taken down 1828.

Section from North to South
Shewing rotary Steam engine
and Eight horse
Pump also main 6 feet Stroke
Wooden Boiler 9 feet Square 15 feet long

41. View of Center (Penn) Square, showing B. H. Latrobe's Pump House and William Rush's Fountain. *c.*1812.

42. Bank of Pennsylvania. Benjamin Henry Latrobe. Built 1798-1801; demolished 1871(?).

44. Ionic Capital of North Porch of the Erectheum, Athens, Greece. From Stuart and Revett's *Antiquities of Athens*.

43. Ionic Capital of the Bank of Pennsylvania.

45. House of Edward Shippen Burd. Benjamin Henry Latrobe. Built 1801-2; demolished *c.*1865.

46. First Chestnut Street Theater. Built 1791-94; remodeled 1801 by B. H. Latrobe; burned 1820.

47. Second Chestnut Street Theater. William Strickland. Built 1820-22; demolished 1856.

48. Arch Street Theater. William Strickland. Built 1826-28; demolished 1936.

49. Walnut Street Theater. Built 1809; remodeled 1828 by John Haviland.

50. Fairmount Bridge (The Colossus). Louis Wernwag, engineer, and Robert Mills, architect. Erected 1809-12; burned 1838.

51. Wire Suspension Bridge, Schuylkill River near Fairmount. Col. Charles Ellet, Jr. Opened 1842; demolished 1874.

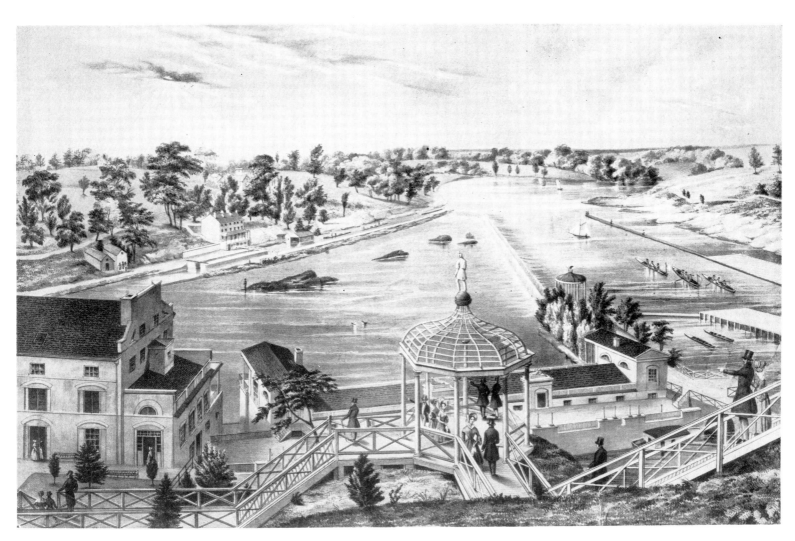

52. Fairmount (Schuylkill) Waterworks from the Mount. Frederick C. Graff. 1812-22.

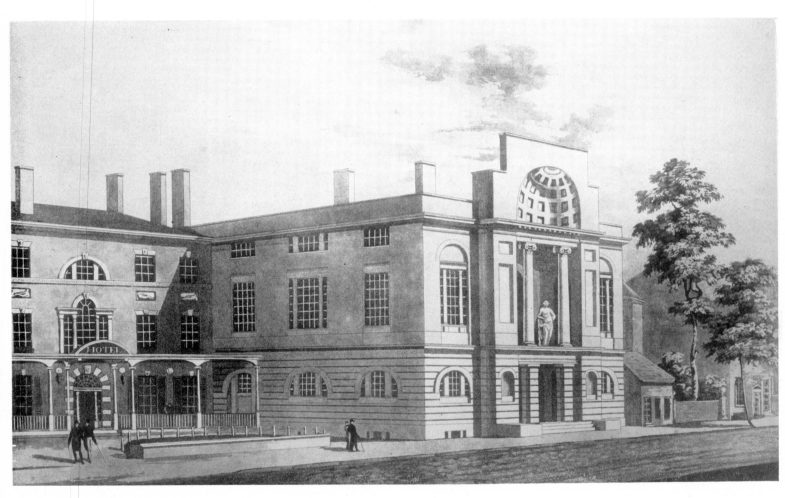

53. Washington Hall. Robert Mills. Completed 1816; burned 1823.

54. Second Bank of the United States. William Strickland. 1818-24.

55. The Parthenon, Athens, Greece, from Stuart and Revett's *Antiquities of Athens.*

56. Naval Asylum (U.S. Naval Home, after 1879). William Strickland. 1827-33.

57. First Congregational Unitarian Church. William Strickland. Built 1828; demolished 1885.

58. United States Mint. William Strickland. Built 1829-33; demolished 1902.

59. Philadelphia (Merchants') Exchange (at left). William Strickland. 1832-34. Bank of the United States (in background). Samuel Blodgett, Jr. 1795-97

60. University of Pennsylvania. William Strickland. Built 1829; demolished c.1874.

61. First Presbyterian Church, Washington Square. John Haviland. Built 1820-22; demolished 1939.

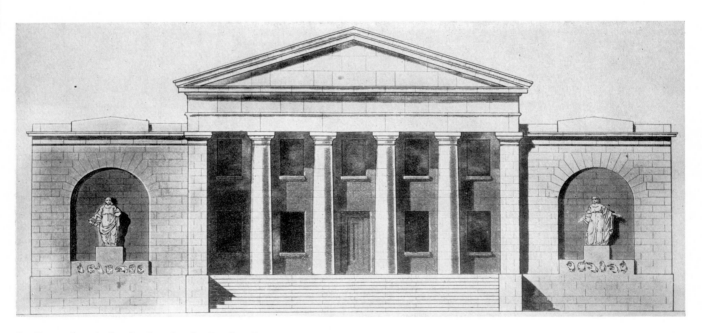

62. Pennsylvania Institution for the Deaf and Dumb (now the Philadelphia Museum College of Art). John Haviland. 1824-25.

63. Philadelphia Arcade. John Haviland. Built 1826-27; demolished 1863.

64. Colonnade Row. John Haviland. Built 1830; partially destroyed 1868 to make way for the Colonnade Hotel (1869-1925).

65. Residence of Charles Blight. John Haviland. Built 1828; no longer standing.

66. Powelton, West Philadelphia. Built *c.*1830 (?); demolished 1885.

67. Girard College. Thomas U. Walter, 1833-47.

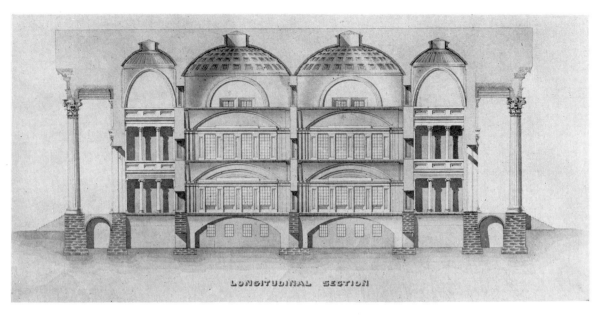

68. Longitudinal Section, Founder's Hall, Girard College. Thomas U. Walter. 1833-47.

69. Mercantile Library. William L. Johnston. Built 1844-45; demolished c.1925.

70. First Reformed Dutch Church. Stephen D. Button. Built 1853-55; no longer standing.

71. Sedgeley. Benjamin Henry Latrobe. Built 1799; demolished 1857.

72. Dorsey's Gothic Mansion. John Dorsey. Built *c.*1810; remodeled 1853.

73. The Philadelphia Bank. Benjamin Henry Latrobe. Built 1807-8; demolished 1836.

74. Masonic Hall. William Strickland. Built 1808-11; tower and interior burned 1819; demolished 1853.

75. New Masonic Hall. Sloan & Stewart. Built 1853-55; burned 1886.

76. Grand Lodge Room, New Masonic Hall. c.1855.

77. Eastern State Penitentiary. John Haviland. Built 1823-36.

78. Philadelphia County Prison, Moyamensing. Thomas U. Walter. 1832-35.

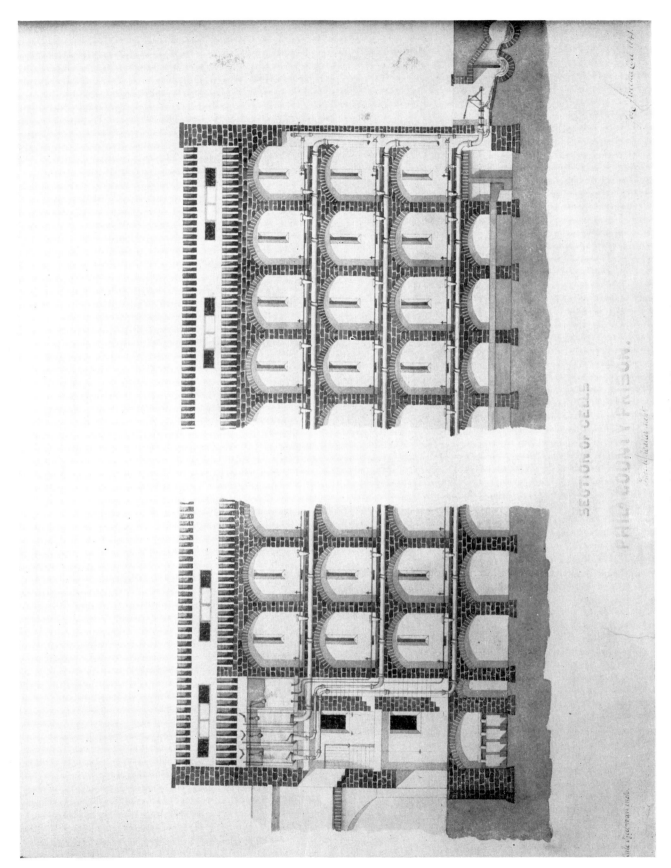

SECTION OF CELLS

PHILA COUNTY PRISON.

79. Section of Cells, Philadelphia County Prison. Thomas U. Walter. 1832–35.

80. Residence of Turner Camac. Built *c.*1825; demolished 1870.

81. St. Stephen's Episcopal Church. William Strickland. 1822-23.

SOUTH FLANK LOCUST STREET.

155 feet

82. St. Mark's Church. Erected under supervision of John Notman. 1848-51.

83. Floating Church of the Redeemer. Clement L. Dennington. Built 1849; burned 1868.

84. Jayne Building. William L. Johnston; completed by Thomas U. Walter. Built 1849-50; demolished 1958.

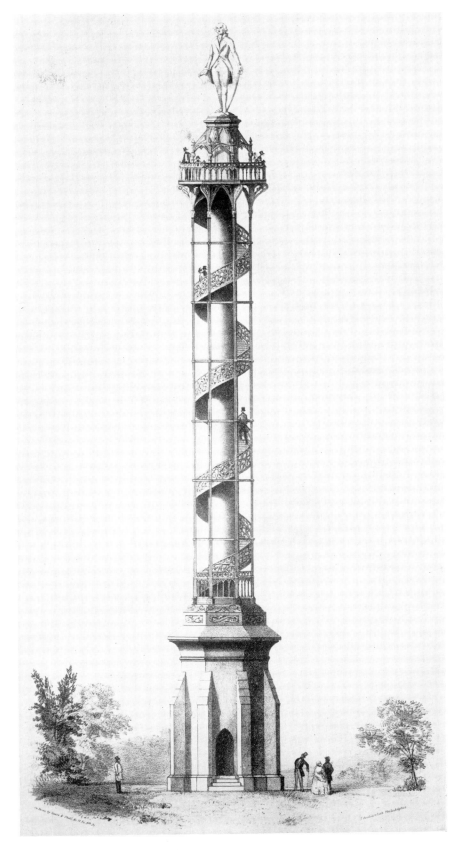

85. Standpipe of the West Philadelphia Waterworks. Birkinbine & Trotter.
Built *c.*1855; demolished *c.*1870.

86. Northern Liberties and Spring Garden Waterworks. Built 1845; no longer standing.

87. Laurel Hill Cemetery. John Notman. 1836.

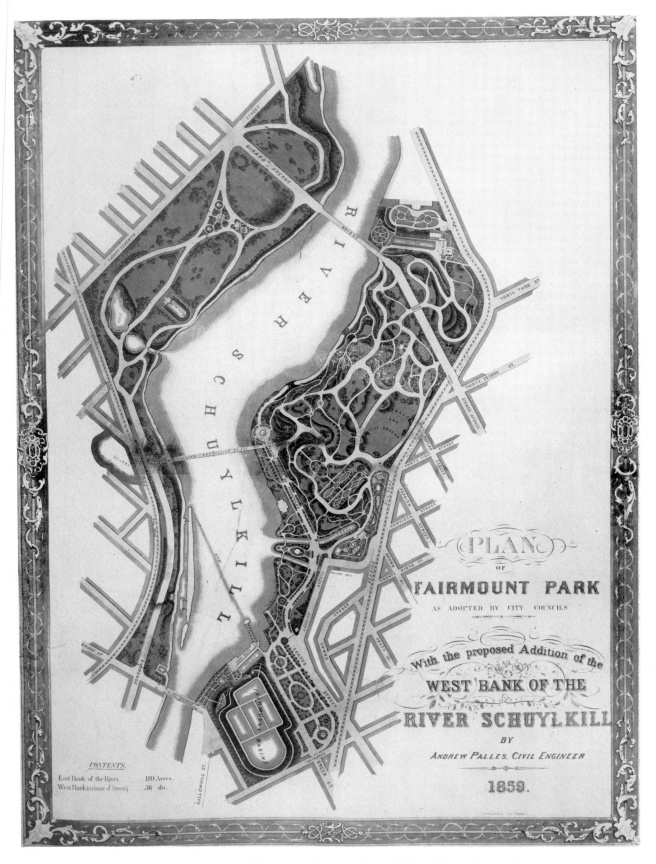

88. Proposed Design of Fairmount Park. Andrew Palles, civil engineer. 1859.

89. Pagoda and Labyrinth Garden. John Haviland. Built 1828; demolished shortly thereafter.

90. Interior of the Chinese Museum. Isaac Holden. Built *c*.1836-38; burned 1854.

91. The Athenaeum of Philadelphia. John Notman. 1845-47.

92. A Symmetrical Italian Villa. From Samuel Sloan's *The Model Architect, c.*1850.

93. Bartram Hall, Residence of Andrew M. Eastwick. Sloan & Stewart. Built 1851; demolished *c.*1895.

94. Joseph Harrison House. Samuel Sloan. Built 1855-57; demolished 1925.

95. Roman Catholic Cathedral of SS. Peter and Paul. 1846-64.

96. Proposed Façade for the Academy of Music. Napoleon LeBrun and Gustav Runge. 1855-57.

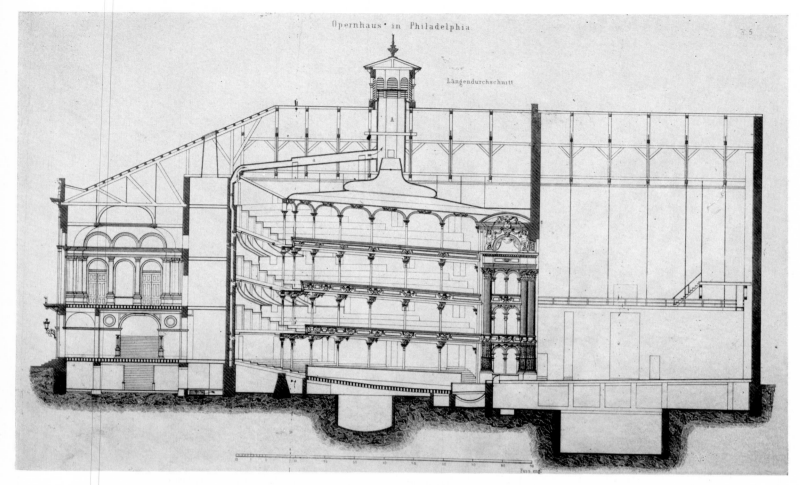

97. Longitudinal Section, Academy of Music. Napoleon LeBrun and Gustav Runge. 1855-57.

98. West Arch Street Presbyterian Church. Joseph C. Hoxie. 1850-55.

99. Department for Males, Pennsylvania Hospital for the Insane. Samuel Sloan. Built 1856-59; demolished 1959.

100. Store of Dale, Ross & Withers. Stephen D. Button. Built *c*.1857; demolished *c*.1955 (?).

101. Charles Oakford's Model Hat Store. Occupied by Oakford 1854-60.

102. Continental Hotel. John McArthur, Jr. Built 1857-60; demolished 1923-24.

103. Business Exchange and Lobby of the Continental Hotel. John McArthur, Jr. Built 1857-60; demolished 1923-24.

104. Sectional Floating Dry Dock. *c.*1855.

105. *Panoramic View of Philadelphia. c.*1855.

106. Rodeph Shalom Synagogue. Fraser, Furness & Hewitt. Built 1869; demolished 1925.

107. College Hall, University of Pennsylvania. Thomas W. Richards. 1870-72.

108. Independence Hall in 1876 with the building of the Philosophical Society on the left and the Ledger Building in the background on the right.

109. Interior of the East (Assembly) Room of Independence Hall in 1856.

110. Girard Avenue Bridge. Henry A. and James P. Sims, architects; Thomas C. Clark, engineer. 1872-74.

111. Balloon View of the Centennial Grounds. 1876.

112. Masonic Temple. James H. Windrim. 1868-73.

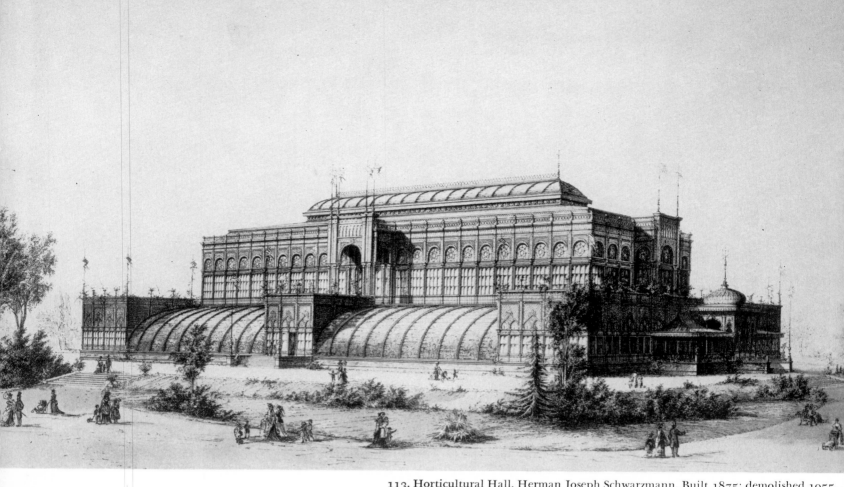

113. Horticultural Hall. Herman Joseph Schwarzmann. Built 1875: demolished 1955.

114. Wanamaker's Grand Depot. Remodeled 1876; demolished 1902.

115. David Jayne Residence. John McArthur, Jr. Built 1865-66; demolished 1922.

116. United States Post Office and Federal Building. Built 1873-84; demolished *c.*1935.

117. Philadelphia City Hall. John McArthur, Jr. 1871-81.

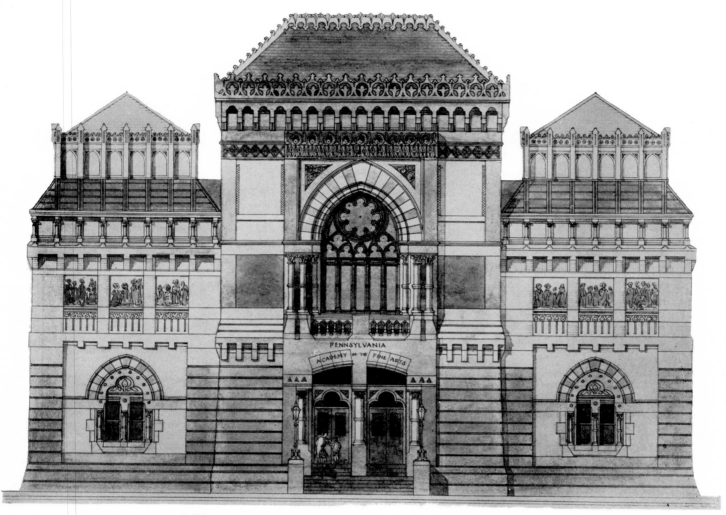

118. The Pennsylvania Academy of the Fine Arts. Frank Furness. 1872-76.

119. "Bank Row," North Side of Chestnut between Fourth and Fifth streets.

120. The Library Company of Philadelphia. Frank Furness. Built 1878-80; demolished 1940.

121. Broad Street Station. Unexecuted design by Furness, Evans & Co. for addition to earlier building (opened 1882) by Wilson Bros. & Co.

122. The Girard Life Insurance, Annuity and Trust Co. Addison Hutton. Built 1888-89; demolished 1926.

123. Drexel Building. Wilson Bros. & Co. Built 1885; enlarged 1887-89; demolished 1955.

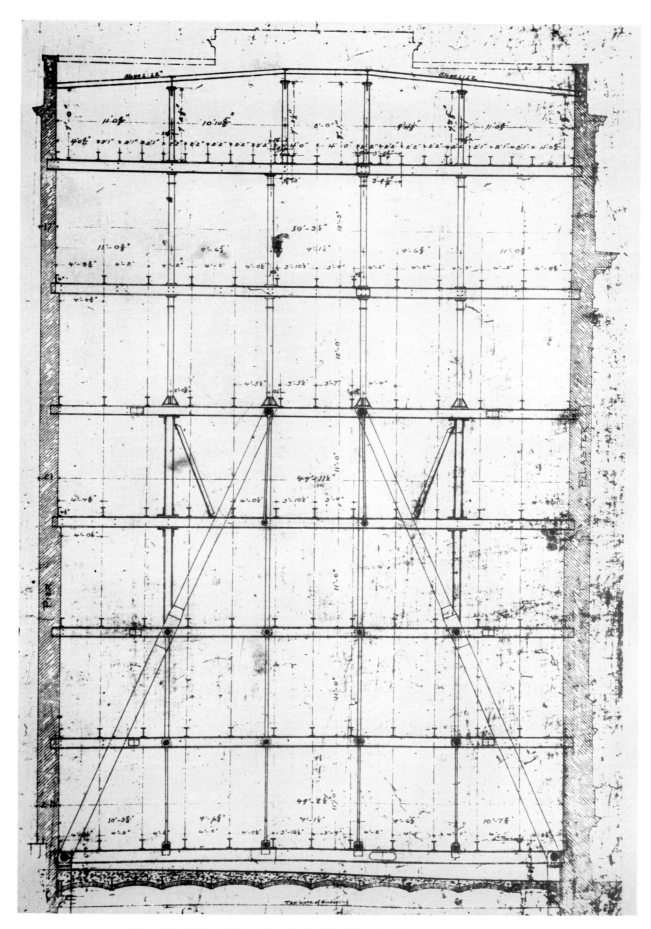

124. Drexel Building. Wilson Bros. & Co. Working drawing showing A-frame. *c.*1887.

125. Bingham House. Built *c.*1876; altered 1890 from designs of Willis G. Hale; demolished 1926.

126. Horticultural Hall. Frank Miles Day. Completed 1896; demolished 1917.

127. Men's Dormitories, University of Pennsylvania. Cope & Stewardson. Begun 1895.

128. House for Messrs. Neil and Mauran. Wilson Eyre, Jr. 1890.

129. University Museum, University of Pennsylvania. Wilson Eyre, Jr., Frank Miles Day & Bro., and Cope & Stewardson. Begun 1893.

130. The Racquet Club of Philadelphia. Horace Trumbauer. 1907.

Club House 215 South 16th St. Occupied in 1907.

131. John Wanamaker Philadelphia Store. Daniel H. Burnham. 1902-10.

132. Girard Trust Corn Exchange Bank. McKim, Mead & White. 1905-8.

133. Plan of the Benjamin Franklin Parkway. Jacques Auguste Henri Gréber. Begun 1917.

134. Federal Reserve Bank of Philadelphia. Paul P. Cret. 1932-34.

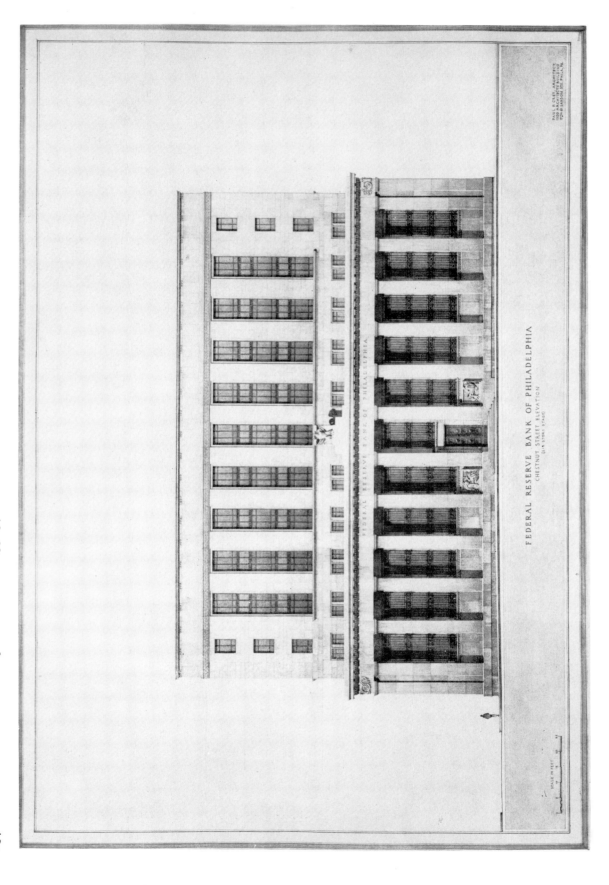

FEDERAL RESERVE BANK OF PHILADELPHIA
CHESTNUT STREET ELEVATION

FEDERAL RESERVE BANK OF PHILADELPHIA

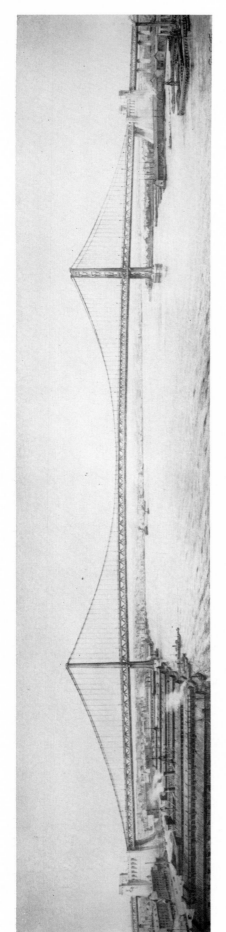

135. Delaware River (now Benjamin Franklin) Bridge. Paul P. Cret, architect; Ralph Modjeski, chief engineer. 1920-26.

136. Philadelphia Saving Fund Society Building. Howe & Lescaze. 1930-32.

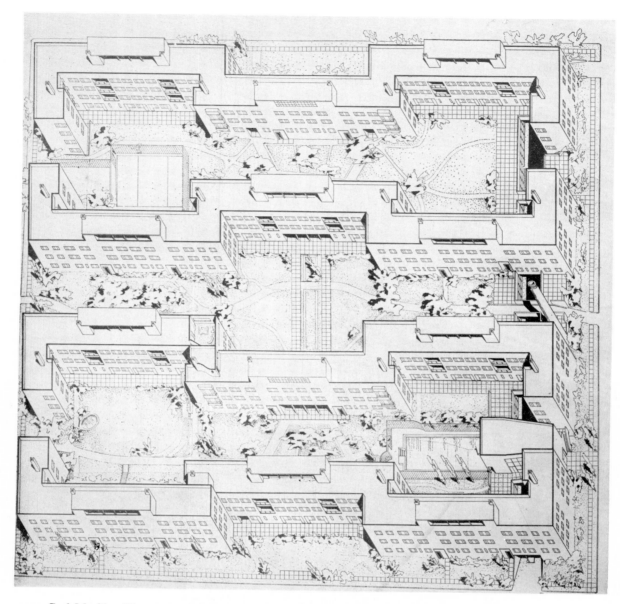

137. Carl Mackley Houses. Designed by Oskar Stonorov and Alfred Kastner; constructed under the direction
of W. Pope Barney. 1933-34.

138. Mercantile Library. Martin, Stewart & Noble. 1953.

139. Lankenau Hospital and Health Center. Vincent G. Kling. 1953-59.

140. Pennsylvania State Office Building. Carroll, Grisdale & Van Alen; Harbeson, Hough, Livingston & Larson; and Nolen & Swinburne.
Completed 1958.

141. Garden of the Pennsylvania State Office Building. Ian L. McHarg. 1958.

142. Extension of the Moore School of Electrical Engineering, University of Pennsylvania. Geddes, Brecher, Qualls & Cunningham. 1958.

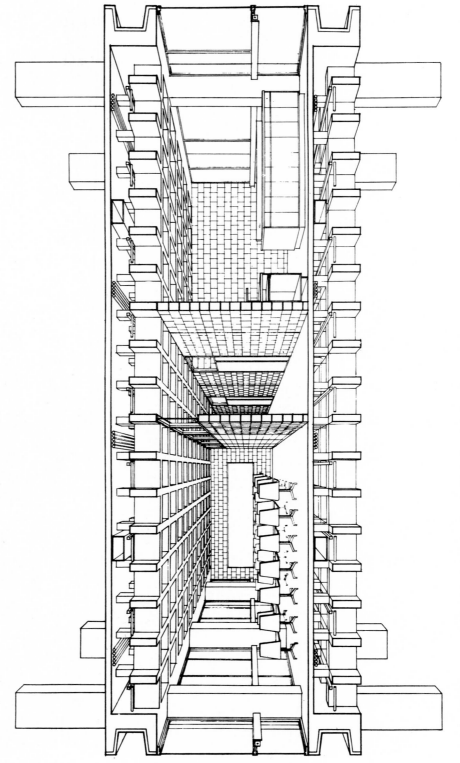

143. Section, Extension of the Moore School of Electrical Engineering. Geddes, Brecher, Qualls & Cunningham. 1958.

144. Washington Square East Urban Renewal, Eastern Section. Design of I. M. Pei & Associates. 1958.

145. Alfred Newton Richards Medical Research Building, University of Pennsylvania. Louis I. Kahn. 1959-60.

GENERAL BIBLIOGRAPHY

IN LISTING BELOW THE BOOKS FOUND MOST USEFUL IN THE PREPARATION OF THIS HISTORY OF
Philadelphia architecture, only those of a general nature have been included; articles or
monographs relating solely, or principally, to a single building or group of buildings have
been mentioned in the notes and are not repeated here. Additional bibliography connected
with prints and printmakers will also be found in the introduction of the Notes to the
Illustrations.

Although it has not seemed practical to include a comprehensive list of the innumerable guide books, almanacs, and directories put out by Boyd, Chapman, Desilver, Macpherson, Westcott, and others, a few representative examples have been cited. On the same
basis the numerous periodicals and newspapers of the period have had to be omitted, however indispensable they may be for the historian. A partial list of the more important titles
in this category would include: *The American Architect, The Analectic Magazine, Ballou's*
(later *Gleason's*) *Pictorial Drawing-Room Companion, The Casket* (later *Graham's Magazine*), *The Columbian Magazine, The Family Magazine, Harper's Weekly, The Literary
Magazine and American Register, Poulson's Daily Advertiser, The Port Folio,* and the
Public Ledger.

Dates given for the architects are based, for the most part, on the standard biographical
dictionaries, principally the *Dictionary of American Biography, The National Cyclopaedia
of American Biography,* and the *Biographical Dictionary of American Architects* (Henry
F. and Elsie R. Withey, Los Angeles [1956]). The dates given for the printmakers and
other artists are mostly those of *The New-York Historical Society's Dictionary of Artists in
America: 1564-1860* (George C. Groce and David H. Wallace, New Haven, 1957).

Since they are not in published form, many of the most fruitful sources of information
about Philadelphia architecture are apt to be overlooked in a general bibliography of this
kind. Among these are the insurance surveys at the Philadelphia Contributionship and the
Mutual Assurance Company, the exhibits of the Atwater Kent Museum, the Samuel
Castner notebooks in the Print and Picture Department of the Free Library of Philadelphia, and the more than one hundred scrapbooks of clippings compiled by Miss Jane Campbell, now in the Historical Society of Pennsylvania. Also in the Manuscript Department of
the Historical Society is David McNeely Stauffer's remarkable 32-volume extra-illustrated
edition of Thompson Westcott's *History of Philadelphia* 1608-1828, a compilation of
articles from *The Sunday Dispatch* (1867-1884), which expand considerably much of the
material to be found in Scharf and Westcott's better-known *History*. And there are few
people or events associated with Philadelphia not mentioned in *The Pennsylvania Magazine*

of History and Biography, easily referred to through its comprehensive *Index* (Eugene E. Doll, ed., Philadelphia, 1954).

Andrews, Wayne, *Architecture, Ambition and Americans,* New York [1955].

Bowen, Daniel, *A History of Philadelphia,* Philadelphia, 1839.

Brandt, F. B., and Gummere, H. V., *Byways and Boulevards In and About Historic Phila-delphia,* Philadelphia, 1925.

Bridenbaugh, Carl, *Cities of the Wilderness,* New York, 1938.

Brown, H. Glenn, and Brown, Maude O., *A Directory of the Book-Arts and Book Trade in Philadelphia to 1820, Including Painters and Engravers,* New York, 1950.

Burt, Maxwell Struthers, *Philadelphia, Holy Experiment,* New York, 1945.

Cousins, Frank and Riley, Phil M., *The Colonial Architecture of Philadelphia,* Boston, 1920.

Dallett, Francis James, "John Notman, Architect," *The Princeton University Library Chronicle,* Spring, 1959.

Eberlein, Harold Donaldson, and Hubbard, Cortlandt Van Dyke, *Diary of Independence Hall,* Philadelphia [1948].

———, *Portrait of a Colonial City: Philadelphia 1670-1838,* Philadelphia [1939].

Faris, John T., *Old Churches and Meeting Houses In and Around Philadelphia,* Philadel-phia, 1926.

———, *Old Gardens In and About Philadelphia,* Indianapolis [1932].

———, *Old Roads Out of Philadelphia,* Philadelphia [1917].

———, *The Romance of Old Philadelphia,* Philadelphia, 1918.

Freedley, Edwin T., *Philadelphia and Its Manuacturers,* Philadelphia, 1858.

Gallagher, H. M. Pierce, *Robert Mills,* New York, 1935.

Gilchrist, Agnes Addison, *William Strickland: Architect and Engineer, 1788-1854,* Phila-delphia, 1950; additions published as a supplement to the *Journal of the Society of Architectural Historians,* October, 1954.

Godcharles, Frederic A., *Daily Stories of Pennsylvania,* Milton (Pennsylvania), 1924.

Gray, William F., "Philadelphia's Architecture," *Publications of the City History Society of Philadelphia,* Vol. I, Philadelphia, 1915.

Guide to the Lions of Philadelphia, Philadelphia, 1837.

Hamlin, Talbot F., *Benjamin Henry Latrobe,* New York, 1955.

———, *Greek Revival Architecture in America,* New York, 1944.

Harbeson, John, "Philadelphia's Victorian Architecture," *The Pennsylvania Magazine,* July, 1943.

Harbeson, William, "Mediaeval Philadelphia," *The Pennsylvania Magazine,* July, 1943.

Hazard, Samuel (ed.), *The Register of Pennsylvania,* 16 vols., Philadelphia, 1828-1835.

Hazard, Willis P., *see* Watson, J. F., *Annals.*

Historic Philadelphia From the Founding Until the Early Nineteenth Century, Vol. 43, Part 1, *Transactions of the American Philosophical Society* (Luther P. Eisenhart, ed.), Philadelphia, 1953.

Hitchcock, Henry-Russell, *American Architectural Books*, 3d ed., Minneapolis, 1946.

——, *Architecture: Nineteenth and Twentieth Centuries*, Baltimore, 1958.

Illustrated Philadelphia: Its Wealth and Industries, New York, 1889.

Jackson, Joseph, *America's Most Historic Highway: Market Street, Philadelphia*, new ed., Philadelphia [1926].

——, *Early Philadelphia Architects and Engineers*, Philadelphia, 1923.

——, *Encyclopedia of Philadelphia*, 4 vols., Harrisburg, 1931-1933.

——, *Iconography of Philadelphia*, Philadelphia, 1934.

Kimball, Fiske, *American Achitecture*, New York [1928].

——, *Domestic Architecture of the American Colonies and of the Early Republic*, New York, 1922.

King, Moses, *Philadelphia and Notable Philadelphians*, New York, 1902.

Larkin, Oliver W., *Art and Life in America*, New York [1949].

Lippincott, Horace Mather, *Early Philadelphia, Its People, Life and Progress*, Philadelphia, 1917.

Marceau, Henri, *William Rush: 1756-1833*, Philadelphia, 1937.

McIntire, Henry B., *Philadelphia Then and Now*, Philadelphia, 1936.

Mease, Dr. James, *The Picture of Philadelphia*, Philadelphia, 1811; continued by Thomas Wilson, Philadelphia, 1824, and Thomas Porter, Philadelphia, 1831.

Moore, S. S., and Jones, T. W., *The Traveller's Directory*, Philadelphia, 1802.

Morrison, Hugh, *Early American Architecture From the First Colonial Settlements to the National Period*, New York, 1952.

Murtagh, William, "The Philadelphia Row House," *Journal of the Society of Architectural Historians*, December, 1957.

Myers, Albert Cook, *Narratives of Early Pennsylvania, West New Jersey and Delaware, 1630-1707*, New York, 1912.

Oberholtzer, Ellis Paxson, *Philadelphia: A History of the City and Its People*, 4 vols., Philadelphia, 1911.

One Hundred Years of Philadelphia: the Evening Bulletin's Anniversary Book, 1847-1947, Philadelphia, 1947.

Philadelphia and Her Merchants, Philadelphia, 1860.

Philadelphia and Its Environs, Philadelphia, 1875.

Philadelphia and Popular Philadelphians, Philadelphia, 1891.

Philadelphia in 1830, Philadelphia, 1830.

Porter, Thomas, *see* Mease, Dr. James.

Powers, Fred Perry, "The Historic Bridges of Philadelphia," *Publications of the City History Society of Philadelphia*, Vol. I, Philadelphia, 1914.

Prime, Alfred Coxe, *The Arts and Crafts in Philadelphia, Maryland and South Carolina, 1721-1800*, 2 vols., Topsfield (Massachusetts), 1929, 1932.

Proud, Robert, *The History of Philadelphia*, 2 vols., Philadelphia, 1798.

Raymond, Eleanor, *Early Domestic Architecture of Pennsylvania*, New York, 1931.

Repplier, Agnes, *Philadelphia, the Place and the People*, New York, 1925.

Richardson, A. E., *Georgian Architecture,* New York, 1949.

Rutledge, Anna Wells, *Cumulative Record of the Exhibition Catalogues: The Pennsylvania Academy of the Fine Arts, 1807-1870, The Society of Artists, 1800-1814, The Artists' Fund Society, 1835-1845,* Philadelphia, 1955.

Scharf, J. T., and Westcott, T., *History of Philadelphia 1609-1884,* 3 vols., Philadelphia, 1884.

Simon, Grant Miles, *Some Account of the Singular Beginnings of Philadelphia,* 1957.

Smith, R. A., *Philadelphia As It Is In 1852,* Philadelphia, 1852.

——, *New Guide to Philadelphia,* Philadelphia, 1870.

Stokes, I. N. Phelps, and Haskell, Daniel C., *American Historical Prints, Early Views of American Cities etc.,* New York, 1932.

Strathan, Edward (ed.), *A Century After, Picturesque Glimpses of Philadelphia and Pennsylvania,* Philadelphia, 1875.

Tanner, H. S., *A New Picture of Philadelphia, (Stranger's Guide),* Philadelphia, 1840, 1841, 1844, etc.

——, *Index to the New Plan of the City of Philadelphia and Adjoining Districts,* Philadelphia, 1830.

Tinkcom, Harry M., and Tinkcom, Margaret B., with Simon, Grant M., *Historic Germantown,* Memoirs of the American Philosophical Society, Philadelphia, 1955.

Thomas, Gabriel, *An Historical and Geographical Account of the Province and County of Philadelphia and of West-New-Jersey in America,* London, 1698.

Wainwright, Nicholas B., *Philadelphia in the Romantic Age of Lithography,* Philadelphia, 1958.

Wallace, Philip B., *Colonial Houses, Philadelphia, Pre-Revolutionary Period,* New York [1931].

Waterman, Thomas T., *The Dwellings of Colonial America,* Chapel Hill [1950].

Watson, John F., *Annals of Philadelphia and Pennsylvania,* Philadelphia, 1 vol., 1830; 2 vols., 1850; 3d vol. added 1877 by Willis P. Hazard.

Westcott, Thompson, *The Historic Mansions and Buildings of Philadelphia,* Philadelphia, 1877.

Wilson, Thomas, *see* Mease, Dr. James.

Wise, Herbert C., and Beidleman, H. Ferdinand, *Colonial Architecture for Those About to Build,* Philadelphia, 1913.

White, Theo. B. (ed.), *Philadelphia Architecture in the Nineteenth Century,* Philadelphia, 1953.

Young, John Russell (ed.), *Memorial History of the City of Philadelphia,* 2 vols., New York, 1895.

ACKNOWLEDGMENTS

A GENERAL HISTORY OF THIS KIND COULD NOT HAVE BEEN WRITTEN IN THE TIME ALLOTTED without the assistance of numerous scholars and specialists in many fields. The obligation of the author to published sources has, it is hoped, been fully acknowledged through the Notes and General Bibliography, but a further word of appreciation for the informal aid and counsel of many other persons is also in order here.

A particular debt is owed to several members of the Committee on Architecture of the Philadelphia Art Alliance. Its chairman, Theo. B. White, has afforded invaluable assistance in many ways and at every stage in the preparation of this volume: all the financial arrangements have been his responsibility; a number of the illustrations were secured by him, and his advice has been especially relied upon in the selection of the buildings for inclusion in the section on contemporary Philadelphia. The other member of the sub-committee, David M. Robb, for many years Chairman of the Department of the History of Art at the University of Pennsylvania and currently President of the College Art Association, not only assumed a number of the author's teaching obligations in order to allow him more time to work on the manuscript, but also kindly took the preliminary draft in hand, contributing considerably thereby to the literacy of the final result.

Throughout the latter stages of the preparation of the manuscript, the author had the constant assistance of Robert B. Ennis, a graduate in architecture of the University of Pennsylvania and presently a candidate for the doctorate in the history of art. He sought out and verified many references, checked and criticized portions of the text, conducted personal interviews with contemporary architects, and prepared several very full memoranda that were used extensively in developing the last two sections of the book. Without Ennis' assistance the manuscript could never have been completed in time for the opening of the exhibition at the Philadelphia Art Art Alliance in April, 1961, and he shares fully in whatever merit the finished product may prove to have.

In spite of the best efforts of the author, errors inevitably creep into a book of this kind. That there are not more in this case is due largely to those persons mentioned above as well as to the kindness of several other scholars who took time from busy schedules to examine and criticize portions of the text. Charles E. Peterson read the earlier sections and made a number of very helpful suggestions; it was he who first brought to the author's attention the Neave and Abercrombie houses, supplied information concerning them, and added several details of the remarkable career of John Dorsey. In this connection, special thanks are also due the staff of the Philadelphia Historical Commission. Most of the specific insurance surveys mentioned here were brought to the author's attention by Mrs. Earle R. Kirkbride, historical assistant, who also offered a number of pertinent criticisms. And to few persons is the author more indebted than to Dr. Margaret B. Tinkcom, historian of the Commission, who very generously undertook to read large parts of the manuscript and to offer detailed criticism based on her own wide acquaintance with the subject. Without her assistance the text would have been far less full or accurate.

Every teacher has had the experience of learning from his students—frequently when he is least aware of it. At the risk of inadvertently overlooking some of those who have perhaps helped the most, it is a pleasure to include at least a partial list of students, past and present, who directly or indirectly have contributed to this survey of Philadelphia architecture: Tracy Atkinson for his work on the rural cemetery in America; Matthew Baigell for his paper on the Federal period in Philadelphia; Gerald S. Bernstein for his investigation of the Moorish Revival; William Bertolet for his study of Cope & Stewardson; (Mrs.) Joan Buchman for her work on American hotels; David J. Crownover for his careful examination of the records of early Philadelphia churches made under the direction of Prof. Robert C. Smith; William J. Elder for pointing out the similarity of the Baltimore Athenaeum to that of Notman; Charles P. Graves for his work on the Philadelphia theaters, especially the Academy of Music; Bernard Hanson for his paper on the use of the French Renaissance style in America; Melvin E. Meyers for his study of museums in the United States; William J. Murtagh for his pioneer analysis of the Philadelphia city house; Julia Jane Nash for her investigation of cast iron made in Philadelphia; (Mrs.) Ann Sue Hirshorn for her work on Lemon Hill (prepared originally for Prof. Smith) and for bringing to the attention of the author Thomas Hamilton's description of the plan of Philadelphia; Kenneth Wilson for his research on the Centennial. Special dependence has been placed upon the advice of those who have selected some aspect of Philadelphia architecture for their doctoral dissertations, now in progress: Matthew Baigell (John Haviland); Harold N. Cooledge, Jr. (Samuel Sloan); Robert B. Ennis (Thomas U. Walter).

In his Foreword, Theo. B. White, on behalf of all those connected with the Exhibition and resultant book, has thanked the directors of museums and libraries for their interest and assistance in the assembling of the prints and drawings of Philadelphia architecture. An additional word of appreciation is also due those who have borne with such good grace the author's many requests for aid and information, especially: J. Harcourt Givens and the staff of the Manuscript Department of the Historical Society of Pennsylvania; Barney Chesnick, Curator, and Mrs. Lillian Tonkin of the Library Company of Philadelphia; Miss Dorothy Hale Litchfield and the staff of the Print and Picture Department and Miss Ellen Shaffer, Librarian of the Rare Book Department, all of the Free Library of Philadelphia; Miss Eleanor Worfolk and the staff of the Library of the School of Fine Arts of the University of Pennsylvania; Miss Janet S. Byrne, Associate Curator of the Department of Prints of the Metropolitan Museum; Miss Elizabeth E. Roth, First Assistant in the Print Room of the New York Public Library, and Miss Marna Feldt, Assistant to the Director of the American Swedish Museum in Philadelphia. To the author's hurried calls for information, M. Joseph McCosker, Director of the Atwater Kent Museum, and the members of his staff have also replied with helpful information and great forbearance.

On a variety of matters, large and small, persons in many positions and capacities have generously shared their special knowledge and experience; credit is especially due Mrs. Frederic L. Ballard for assistance in piecing together the history of Fairmount Park; Frank M. Boeshore for information on the Drexel Building; Boyd T. Barnard for a number of the facts concerning the Lincoln-Liberty Building; Mrs. Henry Peter Borie for help in untangling the history of the Philadelphia Museum; H. Tatnall Brown for information on the buildings of the Girard Trust Co.; Alan Burnham for permitting the author to read his paper on Wilson Eyre, Jr.; R. Damon Childs for assistance in running down a number of facts, especially concerning Moyamensing Prison; Francis James Dallett for suggestions concerning the Camac residence; John Harbeson for his advice concerning the buildings to be included in this survey of Philadelphia architecture; Penelope Hartshorne for information on Franklin Court; William J. H. Hough for additional facts relating to the Delaware River Bridge; Norman B. Johnston for his advice concerning the prisons of Philadelphia; George S. Koyl for information on the Stewardson Scholarships; Miss Frances Lichten for making available the records of the Pennsylvania Academy of the Fine Arts; William H. Livingston for sharing his recollections of Paul P. Cret; James C. Massey for information on the work of Frank Furness, a subject of which he is making a special study; Sidney E. Martin for assistance with the history of the Benjamin Franklin Parkway; Louis E. McAllister for his helpful discussion of his association with Howe & Lescaze; Kneeland McNulty for advice concerning the technique of prints; Lee Nelson for bibliography on bridges; James H. O'Gorman for the results of his research on the Neave House made as part of the Historic American Buildings Survey; J. D. Otley for information on brickmaking in Philadelphia; Martin P. Snyder for facts about W. L. Breton based on his forthcoming article; Walter M. Stawuszewski for information on the John Wanamaker Philadelphia store; the Rev. Percy Stockman for the later history of the Floating Church of the Redeemer; the Rev. G. Hall Todd for information about the Arch Street Presbyterian Church and J. C. Hoxie, its architect; Wilhelm Viggo von Moltke for making available material on the rehabilitation of the Society Hill area; and Winston Weisman, head of the Art Department of the Pennsylvania State University, for advice concerning commercial architecture in Philadelphia and for several of the references to Hoxie and Button. The author and his associates are particularly appreciative of the cooperation which they received from the architects whose work is illustrated in the last section of this volume. Miss Barbara Muhs was especially helpful in assembling references to the work of Vincent Kling, as was Thomas R. Vreeland in connection with that of Louis Kahn. The Rev. Joseph Koci, Jr., kindly took the author on a tour of St. Peter's and supplied information concerning the history of the church; Mr. William J. Wallace, Chairman, Committee on the Temple, and Dr. William J. Paterson, Librarian, were of material assistance in securing a suitable drawing of the Masonic Temple at Broad and Filbert streets. Mr. Joseph T. Fraser, Jr., and Mrs. Loren C. Eiseley supplied information concerning the Pennsylvania Academy of the Fine Arts, as did Mr. Harold Mason for the Academy of Music. The staff of the library of *The Evening Bulletin* patiently answered many inquiries. And to John H. Norton much is owed for many favors, too numerous to be detailed, but which at the time made all the difference.

The photographs of prints and drawings in collections outside the city were supplied by the lending institutions. Most of the material in the Philadelphia area was photographed by the Kean Studios under the direction of Manuel Kean to whom the author is indebted for his personal interest and helpful counsel. The detail of the capital from the Erectheum illustrated in Stuart and Revett was photographed by George Pohl; the photograph of E. L. Henry's Battle of Germantown was made by Charles P. Mills & Son; that of the Pennsylvania State Office Building by Alfred A. DeLardi; Lawrence S. Williams was the photographer of the project of I. M. Pei & Associates.

And last, but certainly not least, the author is deeply indebted to his "personal staff": to his friend and neighbor, Mrs. Elizabeth F. Jones, who devoted much of her summer to typing the several drafts of the text of this book, and especially to his wife for her willingness to assume his family duties along with her own, while at the same time serving as his typist, filing clerk, proofreader, and general secretary. At last it is entirely clear what authors mean when they end their acknowledgments by saying of their wives: "Without her constant encouragement and assistance this book could not possibly have been written."

INDEX

Unless otherwise indicated, all references are to Philadelphia. Most buildings in other cities are listed by location. With a few exceptions, the names of authors included in the General Bibliography are not repeated in the Index. The owners of the prints and drawings used as illustrations are not indexed but may readily be found by consulting the Notes. Numbers in parentheses, when used in conjunction with other numbers, refer to notes; those in italics to illustrations.